PANZERS
IN NORMANDY
THEN AND NOW

Eric Lefèvre

© *After the Battle* magazine 1983
Second edition 1990
Reprinted 1993
ISBN 0 900913 29 0
Printed in Great Britain.

Translated from the French by Roy Cooke and edited by Andrew Holmwood.

Designed by Winston G. Ramsey
Editor *After the Battle* magazine.

Technical adviser: Jean Paul Pallud.

PUBLISHERS
Battle of Britain Prints International Limited,
Church House, Church Street,
London E15 3JA, England.

PRINTERS
Plaistow Press Limited,
Church House, Church Street,
London E15 3JA, England.

ACKNOWLEDGEMENTS

The author would like to express his gratitude to all those who have given him the benefit of their knowledge or access to material in their possession: firstly to Loïc Le Guen and Jean de Lagarde, also to Dr Haupt, General Graf von Schwerin, Dr Weiss, Paul-Charles Steinmetz-Lange, Dr Meyer, Michel Danin and, above all, to Robert Soulat and Georges Bernage. The help and advice of Peter Chamberlain, Jean Paul Pallud and Gary Simpson was invaluable in compiling the English language edition. The illustrative material for Panzer Regiment '44' and the organisational charts were compiled and drawn by Jean Paul Pallud.

EDITOR'S NOTE

Of necessity the German army had to use abbreviations for their units. The company (Kompanie), regiment, brigade, division and army was always designated by an Arabic figure, the battalion (Abteilung) and corps (Korps) by a Roman numeral. Thus: 5./Pz.Rgt. 3 means the 5th Company of the 3rd Tank Regiment. Likewise II./Pz.Rgt. 16 is short for the 2nd Battalion of the 16th Tank Regiment, 'Panzer' being the German for 'armour' but also used for 'tank'. The style adopted in this book, while not adhering strictly to the hieroglyphics of the German abbreviations is, nevertheless, 'Germanic' in flavour while being more readily understood in English.

MAPS

Unless stated to the contrary, all maps are reproduced from GSGS 4249 1:100,000 — either from Sheet 6F St Lô-Vire 1942 Edition or Sheet 7F Caen-Falaise 1943 Edition and are Crown Copyright. All extracts are reproduced to the same scale of 1:100,000, i.e. 1cm = 1km. Distance scales have been omitted on some pages in the interest of clarity. It is important to remember that the majority of roads in France have been reclassified and/or renumbered since the war. The numbers overlaid on the maps are those in current use. (See also pages 186-187.)

PHOTOGRAPHS

Copyright is indicated on all contemporary photographs where known (Imperial War Museum is abbreviated IWM). All present day photographs copyright *After the Battle* magazine.

FRONT COVER

Reproduced from a painting by George A. Campbell of SS-Obersturmführer Michael Wittmann of schwere SS-Panzer Abteilung 101 before his promotion and the award of the swords to his Ritterkreuz. His unmarked field grave, dating from August 1944, was found as a result of the research undertaken for this edition (see page 183).

BACK COVER

Panther from the 6. Kompanie, II. Abteilung, Panzer Regiment 33 which fought in Normandy in August 1944. The loader has emerged from the rear hatch, his eyes protected by dark goggles, in order to spot any Allied fighter-bombers attacking from out of the sun. (Bundesarchiv)

FRONT ENDPAPER

In victory. A crew from schwere SS-Panzer Abteilung 101 with their well camouflaged Tiger Ausf E photographed shortly after their successful battle against the advance of the British 22nd Armoured Brigade at Villers-Bocage on June 13. They wear a mixture of clothing often seen during active service. Each crew member was issued with a P.38 semi-automatic pistol apart from the gun-layer who was given an MP40 sub-machine gun. (Bundesarchiv)

The Panther — these are Ausf Gs — served in Normandy with the majority of the panzer regiments although rarely at the theoretical strength of 17 per Kompanie. (Bundesarchiv)

REAR ENDPAPER

In defeat. Panther Ausf A abandoned in St Lambert-sur-Dive outside the Mairie photographed by Captain Derrek Knight on August 23, 1944. (Imperial War Musuem)

PAGES 4-5

The 8. Kompanie of Panzer Regiment 3 in battle formation on the Picardy plain before the invasion. (Bundesarchiv)

PAGES 60-61

An SS-Panzer Regiment 12 Panther commander attired in the camouflage-style uniform which had been manufactured from cloth obtained from Italy when he was stationed there in 1943, probably as a member of the Liebstandarte Adolf Hitler. (Bundesarchiv)

PAGES 76-77

A Panther Ausf G of the II. Abteilung of Panzer Regiment 33 being transported from Mailly-le-Camp eighty miles east of Paris to Normandy by rail. The fir branches used for camouflage are indigenous around the tank training area and would have to be renewed during the long journey to the front. The summer dress of the crew is typical of the period: pre-1943 shirts with rolled up sleeves and canvas trousers. The standard black peaked caps outnumber the forage cap. (Bundesarchiv)

PAGES 124-125

Tiger Is of schwere SS-Panzer Abteilung 101 climb the hill on the N316 north-east of Morgny en route to Normandy. Note the wide battle tracks on this late production Ausf E. (Bundesarchiv)

PAGES 208-209

The sole panzer remaining in Normandy today — the Tiger Ausf E beside the Route Nationale 179 outside Vimoutiers.

CONTENTS

INTRODUCTION

On June 6, 1944 Hitler's so-called Atlantic Wall delayed the Allied landings in Normandy only by a few hours. The Luftwaffe and Kriegsmarine were no longer forces to be reckoned and the German infantry divisions defending the coastal area were still using horses as their main means of transport. Once ashore, the invading troops could rely on permanent air support that was limitless and devastating. Allied aircraft were able to harass enemy columns hundreds of kilometres in the rear, paralysing all movement, and preventing men, shells, and petrol from arriving at the front. The Allies, on the other hand, were assured of permanent supplies, far in excess of their effective requirements, and were able to rely on massive artillery support and on the heavy guns of warships firing from out at sea for dozens of kilometres inland.

There were, however, the panzers. They could move by night, when what the Germans called 'Jabos' (fighter-bombers) could no longer intervene, and, face to face with Allied tanks, the panzers often had the upper hand, even when it was a case of one against five. But they were comparatively few in number and most of them a long way from Normandy. They were to arrive piecemeal, right up to the final days of the battle . . . and their hulks were to be abandoned right across the Normandy countryside.

This book deals specifically with the tank regiments of the panzer divisions in Normandy and with the independent heavy tank battalions. Ten panzer divisions took part in the battle, the same number as in the Blitzkreig of 1940, although then they had been deployed in concerted action, whereas in the summer of 1944 the German High Command had first to be convinced that the landings were the real thing before striving to assemble divisions from the four corners of Europe. Controversy over the deployment of the panzer reserve was considerable. A crucial factor was the question of where the invasion would take place — something which the Allied deception plans exploited to the full. In the spring of 1944, though, it was fairly obvious that it could be Normandy. Hitler was rather in two minds about it — insisting on the need to keep a careful eye on the sector but, at the same time, retaining panzer divisions in north-west France.

On top of everything, the High Command was at that moment divided among itself and in a state of paralysis. Generalfeldmarschall Gerd von Rundstedt, the Commander-in-Chief West, was in favour of keeping the panzer divisions back from the coast so that once the enemy's intentions became clear the armour could be launched in a well-laid conventional counter-attack. The same aims prevailed within Panzergruppe West — the headquarters made up of experienced panzer officers under General der Panzertruppen Geyr von Schweppenburg and entrusted with the training of the panzer divisions — with the General resolutely in support of von Rundstedt's views.

On the other hand Generalfeldmarschall Erwin Rommel, commanding Army Group B stretching from the Dutch-German border to the Loire, believed in a very different approach to that of his superior, and wanted to position the armour as close as possible to the coast in order to throw an assault back into the sea as rapidly as possible. Subsequently Rommel was shown to be right in his assessment of the dominating role of Allied air power, which his superiors had clearly underestimated, yet the presence of the panzer divisions right up on the coast might well have led the Allies to have changed their plans accordingly.

The argument was won by neither side but resulted in a compromise. North of the Loire, Rommel's Army Group B was given command of 2., 21. and 116. Panzer Divisions while 1. and 12. SS-Panzer Divisions and the Panzer Lehr remained under von Rundstedt's authority but with the proviso that they were not to be committed without Hitler's approval. This order was to prove fatal, for the delay in obtaining their release in the first few days could never afterwards be made good. Had the panzer divisions been able to intervene in force, and at once against the troops coming ashore, it could have proved decisive.

Individually, German tanks were superior to those they faced because of their more powerful armament and better armour. Numerically inferior, they faced greater supply difficulties, being dependent on poorer lines of communication, and spares were less standardised. One important point in their favour was that many of their crews had years of ex-perience behind them and were already old hands at tank warfare and more than ready to take on whatever lay in store.

After the invasion, large-scale German tank offensives failed to materialise. On June 8 the staff of Panzergruppe West moved to the château at La Caine, six kilometres north-west of Thury-Harcourt. Allied intelligence monitoring enemy radio traffic learned of the new location and a carefully directed bomb and rocket attack on the evening of the 10th killed eighteen officers, among them the Chief of Staff Generalmajor Ritter und Edler von Dawans. General Geyr von Schweppenburg was wounded. Within two days Allied Ultra intelligence had decoded a German radio message reporting the casualties and stating that all communications of Panzergruppe West were out of action — a grievous blow to the German panzer command staff on its first day of commitment to the Normandy battlefront.

Panzergruppe West was entrusted with operations on the right flank of 7. Armee and in August was renamed 5. Panzer Armee, Geyr von Schweppenburg having been replaced by General der Panzertruppen Heinrich Eberbach. Mostly, German tanks fighting in Normandy were engaged in small numbers in local operations, often in defensive roles, some units having to fight hull-down such as elements of Panzer Regiment 22 north of Caen early in the battle. One by one they met their fate. They managed to repulse a number of attacks and there were many tank commanders who made a name for themselves by their prowess but, in the end, their efforts were not sufficient to really tip the balance.

ORGANISATION OF PANZER REGIMENT '44'

The majority of panzers in Normandy were used on the battlefield by the panzer regiment of a panzer division, and these regiments form the central basis for this book. The panzer regiment was the heart of the panzer division, and consisted of two battalions: I. Abteilung and II. Abteilung. The term 'Abteilung' used in the sense of 'battalion' within a panzer regiment is also a common designation for German units generally and can denote, according to context, unit, battery, battalion, detachment, department, even division, etc — without necessarily corresponding to the British or American equivalent. The panzer division possessed a Sturmgeschutz Abteilung and/or Panzerjäger Abteilung as its main tank destroyer element. The panzergrenadier division (which did not have a tank regiment) possessed a Panzer Abteilung, but this was normally equipped with Sturmgeschutz or Panzerjäger instead of tanks.

The heavy tank units with their Tigers — schwere Panzer Abteilung — were not integral divisional units but came under the category of 'Heerestruppen': units allotted to the army groups and sub-allotted to armies, corps and divisions according to requirements as was standard German practice. Likewise the heavy tank destroyer units — schwere Panzerjäger Abteilung. Both could belong either to the Heer or the Waffen-SS although apart from the designation, the units had more or less the same composition.

Panzer regiments of the Heer (Army) and Waffen-SS were similar in structure, and the theoretical composition of a panzer regiment as set out here is based on the Kriegsstärkenachweisung and Kriegsausrüstungsnachweisung issued by the organisation branch of the OKH on April 1, 1944.

The nominal establishment of a panzer division, in addition to its panzer regiment, included the divisional headquarters, two panzergrenadier regiments (one motorised, the other armoured), an armoured reconnaissance group, tank destroyer battalion, motorised/armoured artillery regiment, flak unit, armoured engineers battalion, armoured signals battalion, instruction battalion, supply battalion, motor vehicle repair battalion, organisation battalion and medical battalion.

The characteristic feature of a panzer regiment in 1944 was the extent of its own means of logistical support at both battalion and regimental level. This was to increase with the appearance of the Panther, which required a great deal of manpower to be maintained properly — the theoretical strength of a Panther battalion service company numbering nearly a hundred more men than a PzKpfw IV battalion (see pages 14 and 15).

Its integral means of logistic support gave a panzer regiment

the appearance of being virtually self-supporting other than in river-crossing (when it was dependent on the divisional engineers battalion) but, in practice, this was not often the case. Service companies, for instance, were lacking in half the tank battalions at the outbreak of the battle, whilst half the panzer regiments were without a repair company.

The regiment depicted on the following pages gives the theoretical top-line strength for a panzer regiment as given in the German document of April 1944. This provided for two possible strengths for each panzer company: either 17 or 22 tanks which in turn affected the number of personnel.

The drawings which follow are based on the most commonly found structure of the panzer regiment in June 1944: the I. Abteilung with seventeen Panthers per company and the II. Abteilung with twenty-two PzKpfw IVs per company. The regiment depicted does not have a band. It is equipped with motorcycles (with sidecars) instead of tracked motor-cycles (Kettenkrads) which were given to divisions fighting on the Eastern Front. In the same way, half-tracked 'Maultiers' would have replaced some trucks in an eastern division.

Transport had become much more standardised than at the beginning of the war. In October 1943 the tremendous variety of models being turned out was reduced to a few standard types for the whole army. In a typical panzer regiment, eighty-five per cent of its lorries were nominally four-wheel drive Type A cross-country vehicles (normal drive being designated Type S).

It should be noted that the illustrations standardise the regiment to an extent never seen in reality and cover only thirty-one different vehicle types. Many makes of vehicle were employed and one particular truck, for example, could have had a different internal configuration according to its function, i.e. signals, engineer, supply, and so on. One important point concerns the Bergeschlepper 35 t which is envisaged in the German document but which was never built as such. Instead the panzer units were issued with a tank recovery vehicle built on the Panther chassis which is the vehicle illustrated.

So much for the theory. The reality was an assortment of transport in which even among smaller units there was little uniformity. Alongside sundry German makes stood those built by foreign firms and others that had been captured and pressed into service.

From February 1943 German military vehicles came out of the factories painted in the dark sand colour that had shown itself to be less conspicuous out in the open than dark grey. At the same time a summer camouflage was adopted incorporating olive green and reddish brown (the olive green coming from Luftwaffe stocks intended for ground in-

The trident insignia of the 2 Panzer Division emblazoned on tank No. 4 of the 8th Kompanie, 3rd platoon, defined by 834 on the turret, of this PzKfw IV of Panzer Regiment 3.

stallations). The paint came in 2 or 20kg tins of concentrated paste and had to be diluted with water or petrol and applied with a spray gun. The job was normally undertaken by maintenance units but very often by the crews themselves. Mixed with water the paint was not very stable, but petrol was hard to come by. Sump oil and diesel fuel were also used, and when time was short the paint was put on with a brush without being diluted: all of which contributed towards widely differing shades of colour and, since there were no overall colour schemes laid down, the variety of camouflage was infinite.

In March 1943 regulations stipulated that all armoured vehicles had to carry details of their category (the Sd.Kfz number), overall weight (Ge.Gew.) and weight category (Ve.Kl.) painted externally within a border in letters up to 10mm wide and 22mm high. This information had to be appear in black on the left-hand side in a prominent position. It was omitted, however, when such details were of a confidential nature — hence hardly ever being seen on tanks except for the PzKpfw IV (on the left of the turret skirts). Non-armoured vehicles were required to carry details of their unloaded weight and total carrying capacity.

Although most divisions and lesser units used their own insignia on vehicles and signboards, they were somewhat rarer on tanks. The choice of emblem was up to the divisional or unit commander and could eventually change with him although the overall motif usually remained basically the same. At the beginning of the war white insignia were reserved for the infantry and yellow for the armour, though by 1944 almost all were in white. It was quite possible to come across signs in more than one colour, and even different signs in the same division. Waffen-SS divisional emblems were in the shape of a shield — panzer divisions having the top right-hand corner of the shield cut away; the panzergrenadier divisions the top left.

Of the large figures painted on the sides and sometimes the rear of a tank's turret, generally the first denoted the company to which it belonged, the second its platoon (Zug), and the third the number of the tank within the platoon. (A tank with the number 723, for example, belonged to No. 2. Zug of the 7. Kompanie in which it was tank number 3.) Sometimes only one or two figures appeared on the turret, particularly on tanks from the local defence battalions (Panzer Ersatz und Ausbildungs Abteilung 100 and Panzer Abteilung 206 in Normandy), which merely indicated the tank's number within its unit. The letter R in place of the first figure indicated that a tank belonged to the regimental headquarters company — R 01 denoting regimental commander and R 02 the second in command. Arabic numerals indicated that a tank came from a battalion headquarters company — II 01 belonging to the commander of II. Abteilung. Some units had a non-standard numbering system starting with R 00, I 00 and II 00 instead of R 01, I 01 and II 01.

An order issued in April 1944 to standardise the system for numbering regimental and battalion command vehicles instituted a two-digit code number in place of the R, I and II designations. As this system was intended to start in June 1944 and seems not to have been used consistently, we have chosen to number our panzer regiment with the old R, I and II system.

The abbreviation SdKfz, which up to 1943 normally came after a vehicle's designation, was short for Sonderkraftfarzeug: literally 'special purpose motor vehicle'. The number that followed was the ordnance number given on the type's acceptance into service. The abbreviation Kfz (Kraftfahrzeug) stood for a non-armoured motor vehicle. The prefix PzKpfw was an abbreviation of Panzerkampfwagen: 'armoured fighting vehicle' or tank. The six types of battle tank that were developed over a period of ten years were numbered with an arabic numeral, with each successive model (Ausführung or Ausf for short) being denoted alphabetically: e.g. PzKpfw IV Ausf B to Ausf F; the Ausf A usually being the first production vehicle.

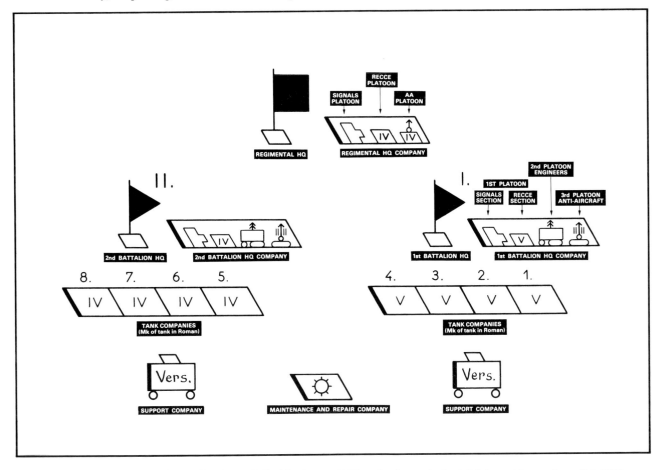

The organisation chart for the Panzer Regiment '44' tables (pages 9-16) — the theoretical establishment for such a unit in 1944.

PANZER REGIMENT '44'

KEY TO THE ORGANISATION TABLES ON PAGES 9-16

Victoria KR 35
le. Krad 350 cm
(light motorcycle)

Zündapp KS 750
Krad mit seitenwagen
(motorcycle with sidecar)

NSU HK 100, SdKfz 2
Kettenkraftrad
(tracked motorcycle)

Volkswagen Typ. 82, Kfz 1
le. Personenkraftwagen gl.
(light personnel carrier, cross-country)

Volkswagen Typ. 166, Kfz 1/20
le. Personenkraftwagen gl. schf.
(light car, cross-country, amphibian)

Horch Kfz 17
Lastkraftwagen 2 t., Funkwagen
(wireless truck)

m. Zugkraftwagen 8-ton, SdKfz 7/1
2 cm Flak Vierling Selbstfahrlafette
(self-propelled quadruple 20mm AA guns)

SdKfz 161/2 Ausf J
Panzerkampfwagen IV
(main battle tank)

SdKfz 251/7 Ausf D.
m. Pionierpanzerwagen
(medium, armoured engineer vehicle)

Horch Kfz 15
m. Personenkraftwagen, gl.
(medium personnel carrier, cross-country)

SdKfz 161/3 'Möbelwagen'
Flakpanzerkampfwagen IV, 3.7 cm Flak 43
(37mm AA gun on PzKpfw IV)

SdKfz 171 Ausf G
Panzerkampfwagen 'Panther'
(main battle tank)

SdKfz 251/8 Ausf D
m. Krankenpanzerwagen
(medium, armoured ambulance)

Phänomen Granit 1500 S
Lastkraftwagen 2 t., Krankenkraftwagen
(truck, ambulance)

Opel-Blitz Typ. 3.6-36 S
Lastkraftwagen 3 t., offen
(truck, open)

Opel-Blitz Typ. 3.6-6700 A
Lastkraftwagen 3 t., gl, offen
(truck, cross-country, open)

Opel-Blitz Typ. 3.6-36 S
Lastkraftwagen
(truck)

Opel-Blitz Typ. 3.6-6700 A
Lastenkraftwagen 3 t., gl
(truck, cross-country)

Opel-Blitz Typ. 3.6-36 S
Lastkraftwagen 3 t., Feldkochherd
(truck, field-kitchen)

Opel-Blitz Typ. 3.6-6700 A
Lastkraftwagen 3 t., gl, Feldkochherd
(truck, field-kitchen, cross-country)

Steyr Typ. 1500 A
Lastkraftwagen 2 t., offen, gl.
(truck, open, cross-country)

'Maultier' Ford Typ. V 3000 S/SSM
Gleisketten Lastkraftwagen 'Maultier'
(semi-tracked truck)

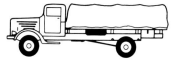

Büssing-NAG 4500 S-1
Lastkraftwagen 4.5 t., offen
(truck, open)

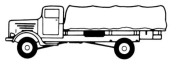

Büssing-NAG 4500 A-1
Lastkraftwagen 4.5 t., gl, offen
(truck, cross-country, open)

Demag D7, SdKfz 10
le. Zugkraftwagen 1 t.
(tractor, 1 ton)

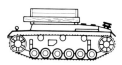

Bergepanzer III
Bergeschlepper, Fahrgest.PzKpfw III
(armoured recovery vehicle)

Famo F3, SdKfz 9/1
Drehkrankraftwagen, Hebekraft 6 t.
(revolving crane, 6 tons, on SdKfz 9 chassis)

Kfz 100
Drehkrankraftwagen, Hebecraft 3 t.
(revolving crane, 3 tons, on a Büssing-NAG 4500 A chassis)

Bergepanther, SdKfz 179
Bergeschlepper 35 t.
(armoured recovery vehicle)

Famo F3, SdKfz 9
s. Zugkraftwagen 18 t.
(tractor, 18 tons)

Tiefladeanhänger, SdAk 116
(22-ton tank transporter trailer)

Panzer-Regiment

Stabskompanie (Staff Company)

a)

b)

c)
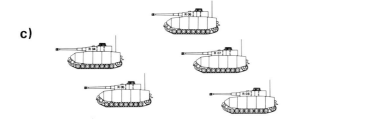

d)

e)

f)

g)

Fliegerabwehrzug (Anti-Aircraft Platoon)

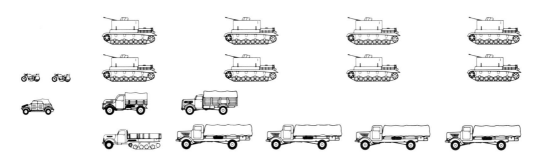

(a) Gruppe Führer (Command Staff); (b) Nachrichtenzug (Signals Platoon); (c) Aufklärungszug (Reconnaissance Platoon); (d) Kfz.Instandsetzungsgruppe (Vehicle Maintenance Squad); (e) Gefechtstross (Combat Train); (f) Verflegungstross (Supply Train); (g) Gepäcktross (Baggage Train). Fliegerabwehrzug (Anti-Aircraft Platoon): one command staff, four squads with two Flakpanzers each, one vehicle and gun maintenance squad (Kfz. und Geschütz-instandsetzungsgruppe) and one combat train (Gefechtstross).

I. Abteilung (1st Battalion)

Stabskompanie (Staff Company)

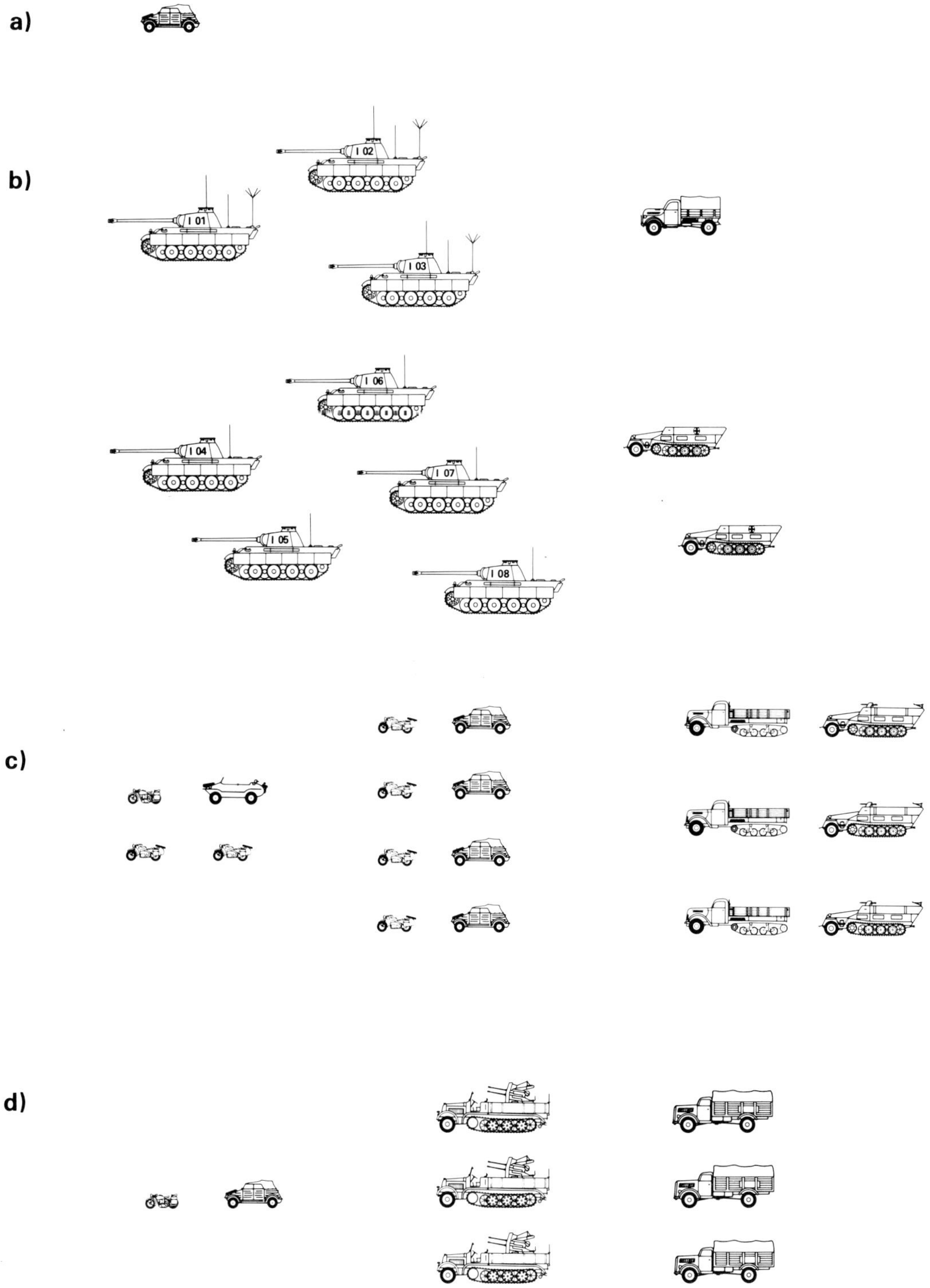

a)

b)

c)

d)

(a) Gruppe Führer (Command Staff); (b) 1. Nachrichten und Aufklärungszug (1st Platoon, Signals and Reconnaissance); (c) 2. Erkunder und Pionierzug (2nd Platoon, Reconnaissance and Engineers); (d) 3. Fliegerabwehrzug (3rd Platoon, Anti-Aircraft).

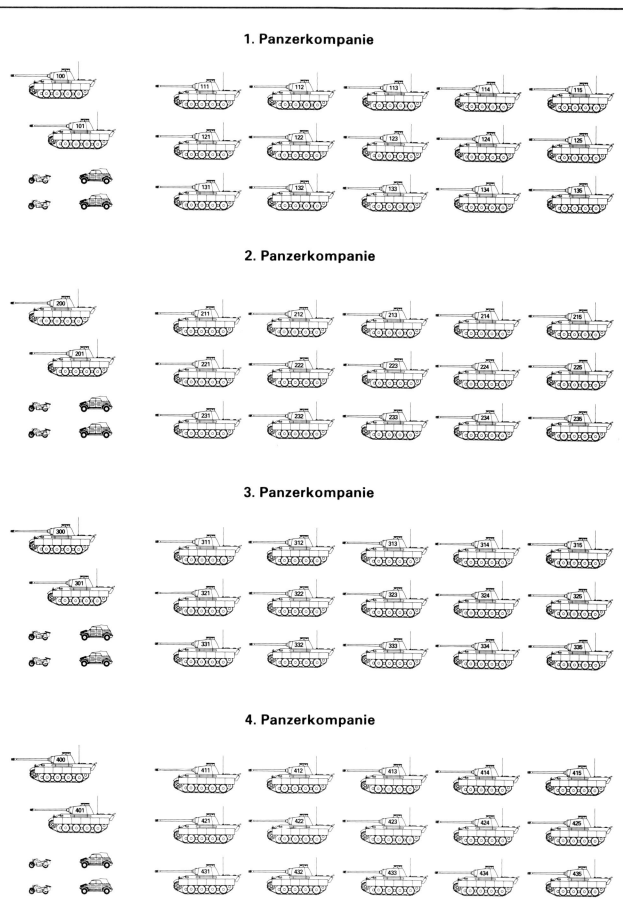

1. Panzerkompanie

2. Panzerkompanie

3. Panzerkompanie

4. Panzerkompanie

1., 2., 3. und 4. Panzerkompanie (1st, 2nd, 3rd and 4th Tank Companies). There are seventeen Panthers in each company —
two with the Gruppe Führer (Command Staff), five with the 1. Zug (1st Platoon), five with 2. Zug (2nd Platoon) and five with
the 3. Zug (3rd Platoon). There are no tanks with the 4. Zug but two panzer crews as personnel reserve.

II. Abteilung (2nd Battalion)

Stabskompanie (Staff Company)

a)

b)

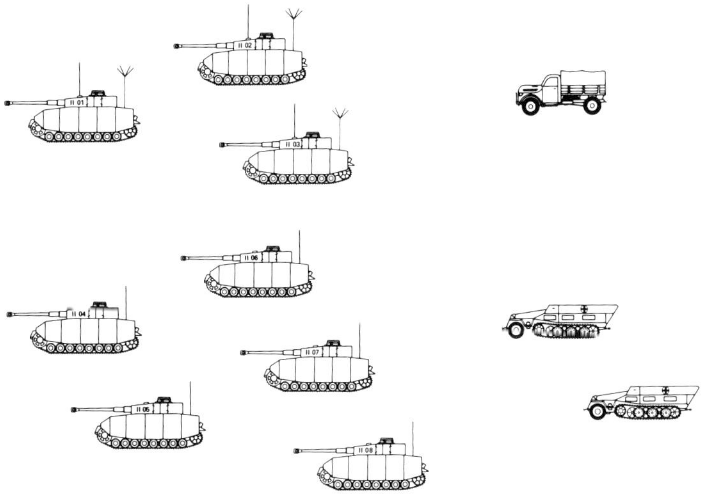

c)

d)

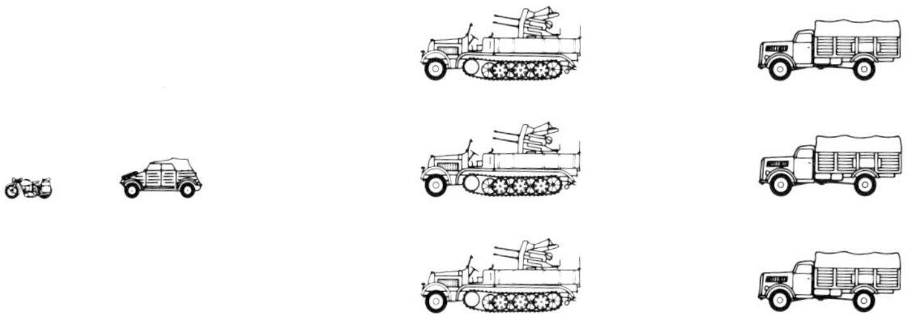

(a) Gruppe Führer (Command Staff); (b) 1. Nachrichten und Aufklärungszug (1st Platoon, Signals and Reconnaissance); (c) 2. Erkunder und Pionierzug (2nd Platoon, Reconnaissance and Engineers); (d) 3. Fliegerabwehrzug (3rd Platoon, Anti-Aircraft).

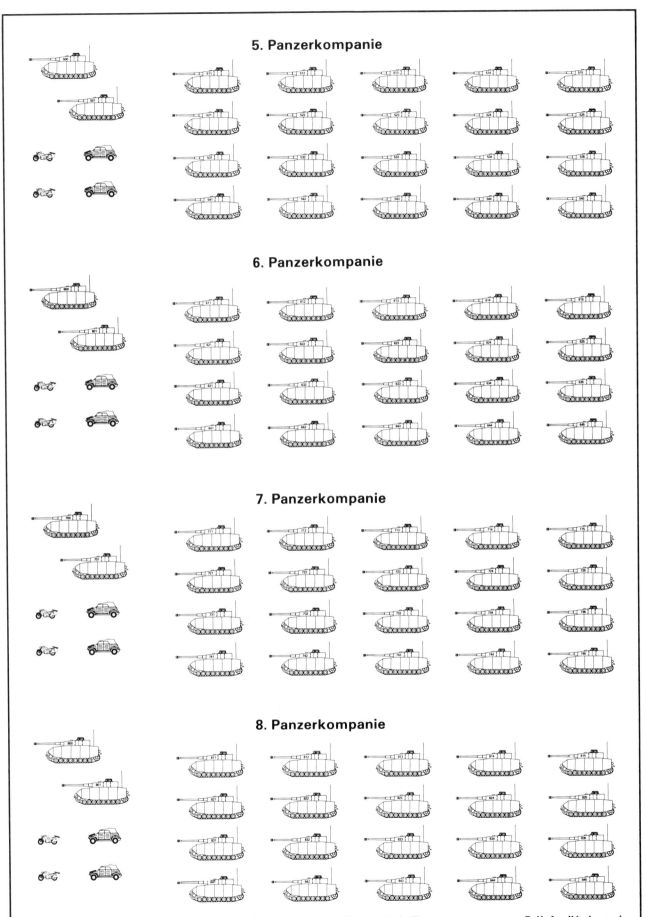

5. Panzerkompanie

6. Panzerkompanie

7. Panzerkompanie

8. Panzerkompanie

5., 6., 7. und 8. Panzerkompanie (5th, 6th, 7th and 8th Tank Companies). There are twenty-two PzKpfw IVs in each company — two with the Gruppe Führer (Command Staff) and five with each of the 1. Zug (1st Platoon), 2. Zug (2nd Platoon), 3. Zug (3rd Platoon) and 4. Zug (4th Platoon).

Versorgungskompanie (Supply Company) I. Abteilung

a)

b)

c)

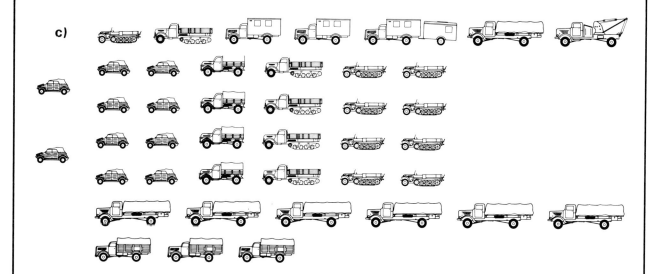

d)

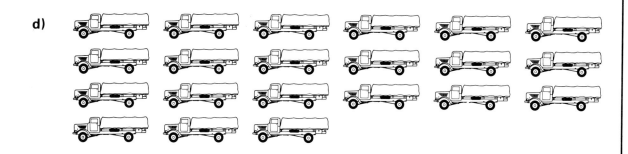

e)

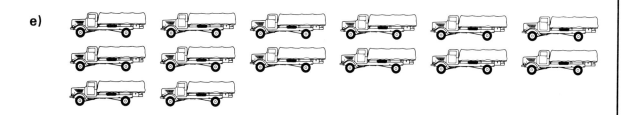

f)

Versorgungskompanie-Panzerabteilung 'Panther' (Supply Company for a Panther battalion): (a) Gruppe Führer (Command Staff); (b) Sanitätsstaffel (Medical Echelon); (c) Instandsetzungsdienst (Maintenance Service) with four squads for vehicle maintenance, one for spare parts and one for radios and weapons maintenance; (d) Betriebsstoffstaffel (Fuel Echelon); (e) Munitionsstaffel (Ammunition Echelon); (f) Verwaltungsstaffel (Administrative Echelon).

Versorgungskompanie (Supply Company) II. Abteilung

a)

b)

c)

d)

e)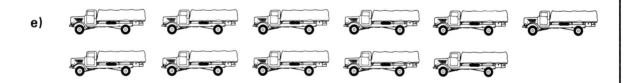

f)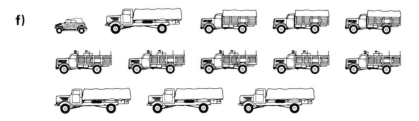

Versorgungskompanie-Panzerabteilung IV (Supply Company for a PzKpfw IV battalion): (a) Gruppe Führer (Command Staff); (b) Sanitätsstaffel (Medical Echelon); (c) Instandsetzungsdienst (Maintenance Service) with four squads for vehicle maintenance and one for radio and weapons maintenance; (d) Betriebsstoffstaffel (Fuel Echelon); (e) Munitionsstaffel (Ammunition Echelon); (f) Verwaltungsstaffel (Administrative Echelon).

Werkstattkompanie (Workshop Company)

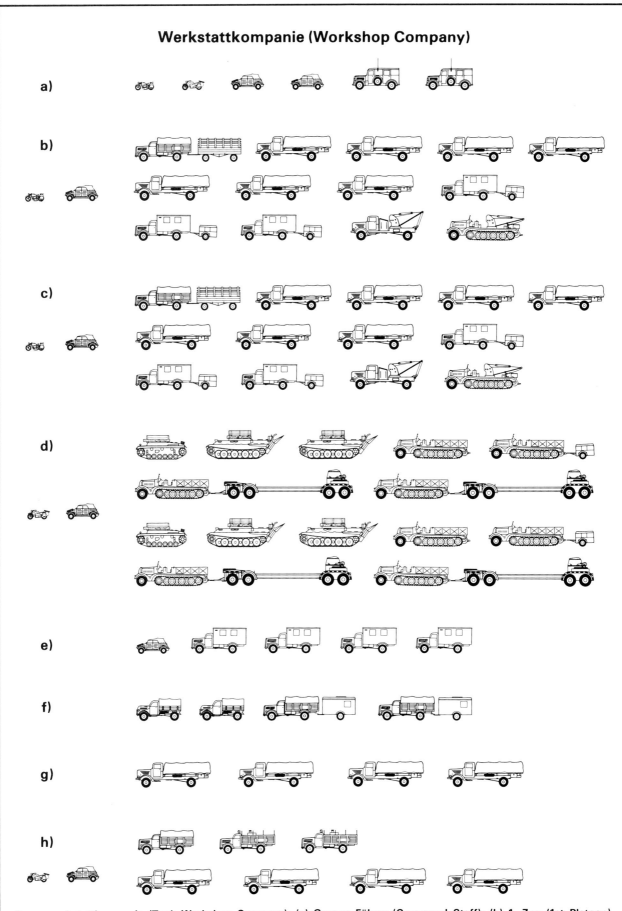

Panzerwerkstattkompanie (Tank Workshop Company): (a) Gruppe Führer (Command Staff); (b) 1. Zug (1st Platoon), (c) 2. Zug (2nd Platoon); (d) 3. Zug-Bergezug (3rd Platoon — Recovery Platoon); (e) Waffenmeisterei (Armoury); (f) Werkstatt für Nachrichtengerät (Signals Workshop); (g) Ersatzteilgruppe (Spare Parts Squad); (h) Tross (Transport column).

THEORETICAL TOP LINE STRENGTH BASED ON PANZER REGIMENT '44'

PERSONNEL

Panzer-Regiment	Officers	Beamt	NCOs	Troops	Hiwi	Total
Panzer-Regiment (Staff plus AA platoon)	8	–	63	97	8	176
I. Abteilung (Staff)	7	–	41	111		159
Panzerkompanie (Four companies, each having 17 tanks)	12	–	228	172	–	412
Versorgungskompanie (for a Panther battalion)	5	2	59	188	23	277
II. Abteilung (Staff)	7	–	41	111	–	159
Panzerkompanie (Four companies, each having 22 tanks)	12	–	264	196	–	472
Versorgungskompanie (for a PzKpfw IV battalion)	5	2	51	103	20	181
Panzerwerkstattkompanie	3	3	39	164	21	230
Total Panzer-Regiment	59	7	786	1,142	72	2,066

Panzer-Division	Officers	Beamt	NCOs	Troops	Hiwi	Total
Panzer-Regiment (Tank Regiment)	59	7	786	1,142	72	2,066
Panzergrenadier-Regiment (gp.) (Armoured Infantry Regiment)	56	7	428	1,726	70	2,287
Panzergrenadier-Regiment (Motorised Infantry Regiment)	54	6	383	1,716	60	2,219
Panzer-Aufklärungs-Abteilung (Reconnaissance battalion)	24	3	222	668	28	945
Panzer-Jäger-Abteilung (Tank destroyer battalion)	17	3	145	289	21	475
Panzer-Artillerie-Regiment (Artillery Regiment)	56	11	349	972	63	1,451
Flak-Artillerie-Abteilung (Anti-Aircraft battalion)	18	3	131	453	30	635
Panzer-Pionier-Bataillon (Engineers battalion)	19	5	120	698	32	874
All other sub-units (signals, medical, administrative, replacement echelon, etc.)	105	39	618	2,735	338	3,835
Total Panzer-Division	408	84	3,182	10,399	714	14,787

EQUIPMENT

	Tanks	Panzer-Jägers	Armoured Cars	Armoured Personnel Carriers	AA Guns SP/mounted/towed	Mounted Guns 20/75mm	Artillery Guns SP/towed	Towed Anti-tank Guns	Motor-Cycles	Cars	Trucks	Half-track Prime Movers	Other Vehicles
Panzer-Regt. (total)	151 plus 9 Bef.	–	–	10	14/–/–	–/–	–/–	–	57	70	187	27	39
Panzer-Division (total)	151 plus 11 Bef.	21	35	287	21/32/55	29/25	30/25	13	468	641	1,443	121	389

Beamt: An official or administrator with no precise equivalent in Allied combat units. Almost a civil servant.

Hiwi: Hilfswillige (Russian auxiliary in the German army). Note in the Panzer-Regiment how the Hiwis appeared only in the support units, not in combat units.

Bef.: Befehlspanzer (command tank).

Artillery guns: Twelve self-propelled Infanterie-Geschütz (infantry guns) are included in total of 30.

SP: self-propelled, means specialised vehicles, i.e. self-propelled AA guns or self-propelled artillery guns.

Mounted: defines pieces carried by a vehicle (usually by an armoured personnel carrier) which is not its specialised function having often retained its former role.

Towed: indicates these pieces are towed into position by a prime mover.

Other vehicles: These figures include the various vehicles that do not come under other headings i.e. ambulances, half tracked 'Maultier' trucks, specialised artillery vehicles, etc.

PzKpfw IV (SdKfz 161)

Numerically, the PzKpfw IV was the most important German tank of the war and of the fighting in Normandy, where the latest Ausf H and Ausf J were the most common. Among the units in Normandy there were two exceptions to the tank's usual allocation to the II. Abteilung of a panzer regiment: in Panzer Regiment 33, where I. Abteilung was equipped with the PzKpfw IV, and in Panzer Regiment 22, where both I. and II. Abteilung were equipped with it.

On paper, seven of the eleven Abteilung were at normal strength, with 22 tanks per Kompanie; but no more than six Abteilung went into action with a full complement of between 17 and 22 tanks per Kompanie.

From 1934 the Armaments Ministry had been thinking of a medium tank with a 7.5cm gun, and the first design, perfected by Krupp, appeared in 1936 under the codename 'I/BW.' This was the PzKpfw IV Ausf A, which was followed by Ausf B, C and D in small numbers up till 1939.

It was not until after the Polish campaign, at the end of 1939, that the PzKpfw IV made its real debut — with the introduction of the Ausf E. Almost 300 PzKpfw IVs took part in the blitzkreig of 1940 and 280 came off the assembly lines that year, rising to 480 in 1941. At this time it was the Germans' heaviest operational tank but, as yet, it

Previous pages: The crew of this PzKpfw IV stop for a breather en route to the 'Invasionsfront'. The insignia identifies the tank as belonging to the 12. SS-Panzer Division 'Hitlerjugend' which was committed to the battle right from the beginning. (Bundesarchiv) *Top:* Some three months later German forces in Normandy were in retreat. Here a PzKpfw IV of an unknown division has reached Bourgtheroulde, just seven kilometres from the Seine near Rouen (see pages 192-196). (Bundesarchiv) *Above:* On this model, most probably an Ausf H, the side skirts (schürzen) have been lost in battle, so exposing the paired road wheels, four pairs per side. It appears that the crew have replaced the support rail with a length of wood. From the eagle on the driver's cap, it is evident that this tank is from an SS division.

SPECIFICATION

PANZERKAMPFWAGEN IV AUSF H AND J (SdKfz161)

GENERAL
Crew: five
Battle weight: 25 tonnes
Dry weight: 23.5 tonnes
Ground pressure: $0.89g/cm^2$

DIMENSIONS
Overall length: 7.02m
Hull length: 5.90m
Width
   without skirts: 2.88m
   with skirts: 3.33m
Height: 2.68m
Turret ring diameter: 1.65m
Tracks
   length on the ground: 3.52m
   width: 40cm
   links per track: 99
Ground clearance: 40cm

PERFORMANCE
Maximum road speed: 38km/h
Operational Range
   roads
      Ausf H: 210 km
      Ausf J: 320 km
   cross-country
      Ausf H: 130 km
      Ausf J: 210 km
Turning circle: 5.92m
Gradient ability: 30°
Fording depth: 1.20m
Vertical step: 60cm
Trench crossing: 2.20m

ARMOUR
Hull
   nose
      upper: 80mm at 80°
      lower: 80mm at 78°
   sides: 30mm at 90°
   rear: 20mm at 78°
   decking: 15mm
   belly: 10mm
Turret
   front: 50mm at 79°
   sides: 30mm at 64°
   rear: 30mm at 74°
   roof: 16mm
Gun mantlet: 50mm

ENGINE
Make and type: Maybach HL 120 TRM petrol, V12-cylinder, water-cooled.
Bore size: 105 x 115mm
Cubic capacity: 11.867 litres
Compression volume: 6.5:1
Output
   maximum: 300bhp at 3,000rpm
   normal rating: 265bhp at 2,600rpm
Maximum torque: 80m.kg at 2,150rpm
Carburettors (reversed): 2 x Solex 40 JFF II

FUEL CAPACITY:
Ausf H: 470 litres (3 tanks)
Ausf J: 680 litres (4 tanks)

ELECTRICAL SYSTEM
Bosch dynamo, GTLN 600/12-1500, 600 watts
Four 12v batteries, 105Ah

TRANSMISSION
Clutch: triple dry-plate
Gearbox: ZF SSG 77, synchromesh; six forward and one reverse speeds
Final drive: 3.23:1

STEERING
Epicyclic clutch and brake

SUSPENSION
Four pairs of road wheels per side with leaf springs. Front drive sprocket, rear idler wheel and four return rollers.

TURRET TRAVERSE
Ausf H: electric, powered by two-stroke DKW 500cc engine
Ausf J: two-speed handwheel

ARMAMENT
Main: 7.5cm KwK 40 L/48 gun
Sighting telescope
   Ausf H: TZF 5 or 5 f/1
   Ausf J: TZF 5 f/10 or 5 f/2
Effective range
   armour-piercing: 2,286m
   high explosive: 3,200m
Auxiliary armament
   mantlet: coaxial 7.92mm MG 34
   driver's front plate: ball-mounted 7.92mm MG34
   cupola: demountable 7.92mm MG34
Effective range: 1,100m

AMMUNITION STOWAGE
Main: 87 rounds
MG: 3,150 rounds

COMMUNICATIONS
WT set (transmitter/receiver/intercom): Fu 5 and Fu 2.

---

had a 7.5cm gun with a 24-calibre barrel.

The Ausf F of 1941 was produced in collaboration between Krupp and Rheinmetall-Borsig, and possessed a modified suspension and wider tracks. The F2 which followed was, at last, armed with a 43-calibre 7.5cm gun which, in 1942, when it was given a muzzle brake, became the Ausf G (SdKfz 161/1). The armour-plate had

been regularly thickened, and an innovation was the way in which warm water in the cooling system was transferred from one radiatior to another to help in starting the engine.

In June 1942 — when it began to be fitted with a 48-calibre gun and the frontal armour of its hull had been supplemented to 80mm thick — the PzKpfw IV had almost reached its definitive form.

The exhaust identifies this model as a late-type Ausf J. Although not visible on a side plan view, the main difference between the Ausf H and J was that the former had a small auxiliary engine at the rear serving as a generator for the electric turret traverse. (The turret was manually driven on the Ausf J.) The gun is a 7.5cm KwK40 L/48 — 48 standing for the length which was 48 times the calibre, i.e. 48 × 75mm.

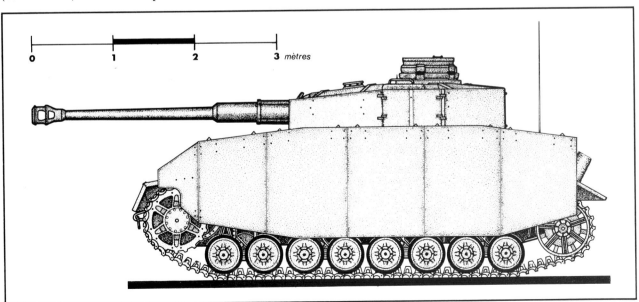

Ausf H (SdKfz 161/2)

1943 was a turning point for the PzKpfw IV, when the backbone of the panzer units, the PzKpfw III, ceased production and it was a question of whether the PzKpfw IV should stop as well. The Tiger was beginning to assert itself and deliveries had started of the Panther.

The proposal to stop producing the PzKpfw IV in favour of the new and larger tanks encountered vehement opposition from several generals, among them the Inspector General of Armoured Troops, Guderian, who maintained that only the PzKpfw IV could be turned out in large numbers. The Tiger was at that time being produced at the rate of just twenty-five a month and the Panther was as yet untested in battle.

The outcome was an order for all-out production of the PzKpfw IV. There were further threats to the tank's existence towards the end of the year when Organisation Todt proposed using the turret for fortification points and another suggestion was that a halt should be called to increase the manufacture of assault guns, but nothing came of this and more than 3,000 were completed by the factories during the year — almost as many as were to be built from then till the end of the war.

Whilst the arguments were being pursued, in March 1943 the Ausf H made its appearance. Mechanically, it differed from previous models by the replacement of the ZF SSG 76 gearbox with the ZF SSG 77 which had earlier been fitted in the PzKpfw III. Externally, the main difference between the

Tankers from an army panzer unit with their Ausf H. The schürzen afforded a measure of protection to the sides of the body and turret. Constructed of 5mm mild steel boiler plate, these skirts would prematurely explode a projectile several inches in front of the armour. The wires have been added for attaching camouflage foliage. The turret machine gun is the 7.92mm MG34. (Bundesarchiv)

Ausf H and the G was the presence of Schürzen — or skirts — on the hull sides, late models of the Ausf G having already been given turret skirts. This soft steel, 5mm-thick armour-plate was intended to explode hollow-charge projectiles prematurely on the outside of the tank itself — between the skirt and the tank — cancelling out the shell's penetrating power. At first the hull plates were fixed soundly onto lengthwise rails; then this was abandoned for slotting them on brackets welded to the rails. This way the plates came away more easily on impact and

with less chance of getting jammed in the tracks and damaging the running wheels.

Observation slits for the loader and aimer at the side of the turret were dispensed with as redundant; the aerial was now fixed on the left at the rear of the hull; a new driving sprocket and idler wheel with 'open' spokes were introduced; 30mm frontal armour-plate was first bolted on but then soon welded on; the driver's and navigator's side observation ports soon disappeared in their turn, and the cupola hatch reverted to a single section.

Schürzen-less, this Ausf H with a broken track was photographed near Caen on July 9 by Sergeant Mapham. (IWM)

Ausf J (SdKfz 161/2)

The last development of the PzKpfw IV — the Ausf J — came out a year later in March 1944. To increase its operational range, the electric turret traversing mechanism was removed and the space saved used for an extra fuel tank. Thereafter the turret was operated by a two-speed handwheel. The external 2-stroke engine that worked the electric generator was also removed — its absence being the clue in identifying the Ausf J.

Possibly some two-thirds of the PzKpfw IV battalions in Normandy were equipped with the Ausf H and the remainder with the Ausf J. There were also around half a dozen ancient Ausf Bs

Left: Abandoned in Putanges, seventeen kilometres south of Falaise, this Ausf H or J is given the once-over by Canadian soldiers on August 20. The hatch on the turret side was used by the loader; a door was provided in the skirt for access. The small sign nailed on the right is that of the 2. SS-Panzer Division Das Reich. (Note the 50th Northumbrian Infantry Division waterpoint arrow on the extreme left.) (IWM) *Above:* M. Grimbert's shoe shop still sports its original inscription 'Cordonnerie'.

or Cs in II. Abteilung of Panzer Regiment 22 which were most likely used for training or as OP tanks but were nonetheless sent into action. Almost certainly, some units must still have possessed a few Ausf Gs; and some Ausf H and Ausf J turrets housed the Ausf G 43-calibre gun which was 38cm shorter

than the 48-calibre. The PzKpfw IV was mechanically well tried and very reliable; it was available in large numbers and had a good operational range — particularly the Ausf J. By this stage of the war, however, its armour was inadequate and its speed was slow in relation to its weight.

The battle is now over for these two PzKpfw IVs pictured near Nécy just east of the Falaise-Argentan road on August 21. They can be identified as Ausf Js by the absence of the auxiliary engine which on previous models was positioned at the rear of the body to the left of the exhaust outlet. See also page 45. (IWM)

PzKpfw V PANTHER (SdKfz 171)

Above: 'Panzer in Marsch von Caen, Juli 1944' reads the original German caption to this shot of a Panther Ausf G. (Bundesarchiv)

Above: It is very unusual to find the factory number stencilled on a Panther. This is a type G. The crew wear the green overalls, originally intended for reconnaissance units, with the black shoulder straps of the Waffen-SS. *Previous pages:* An instant in time frozen on celluloid. Almost like an entry for a photographic competition, an Ausf A thunders down a leafy lane en route to 'Invasionsfront'. (Bundesarchiv)

The Panther was unquestionably the best all round tank the Germans possessed during the last two years of the war — a very happy compromise between the conflicting qualities demanded of a battle tank: powerful armament, thick armour in the appropriate places, relatively high speed, an acceptable operational range, and mechanically dependable — despite suffering considerably from teething troubles.

The I. Abteilung of every panzer regiment was supposed to be equipped with the Panther, but not all were. Among the panzer regiments in Normandy both I. and II. Abteilung of Panzer Regiment 22 were equipped with the PzKpfw IV, and neither Panzer Regiment 16 nor SS-Panzer Regiment 10 possessed Panthers in Normandy. (The I. Abteilung of both regiments were then in the process of being equipped with them.) This meant that the Panther was deployed in only seven of the ten panzer regiments in Normandy and, even then, rarely in the theoretical strength of seventeen per Kompanie, or of twenty-two in June for SS-Panzer Regiment 2, other than in Panzer Regiment 3 and Panzer Lehr Regiment at the onset of the battle.

A common origin could be attributed

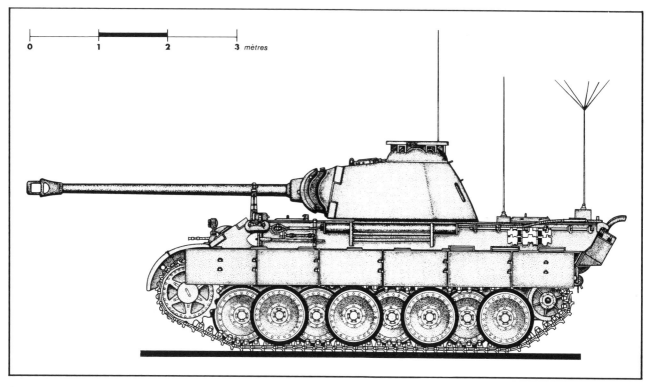

Command version of the Panther, the Befehlspanther (SdKfz 167 or 168). This is an Ausf A.

SPECIFICATION

**PANZERKAMPFWAGEN V PANTHER
AUSF D, A and G (SdKfz 171)**

GENERAL
Crew: five
Battle weight
    Ausf D: 44 tonnes
    Ausf A: 45.5 tonnes
    Ausf G: 44.8 tonnes
Ground pressure: 0.87kg/cm²
Turret weight: 7.5 tonnes

DIMENSIONS
Overall length: 8.86m
Hull length: 6.87m
Width
    without skirts: 3.27m
    with skirts: 3.42m
Height:
    Ausf D: 2.95m
    Ausf A: 3.10m
    Ausf G: 3m
Turret ring diameter: Ausf A: 1.65m
Tracks
    length on the ground: 3.90m
    width: 66cm
    links per track: 86
Ground clearance: 56cm

PERFORMANCE
Maximum road speed: 55km/h
Operational range
    roads
        Ausf D: 169km
        Ausf A and G: approx 200km
    cross country
        Ausf D: 85km
        Ausf A and G: approx 100km
Turning circle: 10m
Gradient ability: 35°
Fording depth: 1.90m
Vertical step: 90cm
Trench crossing: 2.45m

ARMOUR
Type: rolled homogenous plate;
interlocking stepped joints; welded
construction

Hull
    glacis: 80mm at 35°
    nose: 60mm at 55°

sides
    upper
        Ausf D and A: 40mm at 50°
        Ausf G: 50mm at 60°
    lower: 40mm at 90°
    rear: 40mm at 60°

decking
    Ausf D and A: 15mm
    Ausf G: 16mm
belly: 20/13mm

Turret
    front
        Ausf D: 80mm at 80°
        Ausf A: 110mm at 80°
        Ausf G: 100mm at 80°
    sides: 45mm at 65°
    rear: 45mm at 62°
    roof: 15mm

Gun mantlet: 100mm

ENGINE
Make and type: Maybach HL 230 P 30
petrol, V12-cyclinder, water-cooled
Bore size: 130 x 145mm
Cubic capacity: 23.88 litres
Output maximum: 700bhp at 3,000rpm
    normal rating: 600bhp at 2,500rpm
Compression volume: 6.8:1
Carburettors reversed twin: 4 x Solex 52
JFF II D
Fuel capacity: 730 litres (five tanks)

ELECTRICAL SYSTEM
700w dynamo. Two 12v batteries 120 or
150Ah

TRANSMISSION
Clutch: triple dry-plate
Gearbox: ZF AK 7-200, synchromesh;
seven forward and one reverse speeds.

STEERING
Non-continuous regenerative type giving
one radius of turn for each gear engaged.

SUSPENSION
Four pairs of large overlapped and
interleaved road wheels per side,
independently sprung on two torsion bars
connected in series. Small return roller
behind front drive sprocket. Rear idler
wheel.

TURRET TRAVERSE
Hydraulic (pedal operated) and handwheel

ARMAMENT
Main: 7.5cm KwK 42 L/70 gun
Sight telescope:
    Ausf D: TZF 12 binocular
    Ausf A and G: TZF 12a monocular
Auxiliary armament:
    Ausf D: glacis and coaxial, 7.92mm
MG 34
    Ausf A and G: glacis, coaxial and
    cupola (demountable) 7.92mm MG 34

AMMUNITION STOWAGE
Main:
    Ausf D and A: 79 rounds
    Ausf G: 82 rounds
MG:
    Ausf D: 4,104 rounds
    Ausf A and G: 4,200 rounds

COMMUNICATIONS
WT set (transmitter/receiver/intercom).
Fu 5 and Fu 2.

Befehlpanther in action. Theoretically the typical 1944 panzer regiment should have been issued with six of these tanks. Although lacking official confirmation, the '96' may relate to the two-figure numbering system for regimental and command staff introduced in April 1944. This example carries its battle scars: the skirts are torn away, one of the 'Rommelkisten' — the kit lockers at the rear — is missing and the other has lost its lid. The horizontal position for the jack identifies this as an early Ausf A — later it was mounted vertically between the exhausts. (Bundesarchiv)

to the Panther and the Tiger in so far as research projects for a heavy tank undertaken in 1937 by Henschel, Porsche, Daimler-Benz and MAN should have resulted in the Panther rather than in the Tiger. As it was, the concept of the Panther was born in the summer of 1941 when the Germans were confronted by a newcomer on the plains of Russia — the T-34. Urged by Guderian, a commission was sent to the Eastern Front at the end of the year to examine the new Russian tank; after which, Daimler-Benz and MAN were each to undertake the design of an equivalent. A 30-tonne tank was specified, with a 7.5cm gun, a maximum speed of 60km/h and frontal armour of 60 to 100mm thick.

By April 1942, the two projects numbered VK3002 were ready; then another clash developed between Hitler and the Armaments Ministry. For whilst Hitler's intention was to replace the planned 48-calibre gun by one with a larger barrel (and he ordered 200 such tanks from Daimler-Benz) the Armaments Ministry expressed its preference for the MAN design. What particularly worried the Ministry was the new MB 507 diesel engine, which had not undergone trials, intended for the Daimler-Benz tank. Moreover the new gun which Hitler insisted upon would have proved difficult to adapt to its turret, and subsequently the Daimler-Benz project (an almost exact copy of the T-34) was suspended.

Brand-new Panther type G, unit unknown, although the crewman wears an army uniform and the 432 (most probably painted in yellow) identifies it as Tank No. 2 in the 3rd Zug (platoon) of the 4th Kompanie. The stripey camouflage pattern is unusual on a Panther. As well as providing spares, the track wheel and links on the sides of the turret gave additional protection. Below can be seen a coiled towing cable, the tool kit and fire extinguisher. (Bundesarchiv)

Absolute priority was given to the Panther project and at this stage the chief engineer of the Trials and Development Section of the Armaments Ministry took personal charge of the assembly lines at MAN. At the same time Rheinmetall-Borsig were entrusted with the job of perfecting the turret, and the one they decided upon was inspired by a design ordered from them by Henschel — but never built — for the VK 4501 project: the Tiger.

At MAN work went ahead rapidly, so that the prototype was ready in September 1942. In the meantime however, came a change of gun for the Rheinmetall-Borsig turret — from 60 to 70-calibre — and this was followed in June by instructions from Hitler that the frontal armour had to be thickened from 60 to 80mm, both of which resulted in an increase in weight.

During this period work had begun at MAN on the hull for a 35-tonne tank. A great saving in weight was gained from choosing torsion-bar suspension — fifteen times lighter than leaf springs and interchangeable (although the longitudinal placement of the torsion bars meant that escape hatches could not be included in the belly of the tank). The torsion bars and various key components, tracks, wheels, etc., were ordered from other firms. In the end, the prototype greatly exceeded 35-tonnes. The HL 210 engine had to be replaced by a larger bore, 700hp engine — the HL 230 P 30 — and the tank's maximum speed was reduced. MAN also had to develop a new synchronised gearbox, the AK 7-200.

By then, Hitler had increased his demand for 250 Panthers to 600 . . . by the end of May. This was a practical impossibility, and, indeed, to reach the first figure, the Armaments Ministry had to involve Henschel and the firm of MNH from Hanover.

The Ausf D initial production vehicle

Above: **Believed to be from Panzer Lehr Regiment, 'Christel' in the foreground is an Ausf D with an Ausf A turret. (Ullstein)** *Below:* **One of Panzer Lehr's type A Panthers knocked out by an American M-10 tank destroyer in the German counter-attack at le Désert near the Vire-Taute Canal on July 11. (US Army)**

completed at MAN in November 1942 had not received modifications that had been decided upon in the spring. Mass production proper began at MAN and Daimler-Benz in January 1943, when a number of weaknesses rapidly started to show up which were basically due to the increase in weight — ill-fitting tyres on the road wheels, an engine that tended to overheat, with other gearbox and steering deficiencies. The first was got round by provisionally doubling the number of bolts securing the tyres to the rims of the road wheels; the second by modifications to the exhaust outlets, but the gearbox and steering was to remain a weakness in the Panther to the end.

Production at MNH began in February 1943 and at Henschel in March. From February Schürzen skirts were added to the sides of the hull — like those on the PzKpfw IV though somewhat smaller — and by the end of May more than 300 Panthers had been built. Just as in 1942 with the Tiger, the tank experts were again loathe to hurriedly pitch the new tank into battle with its defects not yet ironed out and its crews insufficiently trained. Nevertheless, in July the Panther went into action with 4. Panzer Armee in Operation Zitadelle (the German offensive on the Eastern Front at Kursk) among the elite divisions of the Heer and Waffen SS — including SS Panzer Regiments 1 and 2.

July 19, 1944. US P-47 Thunderbolt pilots have been taken by military police to view two of their victims. Both type As, '215' *above* appears relatively intact. That *below* has been struck by rockets and/or bombs. The rear armour has been pierced and a crater shows where another missile hit the road and blew off the track. A good shot of the engine compartment with the fuel tanks and cooling fans at the sides. (US Army)

The advance continues near Berniers-Bocage beside a disabled Ausf A. (IWM)

The new tank showed itself to be superior to the Russian T-34 but its mechanical weak spots made themselves sorely felt and breakdowns had to be abandoned to the enemy during the German withdrawal. Also the lack of suitable recovery vehicles soon became evident as two 18-tonne half-tracks were required to recover one Panther.

From the end of July production had begun at Daimler-Benz on the new Ausf A. A cupola with episcopes replaced the one with vision slits; hatches for ejecting shell cases and pistol ports for fighting at close quarters were dispensed with; the gunner's binocular sight was replaced by a monocular one (a single aperture at the front to the left of the barrel); the machine gun now had a ball-mounting within a casemate, and the number of bolts on the rims of the road wheels was increased from sixteen to twenty-four. However nothing was done about the gearbox which had been pushed to its limits; beyond, in fact, where engaging first gear was concerned.

The Ausf D continued to come out of the Henschel workshops until November, although a number of tanks were built during this period from components common to both the Ausf A and Ausf D. For 1943, total production of the Ausf D was about 600 and of the Ausf A 1,788.

The third and final Panther, the Ausf G, began to be built at the beginning of 1944. The main external modification was to the upper edges of the hull sides which were extended and had their armour-plate improved to provide increased protection for the fuel tanks. The driver's visor on the glacis plate made way for an episcope; the hatches on the roof of the hull were hinged instead of being a lift-and-swivel arrangement, and idler wheels were newly designed. On the final production versions of the Ausf G the ZF AK 7-200 gearbox was replaced by the ZF AK 7-400.

Towards the middle of 1944, the Panther received a new gun mantlet with a deeper and straighter lower section to prevent shells being deflected onto the less well protected hull roof. By this time production had been speeded up and 3,740 Ausf Gs came out of the combined workshops of MAN, MNH, Daimler-Benz and Demag between the beginning of 1944 and the end of the war.

Although the Ausf D was rarely encountered in Normandy, the Ausf A and Ausf G were deployed in about equal numbers. To summarise, the Panther had the advantages of powerful armament, befitting armour sloped at an angle, relatively high speed and good operational range on the road, though, its road wheels were inadequate in the early days, and there were often problems with its transmission and steering.

During the early days, the Allies recovered German tanks which were little damaged. This type A is almost certainly from I. Abteilung of SS-Panzer Regiment 12. The MG34 has been removed, the driver's porthole opened and his seat raised. (IWM)

PzKpfw VI TIGER AUSF E (SdKfz 181)

By 1944, the Tiger had already become the myth that German propaganda had intended it should become. To Allied soldiers and civilians alike, every German tank at this time became a Tiger on sight — which could possibly be excused due to the slight resemblance in shape between it and the PzKpfw IV. In fact, apart from the handful available with Panzer Kompanie (Fkl) 316 attached to Panzer Lehr Regiment, only the three heavy tank battalions in Normandy — schwere SS-Panzer Abteilung 101 and 102 and schwere Panzer Abteilung 503 had the Tiger (1. Kompanie, schwere Panzer Abteilung 503 having the Königstiger — the 'King' or 'Royal' Tiger). The vast majority of Tigers belonged to the heavy tank battalions, standard Heerestruppen units (Army Troops) allotted in the usual way as required.

In the spring of 1937, when there were only a few dozen PzKpfw IVs in existence, the Armaments Ministry had already asked four firms (Henschel, Porsche, Daimler-Benz and MAN) to develop a heavy tank, but, with the PzKpfw III and IV having come up to expectations, the project was allowed to lapse. Four years later, in the spring of 1941, Hitler, who had been impressed by reports about the armour of the French B-1 bis and British Matilda, once more raised the subject.

In the disagreement that followed between Hitler and the Armaments

Ausf E of the 2. Kompanie of the schwere (heavy) SS-Panzer Abteilung 101 photographed near Villers-Bocage at the time of their commander's famous single-handed battle on June 13. All the crew except for the driver are outside the tank. The unit insignia could be applied to either side of the frontal armour. (Bundesarchiv)

Above: About 50-60 Tiger Is were committed to the Normandy battlefront. This one is from the 3. Kompanie of schwere Panzer Abteilung 101. *Previous pages:* Tank No. 321, the painted number on the turret identifying it as Tank No. 1 of the 2nd platoon of the 3rd company. (Bundesarchiv)

It was absolutely forbidden for the crew of one Tiger to tow another — the engine was simply not designed to take the additional load. The correct procedure was to call up the battalion Berge-panther but as 101 only possessed one of these in Normandy, it is no wonder that short cuts were taken. Picture shows the same tankers of 2. Kompanie *(opposite)* breaking the rules outside Villers-Bocage. (Bundesarchiv)

Ministry over the gun, Hitler favoured an adaptation of the 8.8cm Flak 36 which had shown itself to be a for-midable anti-tank gun in the summer of 1940 whereas the Ministry wanted to install a smaller calibre 6.0cm to 7.0cm gun, which would keep the weight down. To settle the matter, it was decided to go ahead with two projects. Henschel were given responsibility for the Ministry's specification; Porsche for Hitler's. Tur-rets for both were ordered from Krupp.

Because of the lack of tungsten steel for the new gun, the Henschel VK3601 project was scrapped and the firm had to start thinking in terms of a tank weighing the same as the Porsche VK4501, which gave rise to the Henschel VK4501 (H). (VK being an abbreviation of Volkettenfahrzeuge — a fully tracked experimental vehicle — the first two numbers referring to the weight class, and the third and fourth to its prototype requirement.) The hull had to be modified to take the enormous Krupp turret and the tracks widened; and since the VK4501 had been conceived as taking up the full width of a flat-bed railway wagon, the new tank was given two sets of tracks: one for battle and one for transit.

Watched by Hitler, on April 20, 1942 the Henschel and Porsche prototypes both underwent trials at Rastenburg. The Henschel VK4501 (H) proved slightly superior and orders were given to proceed to production, Henschels having, in fact, already completed preparations to build 1,400. From Porsche the new tank inherited the name by which it had officially become known there — the Tiger.

SPECIFICATION

PANZERKAMPFWAGEN VI TIGER AUSF E (SdKfz 181)
Late production model

GENERAL
Crew: five
Battle weight: 57 tonnes approx.
Ground pressure (battle tracks):
1.03kg/cm²

DIMENSIONS
Overall length: 8.45m
Hull length: 6.30m
Width
    without trackguards: 3.56m
    with trackguards: 3.73m
Height: 3.56m approx
Turret ring diameter: 1.79m
Tracks
    length on the ground: 3.61m
    width, battle track: 72.5m
    width, transit track: 52cm
    links per track: 96
Ground clearance: 47cm

PERFORMANCE
Maximum road speed: 38km/h
Operational range
    roads: 195km approx
    cross-country: 110km approx
Turning circle: 7m
Gradient ability: 35°
Fording depth: 170m
Vertical step: 79cm
Trench crossing: 2.50m

ARMOUR
Type: rolled homogenous plate;
interlocking stepped joints; welded
construction
Hull
    nose
        upper: 100mm at 80°
        lower: 100mm at 66°
    sides
        upper: 80mm at 90°
        lower: 60mm at 90°
    rear: 82mm at 82°
    decking: 26mm
    belly: 26mm
Turret
    front: 100mm at 80°
    sides: 80mm at 90°
    roof: 25mm
Gun mantlet: 120mm

ENGINE
Make and type: Maybach HL 230 P45
petrol, V12-cyclinder, water-cooled
Bore size: 130 x 140mm
Cubic capacity: 23.88 litres
Compression volume: 6.8:1
Output
    maximum: 700bhp at 3,000rpm
    normal rating: 600bhp at 2,500rpm
Carburettors reversed twin: 4 x Solex 52
JF II D
Fuel capacity: 540 litres (four tanks)

ELECTRICAL SYSTEM
1,000w dynamo. Two 12v batteries,
150Ah

TRANSMISSION
Gearbox: Maybach Olvar 40 12 16 semi-
automatic, pre-selector; eight forward and
four reverse speeds
Final drive: 10.7:1
Differential: Henschel L 600C fully
regenerative.

STEERING
Regenerative (two radii) controlled
differential and steering wheel controlled
clutches, hydraulic operated. Emergency
steering: by steering levers controlling
disc brakes on each output shaft.

SUSPENSION
Overlapping and interleaved wheels. Eight
independently sprung torsion bar axles on
each side; right-hand axles trailed, left-
hand led forward. Drive sprocket and rear
idler wheel.

TURRET TRAVERSE
Hydraulic (pedal operated) and two-speed
handwheel

ARMAMENT
Main: 8.8cm KwK 36 L/56 gun
Sight Telescope: TZF 9b binocular; later
TZF 9c
Auxiliary armament
    stepped front plate: ball-mounted
    7.92mm MG 34
    mantlet: coaxial 7.92mm MG 34
    cupola: demountable 7.92mm MG 34
    turret roof: grenade projector

AMMUNITION STOWAGE
Main: 92 rounds
MG: 4,500 rounds

COMMUNICATIONS
WT set (transmitter/receiver/intercom):
Fu 5 and/or Fu 2.

Beginning in August 1942, at the rate of 12 per month, production was pushed up to 25 by November. Between that time, at Hitler's insistence and against the advice of his tank experts, who felt that the new tank was not yet fully up to scratch and who wanted to keep it under wraps for the spring offensive of 1943, the first unit to be equipped with the Tiger went into action on the Eastern Front in August 1942. The attack turned out a disaster. Advancing in single file over terrain that was unsuitable for the deployment of heavy tanks, the Tiger's were neutralised by a concentration of well-concealed anti-tank guns firing as if on manoeuvres.

Monthly output continued to increase steadily, reaching a peak of 104 in April 1944, and a final total of 1,355 in August, when production was stopped for the new Königstiger which had started to enter service earlier in the summer — from which point the two Tigers were commonly referred to as the I and II. Meanwhile, on February 27, the Tiger had undergone a change of designation — becoming the PzKpfw Tiger Ausf E.

The Tiger Ausf E encountered in Normandy differed in several respects from the original in that it was no longer submersible in up to thirteen feet of water nor did it have air filters or external grenade launchers. Like the Panther the cupola had five episcopes and a circular rail for an anti-aircraft machine gun. The turret had a ventilator in the centre, an opening at the rear to the right for an anti-personnel grenade launcher (loaded from inside) for defence at close quarters, and an episcope for the loader foward of his hatch.

Unlike previous tanks, in particular the PzKpfw IV, the superstructure was welded and not bolted which gave the entire hull much greater strength. A big innovation were its overlapping road wheels which provided improved weight distribution. The road wheels were dished and their rims were fitted initially with rubber surrounds in the usual way, but problems arose in winter when the ice which inevitably formed with the

A Tiger Ausf E, possibly number 304, (3. Kompanie, schwere SS-Panzer Abteilung 101) on manoeuvres in the spring of 1944 in the fields at the edge of the Fôret de Lyons, east of Rouen. The crossed-keys insignia is that of the I. SS-Panzer Korps — the oak leaves symbolic of the Ritterkreuz (Knight's Cross) awarded its commander, SS-Obergruppenführer Josef 'Sepp' Dietrich. (The 2. Kompanie painted the badge on the right front whereas the 1. and 3. Kompanies carried it on the left.)

mud that accumulated between the rollers simply jammed everything up.

Starting with the 823rd Tiger to be built (chassis no. 250823, the first three figures being standard), the rims of the road wheels no longer had rubber surrounds, the rubber being sandwiched instead between the rim and the hub so that the road wheels still had a certain amount of give to them. This produced savings in rubber through less wear and got round the icing-up problem. On the other hand, the tracks themselves were subject to ten per cent more wear and the din was appalling. The four outside road wheels on either side were eventually eliminated, together with the second set of tracks which had to be taken off each time for transport by rail.

The first 250 Tigers were powered by the HL 210 P 30 used in the Panther Ausf D, which had to be supplanted by the more powerful HL 230 P 45. The steering gear, operated by a steering wheel, was both very complex and very

light and in the hands of inexperienced drivers, accidents tended to mount up.

When it first came out, the Tiger was indisputably the most powerful tank in the world. However, it took twice as long to build as the Panther, at a time when production time had risen to a premium, and three Messerschmitt Bf 109s could have been built for the same amount of money.

The Tiger's fearsome 8.8cm gun (whose panzergranate — or armour-piercing shell — had an initial speed of 810 metres per second) could make light work of the armour of every Allied tank. The tank's frontal protection could not be pierced by the British 6-pdr except at very close range which was unusual in combat. The 17-pdr, on the other hand, was much more effective.

In brief, the Tiger's main qualities were a very powerful gun and very thick armour. Against this should be weighed its delicate steering gear and slow turret traverse.

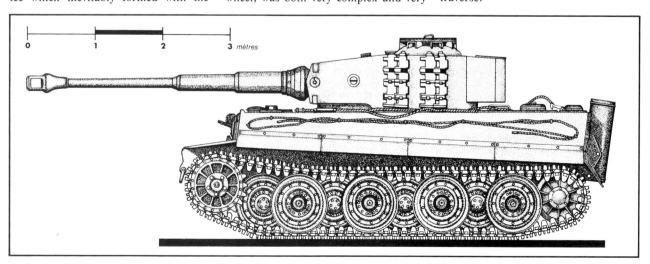

0   1   2   3 *mètres*

Above: The 'Ruckmarsch' to the Seine. Another shot taken of transport piling through Bourgtheroulde during the retreat from Normandy. However, the Tigers, like this one from schwere Panzer Abteilung 503, were unlucky. When they reached the Seine all the bridges were down and there were no rafts large enough to take them across to the northern bank. Below: Four decades later the buildings remain although this breed of tiger is extinct.

PzKpfw VI TIGER AUSF B (SdKfz 182)

Christened the Tiger II, Königstiger or King Tiger by both sides (American literature tends to prefer Royal Tiger), the Tiger Ausf B represented the ultimate in German tanks of the Second World War, having attained what were then the accepted limits in weight and size.

The Tiger Ausf B was still brand new in June 1944, and was present in only one unit during the fighting in Normandy — 1. Kompanie schwere Panzer Abteilung 503. Later, 3. Kompanie was withdrawn to be re-equipped with the Ausf B but did not rejoin the battle. Like the Tiger I, it was allocated to the heavy tank battalions — Heerestruppen (Army

Above and previous pages: **Tiger Ausf Bs, more popularly known as King Tigers, of 3. Kompanie, schwere Panzer Abteilung 503 on the training ground at Mailly-le-Camp in eastern France, north of Troyes. After familiarisation with their new mounts, 3. Kompanie left for Normandy on August 11. The following day their train was set upon by Thunderbolts and most of their Königstigers wrecked. By the time the survivors reached the Seine there was no way across. (Bundesarchiv)**

Troops) units allotted to formations in the normal way according to requirements.

With the original Tiger project proceeding apace, the Armaments Ministry had already began to think along the lines of an even greater development which would surpass in armour and armament the largest Soviet tanks. Porsche and Henschel were once

again approached, and Porsche produced a heavier version of the VK4501 (P) which had previously been turned down in competition with the existing Tiger, the Henschel VK4501 (H). The tank could take either a 37-calibre, 15cm gun or a 70-calibre, 10.5cm gun. Porsche themselves then came up with the VK4502 (P) to take the new 71-calibre, 8.8cm gun. The tank

King Tiger of 1. Kompanie, schwere Panzer Abteilung 503. Like most Tiger IIs in Normandy, it has the Porsche turret. (IWM)

The caption on this print states 'Invasionsfront', which would seem to prove the existence of at least one Henschel-turreted Königstiger in Normandy. The frontal armour is 100mm thick — four inches. Half reassured yet seemingly uneasy, one of the crew points out hits scored by anti-tank rounds. On any other tank, the shell would have gone right through. (Ullstein)

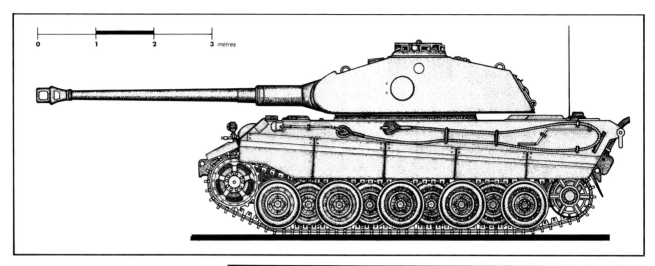

had a redesigned hull and an even larger turret. Its transmission, though, was to have been electric but the shortage of copper ruled this out; not, however, before fifty turrets had already been made.

Having been asked in January 1943, to produce its version of a new heavy tank, Henschel finished work on the VK4503 (H) in October. This was about three months later than anticipated, after the Armaments Ministry had intervened to get features incorporated which would have been standardised with a projected new Panther II. After acceptance, production of the new Tiger began in December — the first fifty hulls being fitted with the ready-built Porsche turret. With possibly one or two exceptions, the twelve Tiger Ausf Bs that fought in Normandy were this version. Henschel's own turret, fitted to the remaining 427, had room for an additional twelve shells.

The new Tiger possessed the same good points and the same defects as the old, but in greater measure. Its armour was even thicker and set at an angle like the Panther, which made it practically invulnerable in normal battle conditions. Its long, 71-calibre, 8.8cm gun was even more deadly, and was considered capable of penetrating armour 20cm thick at 1,000 metres. On the other hand, although it weighed 13 tonnes more than the Tiger Ausf E, the Ausf B was fitted with the same engine as the Panther. Steering and transmission were the same as its predecessor, and had become still more delicate. The engine wore out more quickly and the weight of the gun was poorly counterbalanced with the turret.

The first Königstigers went into action on the Eastern Front in May 1944. Built rather like a mobile bunker, the tank should have felt quite at home in the defensive fighting in Normandy, but the limited numbers engaged do not really allow a proper judgement to be made.

Good points: very powerful main armament, very thick armour. Defects: limited operational range because of high fuel consumption, delicate steering, and too slow a turret movement.

SPECIFICATION

PANZERKAMPFWAGEN VI TIGER AUSF B (SdKfz 182)

GENERAL
Crew: five
Battle weight: 68 tonnes approx
Ground pressure: 1.03kg/cm²

DIMENSIONS
Overall length: 10.28m
Hull length: 7.26m
Width
    without trackguards: 3.62m
    with trackguards: 3.75m
Height: 3.07m
Tracks:
    length on the ground: 4.13m
    width, battle tracks: 80cm
    width, transit tracks: 66cm
    links per track: 92
Ground clearance: 48.5cm

PERFORMANCE
Maximum road speed: 41.5km/h
Operational range
    roads: 170km
    cross-country: 120km
Turning circle: 5m
Gradient ability: 35°
Fording depth: 1.75m
Vertical step: 85cm
Trench crossing (straight sides): 2.50m

ARMOUR
Hull
    glacis: 150mm at 50°
    nose: 100mm at 50°
    sides
        upper: 80mm at 20°
        lower: 80mm at 90°
    rear: 80mm at 25°
    decking: 40mm
    belly: 25/40mm
Turret
    front: 180mm at 80°
    sides
        Porsche: 80mm at 80°
        Henschel: 80mm at 69°
    rear
        Porsche: 80mm at 60°
        Henschel: 80mm at 70°
    roof
        Porsche: 40mm
        Henschel: 44mm
Gun mantlet
    Porsche: 100mm
    Henschel: 80mm

ENGINE
Make and type: Maybach HL 230 P 30 petrol, V12-cylinder, water-cooled
Bore size: 130 x 145mm
Cubic capacity: 23.88 litres
Compression volume: 6.8:1
Output
    maximum: 700bhp at 3,000rpm
    normal rating: 600bhp at 2,500rpm
Carburettors (reversed twin) 4 x Solex 52 JF II D
Fuel capacity: 860 litres (seven tanks)

ELECTRICAL SYSTEM
1,000w dynamo. Two 12v batteries, 150Ah

TRANSMISSION
Gearbox: Maybach Olvar 40 12 16 B semi-automatic, pre-selector; eight forward and four reverse speeds
Final drive: 10.7:1
Differential: Henschel L 600 C, regenerative controlled

STEERING
Henschel L801 giving two radii of turn in each gear (steering wheel acting hydraulically on differential gearbox). Emergency steering: disc brakes hydraulically operated by steering levers and acting in each output shaft.

SUSPENSION
Torsion bar, with overlapped resilient steel disc wheels; nine axles per side. Internal shock absorbers on outer (1st and 9th axles).

TURRET TRAVERSE
Hydraulic (pedal operated) and handwheel

ARMAMENT
Main: 8.8cm KwK 43 L/71 gun
Sight telescope:
    Porsche: TZF 9b1
    Henschel: TZF 9d
Auxiliary armament
    turret front: coaxial 7.92mm MG 34
    glacis: ball-mounted 7.92mm MG 34
    cupola: demountable 7.92mm MG 34
    turret roof: grenade projector

AMMUNITION STOWAGE
Main:
    with Porsche turret: 72 rounds
    with Henschel turret: 84 rounds
MG: 5,850 rounds

COMMUNICATIONS
WT set (transmitter/receiver/intercom): Fu 5 and/or Fu 2

STURMGESCHÜTZ

T/3 Victor J. Porier examines a rare StuG IV near Périers on July 24, most probably belonging to 2. SS-Panzer Division or possibly to 17. SS-Panzer Grenadier Division. (US Signal Corps)

When the battle began, the Sturmgeschütz (or StuG) III assault gun, or more rarely the StuG IV, were standing in for the PzKpfw IV in 5. and 6. Kompanie of SS-Panzer Regiment 2, and in 7. and 8. Kompanie SS-Panzer Regiment 9 and SS-Panzer Regiment 10. These units were mostly equipped with the 7.5cm Sturmgeschütz 40 Ausf G (SdKfz 142/1. The StuG equipped, too, either partly or entirely, the tank destroyer battalions of the panzer divisions. In Normandy the SS-Sturmgeschütz Abteilung 1 of the 1. SS-Panzer Division and the SS-Sturmgeschütz Abteilung 2 of the 2. SS-Panzer Division were equipped entirely with StuG, while all the other divisions (except 9. SS-Panzer Division and 10. SS-Panzer Division which did not have their tank destroyer battalions available in Normandy) had some to supplement the obsolete Marder and the still rarer Jagdpanzer IV.

The main role for the StuG was to equip the Sturmgeschütz Brigades. Although most of these were located on the Eastern Front some were stationed in France, such as Sturmgeschütz Brigade 341 and Sturmgeschütz Brigade 394, and may have been involved in the latter day Normandy battles.

The StuG originated with infantry

demands for an armoured vehicle that could serve as both an infantry artillery support weapon and an anti-tank gun. As the war progressed, however, the StuG was also sometimes used to make up deficiencies in the panzer regiments in addition to generally equipping the tank battalions of panzergrenadier divisions. Basically a turretless tank mounting a limited traverse gun in a

squat superstructure, the early models were built by Daimler-Benz and armed with the short 24-calibre, 7.5cm tank gun supplied by Krupp that was fitted in the PzKpfw IV. Thirty were ordered for troop trials, and a few of these took part in the invasion of France in 1940. Originally allocated to the artillery, it was not until the end of 1943 that assault gun units came under panzer command.

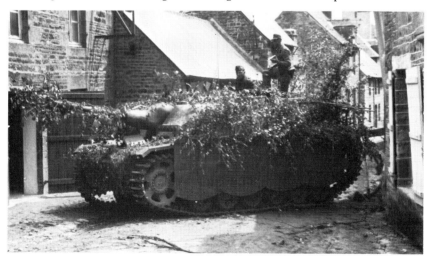

A StuG III of a Panzerjäger battalion of an army panzer division. Note the peculiar scolloped skirts of this Ausf G. (Bundesarchiv)

As a result of Hitler's demands in September 1941 for better anti-tank armament, regardless of weight and speed, by the spring of 1942 the Ausf F was produced with the 43-calibre 7.5cm gun which was then being fitted in the PzKpfw IV. No more than 120 of this model had been built before its L/43 gun was replaced by the StuK L/48 (the equivalent of the KwK L/48 in the PzKpw IV). Designated the Ausf G, this model remained in production — with modifications — until the end of the war.

In 1943 Schürzen were fitted plus a machine gun on the roof. From the end of the year considerably thicker armour included 15cm-thick concrete on the front of the superstructure, and a cast Saukopf mantlet replaced the bolted box version.

When production of the PzKpfw III was halted in August 1943, the chassis continued to be built solely for the StuG III; later models being based on the chassis of the Ausf J, L and M. About 9,000 of the various versions of the StuG Ausf G were built; more than any other German self-propelled gun. Compared with the PzKpfw IV the StuG III Ausf G was armed with the same long-barrelled gun, had armour of a similar thickness and a lower profile. Like all SPGs it was at a disadvantage in not having a manoeuverable turret, though in a defensive role this was less of a handicap.

Pfc. Jim Richie, Pvt. Carmine Calvanico and Staff Sergeant Howard Strella examine another StuG IV near Marigny, five miles south-east of Périers, on July 29. (US Army)

SPECIFICATION

7.5cm STURMGESCHUTZ 40 AUSF G (SdKfz 142/1)

GENERAL
Crew: four
Battle weight: 23.9 tonnes
Dry weight: 21.9 tonnes
Ground pressure: 1.04kg/cm²

DIMENSIONS
Overall length: 6.77m
Hull length: 5.95m
Width
    without skirts: 2.95m
    with skirts: 3.41m
Height: 2.16m
Tracks
    length on the ground: 2.86m
    width: 40cm
    links per track: 93
Ground clearance: 39cm

PERFORMANCE
Maximum road speed: 40km/h
Operational range
    roads: 155km
    cross-country: 95km
Turning circle: 5.85m
Gradient ability: 30°
Fording depth: 80cm
Vertical step: 60cm
Trench crossing: 2.3m

ARMOUR
Hull
    nose:
        50 + 30mm
        or 80mm at 21°
    sides: 30mm at 90°
Superstructure
    front:
        50 + 30mm
        or 80mm at 10°
    rear: 30mm at 0°

ENGINE
Make and type: Maybach HL 120 TRM petrol, V12-cyclinder, water-cooled
Bore size: 105mm x 115mm
Cubic capacity: 11.867 litres
Compression volume: 6.5:1
Output:
    normal: 265bhp at 2,600rpm
    maximum: 300bhp at 3,000rpm
Maximum torque: 80m.kg at 2,150rpm
Carburettors (reversed): 2 x Solex 40 JFF II

ELECTRICAL SYSTEM
Bosch dynamo, GTLN 600/12-1500, 600w. Four 12v batteries, 105Ah

TRANSMISSION
Clutch: triple dry-plate
Gearbox: ZF SSG 77, synchromesh; six forward and one reverse speeds

STEERING
Hydraulically operated epicylcic clutch and brake

SUSPENSION
Six independently sprung, paired road wheels per side, mounted on transverse torsion bars; shock absorbers front and rear. Front driving sprocket; rear idler wheels; three return rollers per side.

ARMAMENT
Main: 7.5cm StuK 40 L/48 gun
Sight telescope: SflZFla/Rb1f36
Auxiliary: 7.92mm MG 34 or MG 42

AMMUNITION STOWAGE
Main: 54 rounds
MG: 600 rounds

COMMUNICATIONS
Fu 15 and Fu 16

Above: On August 21 the Falaise pocket was finally closed. All roads leading towards the Seine were strewn with equipment of every description shot up by Allied fighter-bombers. This StuG III Ausf G on the back road near Nécy has been ripped apart by an internal explosion. (IWM) *Below:* Today the railway on the embankment still runs from Argentan to Caen.

JAGDPANZER IV

A well-camouflaged Jagdpanzer IV provides useful transport for what seems to be a crew of another tank destroyer. Note that one schürzen is missing. (Bundesarchiv)

The Jagdpanzer IV was developed as an improved version of the StuG which it was intended to eventually replace. A soft steel model was shown to Hitler in October 1943 and Vomag started producing the Jagdpanzer by the end of the year. As the name implies, the Jagdpanzer IV was based on the chassis of the PzKpfw IV of which it retained the suspension and drive train. However, the front hull had been modified by replacing the vertical front plate with a double-plate, sharp-nosed front. The armour thickness of the front was 60mm (increased to 80mm in May 1944), the thickness of the sides was 30mm (increased to 40mm in May) with 20mm at the rear.

With a very low silhouette, good mobility, and the hard-hitting 75mm L/48 PaK 39 (later replaced by the even more powerful 75mm L/70 KwK 42), the Jagdpanzer IV was a very efficient design as a tank destroyer. It started entering service at the beginning of 1944, gradually replacing the Marder in the tank destroyer battalions of the panzer divisions. It was still a rare machine in Normandy where the battalions equipped with it had only an average of a dozen available. Among the panzer divisions engaged in Normandy, the following had their tank destroyer battalions at least partly equipped with the Jagdpanzer IV: Panzerjäger Lehr Abteilung 130 (Panzer Lehr Division), Panzerjäger Abteilung 228 (116. Panzer Division), Panzerjäger Abteilung 38 (2. Panzer Division), Panzerjäger Abteilung 50 (9. Panzer Division), and SS-Panzerjäger Abteilung 12 (in fact still named SS-Sturmgeschütz Abteilung 12 at this date) of the 12. SS-Panzer Division.

Just one of the sixty-odd Jagdpanzer IV in Normandy — this one belonging to the Panzerjäger Abteilung 228 of the 116. Panzer Division. (Bundesarchiv)

JAGDPANTHER

Taken at Mailly-le-Camp, this Jagdpanther of the schwere Panzerjäger Abteilung 654 could well be one of the fifteen which saw action in Normandy. (Bundesarchiv)

By October 1942 an order had been issued to develop a heavy assault gun by mounting the potent 88mm L/71 PaK 43 on the Panther chassis. The prototype was shown to Hitler on December 16, 1943, and production started in January 1944. The suspension was the same as that on the Panther, but the drive train was improved by the installation of a new transmission. The fighting compartment was built by extending the hull and side plates of the normal Panther chassis. The armour thickness of the front plate was 80mm and the side plates 60mm. The gun mantlet was the by now well established Saukopfblende. Early production vehicles had the gun mount welded to the superstructure front plate but later models had a new gun mount bolted to the front plate. The perform-

ance of the Jagdpanther was to prove quite in accord with its purposeful design.

The Jagdpanther was a rare machine in Normandy, as only one unit equipped with it was engaged in France, the schwere Panzerjäger Abteilung 654, and only one partly-equipped company of that unit seems to have ever participated in the battle.

MOBILE FLAK

A Flak 38 20mm anti-aircraft gun on a one-tonne halftrack (SdKfz 10/4). It is interesting to see that the crew's helmets have been camouflage painted at the same time as the vehicle. Their rifles are stored in the boxes on the wings. (Bundesarchiv)

By 1943, as Allied air superiority grew steadily greater, a reappraisal of the panzer divisions' air defences had become vitally necessary. Up till then panzer units were equipped with single and quadruple 20mm and single 37mm flak guns mounted on a number of half-tracked vehicles, of which the most widespread was the 1-ton light-duty SdKfz 10/4 mounting a single 20mm Flak 30. The second most widespread was the 8-ton medium-duty SdKfz 7/1 which mounted a quadruple 20mm Flakvierling 38; three per battalion being allowed for on the strength of a 1944 panzer regiment. It would seem that at least half the battalions of the following units were equipped with these two vehicles: schwere Panzer Abteilung 503, schwere SS-Panzer Abteilung 101 and 102; Panzer Regiments 3, 22 and Panzer Lehr; and SS-Panzer Regiments 2, 9, 10 and 12.

The initial response to providing panzer units with an anti-aircraft weapon on a fully tracked chassis was the Flakpanzer 38(t). This was designed around the chassis of the Czech CKD TNHP tank which had been taken into service by the Germans as the PzKpfw 38(t); 1,411 of these tanks having been built between 1940 and 1942 by CKD, as Böhmisch-Mährische AG from 1940. The first Flakpanzer 38(t) was delivered in November 1943, and 140 were built before production ceased in February 1944.

An eight-tonne Zugmaschine with 20mm quadruple Flak (SdKfz 7/1), ex-SS-Panzer Regiment 2, in American hands. The 'Kampfrune' of 'Das Reich' Division appears on the rear left-hand side of the vehicle beside a tactical symbol. The mesh sides are folded out when the gun is in action as shown on page 49. (IWM)

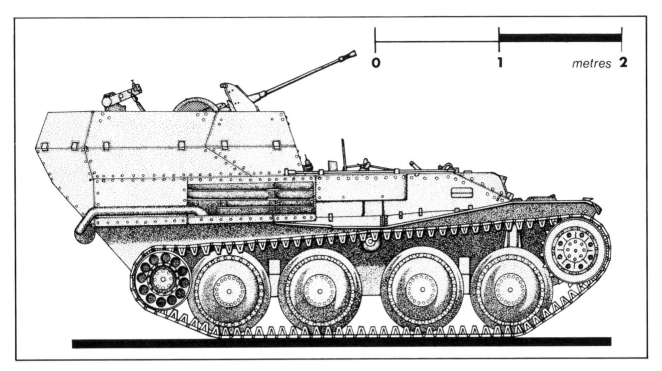

Flakpanzer 38(t) Ausf M mounting the 20mm cannon.

Despite its light armour, the chassis was both rugged and reliable, with excellent cross-country performance. Mounting the already inadequate 20mm single Flak 38 (which had an increased rate of fire compared to the Flak 30) the open-top compartment was thinly armoured and had sides which could be folded outwards in action. In Normandy the Flakpanzer 38(t) was in service instead of the intended Flakpanzer IV with Panzer Regiments 3, 33 and Panzer Lehr, and with SS-Panzer Regiment 1.

The Flakpanzer IV consisted of a 37mm Flakzwilling 43 on the chassis of a PzKpfw IV, and was adopted by Hitler in September 1943 as a result of Guderian's continued demands for an adequately armed and armoured anti-aircraft vehicle. Although the speed at which development work progressed in

Flakpanzer 38(t) of an anti-aircraft platoon of SS-Panzer Regiment 12. (Bundesarchiv).

SPECIFICATION

FLAKPANZER 38(t) AUSF M (SdKfz 140)

GENERAL:
Crew: five
Battle weight: 9.8 tonnes
Ground pressure: 0.57kg/cm²

DIMENSIONS
Overall length: 4.61m
Width: 2.13m
Height: 2.25m
Tracks
    length on the ground: 2.92m
    width: 29.3cm
    links per track: 93
Ground clearance: 38cm

PERFORMANCE
Maximum speed
    roads: 42km/h
Operational range
    roads: 185km
    cross-country: 140km

Turning circle: 5m
Gradient ability: 29°
Fording depth: 90cm
Vertical step: 1.80m

ARMOUR
From 10 to 55mm

ENGINE
Make and type: Praga AC petrol, 6-cylinder, water-cooled
Bore size: 110 × 136mm
Cubic Capacity: 7.75 litres
Compression volume: 7:1
Maximum output: 150bhp at 2,600rpm
Maximum torque: 48m.kg at 2,000rpm
Carburettors: 2 x Solex 46 FNVP

ELECTRICAL SYSTEM
12v battery

TRANSMISSION
Gearbox: Praga-Wilson TN-100 epicyclic pre-selector; five forward and one reverse speeds

STEERING
Praga-Wilson epicyclic clutch and brake

SUSPENSION
Four paired wheels per side, each wheel mounted on a cranked stub-axle and each pair controlled by a semi-elliptic spring freely pivoted. Two return rollers.

ARMAMENT
2cm FlaK 38 L/65 gun
Maximum rate of fire: 480 rounds per min.
Range
    normal: 2,200m
    maximum: 4,800m

AMMUNITION STOWAGE
1,080 rounds

COMMUNICATIONS
Fu 5 transmitter/USW receiver

mating gun and chassis incurred Hitler's displeasure, 150 were ordered from Böhmisch-Mährische Maschinenfabrik of Prague, whilst two further options mounting a quadruple 20mm Flakvierling 38 or single 37mm Flak 43 were developed in the interim.

The chassis was an unmodified PzKpfw IV Ausf H or J; maximum power from the Maybach HL 120 TRM/112 engine being 272bhp at

An SdKfz 7/1 engages a ground target with its quadruple 20mm. (ECP Armées)

2,800rpm. On the move the gun and its crew were protected by four hinged 10mm armoured plates which had to be dropped down to give all-round traverse — and even less protection to the gun crew behind the gun shield. Because of the vehicle's shape with the sides up, and their height (3.10 metres), the Flakpanzer IV was very soon nicknamed the

'Möbelwagen', or furniture van. A total of 240 were produced from March 1944 to March 1945.

Eight Flakpanzer IV 37mm Flak 43 Möbelwagens were allowed for in the anti-aircraft section of a 1944 panzer regiment's headquarters company. On paper, Flak 43 or Flakzwilling 43 Möbelwagens were belatedly allocated to

SPECIFICATION

FLAKPANZER IV

MÖBELWAGEN
Crew: five
Battle weight: 24 tonnes
Ground pressure: 0.89kg/cm²

DIMENSIONS
Overall length: 4.61m
Width: 2.88m
Height: 2.70m

PERFORMANCE
Maximum speed
    roads: 38km/h
Operational range
    roads: 200km
    cross-country: 130km
Turning circle: 5.92m
Gradient ability: 30°
Fording depth: 1.20m
Vertical step: 60cm
Trench crossing: 2.20m

ARMOUR
From 20 to 80mm

ENGINE
Make and type: Maybach HL 120 TRM petrol, V12-cylinder, water-cooled.
Bore size: 105 x 115mm
Cubic capacity: 11,867 litres
Compression volume: 6.5:1
Output
    maximum: 300bhp at 3,000rpm
    normal rating: 265bhp at 2,600rpm
Maximum torque: 80m.kg at 2,150rpm
Carburettors (reversed): 2 x Solex 40 JFF II

ELECTRICAL SYSTEM
Bosch dynamo, GTLN 600/12-1500, 600 watts
Four 12v batteries, 105Ah

TRANSMISSION
Clutch: triple dry-plate
Gearbox: ZF SSG 77, synchromesh; six forward and one reverse speeds
Final drive: 3.23:1

STEERING
Epicyclic clutch and brake

SUSPENSION
Four pairs of road wheels per side with leaf springs. Front drive sprocket, rear idler wheel and four return rollers.

ARMAMENT
3.7cm Flak 43 gun. Some prototypes with 2cm Flakvierling 38

AMMUNITION STORAGE
416 rounds

COMMUNICATIONS
WT set (transmitter/receiver/intercom): Fu 5 and Fu 2.

SS-Panzer Regiment 12 in July 1944, and possibly Panzer Regiment 16.

A new Flakpanzer IV, the Wirbelwind (Whirlwind) appeared in December 1943. This mounted a quadruple 20mm Flakvierling 38 within an open-top revolving turret with 16mm armour, and saw action in very limited numbers in Normandy. Built at the Ostbau Works in Silesia, production ran to some 87.

Above: **Flakpanzer IV Möbelwagen with the 37mm Flak 43 at an unidentified location on the Western Front. (Bundesarchiv)** *Below:* **Another abandoned in September 1944. (US Army)**

RECOVERY VEHICLES

The schwerer Zugkraftwagen 18t or heavy 18-tonne recovery vehicle, SdKfz 9. Although a bulky and powerful prime mover, three of them were required to tow a Tiger! (IWM)

For the most part, the standard tank recovery vehicle remained the heavy-duty 18-ton prime-mover (Zugkraftwagen). The heaviest of the half-tracks, two at least were required for towing a Panther and three for a Tiger. About 2,500 were built by the firm of Famo at Breslau and Warsaw between 1938 and 1944.

Nominally, provision was made in a 1944 tank regiment for two Bergepanzer III recovery tanks and four 35-ton Bergeschlepper towing tanks (probably an early designation for the Bergepanthers). The Bergepanzer III, based on the PzKpfw III Ausf M, N and J, was nevertheless something of a rarity — only to be found in Panzer Regiments 3, 16 and 130 and SS-Panzer Regiment 9 in Normandy. Altogether 271 were built by Alkett of Berlin who were responsible for more than half the production of the PzKpfw III.

From January 1944, all PzKpfw IIIs returned for overhaul were to be converted into Bergepanzer; a box top replacing the turret. (Bundesarchiv)

The heavy tank battalions, with their Tigers, normally had Bergepanthers, which were rarer still. There were two in schwere Panzer Abteilung 503 and one in schwere SS-Panzer Abteilung 101 but none in schwere SS-Panzer Abteilung 102. The Bergepanther (SdKfz 179) was produced by Demag to meet the Armaments Ministry's requirement for a heavy-duty recovery vehicle able to cope with the Tiger and Panther. Between 1943 and 1944, 347 were built by Demag and MNH. The vehicle was a conversion of the Panther Ausf D and G, with the turret removed and housing a winch and its motor in a square open-top compartment with mild steel sides which could be extended upwards with wood flaps and had a tarpaulin cover. At the rear was a massive spade anchor, operated by the winch, to hold the vehicle down during the actual recovery operation. For lifting work there was a jib that could be fixed on either side of the hull roof and on the front plate mount. The fuel capacity of the Bergepanther was increased to 1075 litres.

SPECIFICATION

SCHWERER ZUGKRAFTWAGEN 18t (SdKfz 9)

GENERAL
Battle weight: 18 tonnes
Unladen: 15.1 tonnes

DIMENSIONS
Overall length: 8.3m
Width: 2.6m
Height: 2.9m
Tracks
    length on the ground: 2.9m
    width: 44 cm
Ground clearance: 44cm

PERFORMANCE
Maximum road speed: 50km/h
Operational range:
    roads: 260km
    cross-country: 130km
Gradient ability: 24°
Fording depth: 79cm
Engine: Maybach HL 108 TUKRM V12-cylinder developing 230bhp at 2,600rpm
Fuel capacity: 290 litres

The Bergepanther was the largest of the German WWII tank recovery vehicles. A huge spade anchor was fitted to the chassis of a Panther minus turret, and a 40-ton winch was fitted in the former fighting compartment. The winch cable runs between the exhausts. A 1½-ton derrick could be erected with a dismountable jib on both sides. In the picture *above* the derrick is raised on the left-hand side. *Below:* The Bergepanther in action towing a Panther. (IWM/Bundesarchiv)

HALF-TRACKS

The main armoured half-track of the Wehrmacht — the Mittlerer Schützen-panzerwagen, or m.SPW — that became an intrinsic part of a panzer division, evolved with the concept of mobile warfare, and at the end of the war had appeared in no less than twenty-two variants.

During the mid-1930s Hanomag of Hanover was one of the companies involved in developing a 3-ton half-track tractor, and its type HL Kl 6 went into production in 1937 as the SdKfz 11, which continued to be built until the end of 1944. It was clear that such a vehicle could also provide a suitable chassis for an armoured personnel carrier, and all that was needed were some minor modifications to the Hanomag chassis for it to accept the armoured super-structure designed by Büssing-NAG of Berlin-Oberschöneweide. As the

Above: The squeaking clatter of a German half-track is synonymous with the panzers and their blitzkrieg war. The SPW (pronounced in German as 'ess-pay-vay') was produced for a variety of roles — that above, the SdKfz 151/8, being the ambulance version. (Bundesarchiv) *Below:* The timeless stonework of Bourgtheroulde church.

SPECIFICATION

MITTLERER PIONIERPANZERWAGEN AUSF D (SdKfz 251/7)

GENERAL
Battle weight: 8.87 tonnes
(SdKfz 251/8 ambulance: 7.47 tonnes)
Dry weight: 7.4 tonnes

DIMENSIONS
Overall length: 5.98
Width: 2m
Height: 1.75m
Tracks
    length on the ground: 1.8m
    width: 28cm
    links per track
        left: 55
        right: 56
Ground clearance: 32cm

PERFORMANCE
Maximum road speed: 50km/h
Operational range:
    roads: 300km
    cross-country: 150km
Turning circle: 13.5m
Gradient ability: 24°
Fording depth: 50cm
Trench crossing: 2m

ARMOUR
Hull
    nose: 14.5mm at 14°
    sides and rear: 8mm at 35°

ENGINE
Make and type: Maybach HL 42 TUKRM petrol, 6-cylinder, water-cooled
Bore size: 90 x 110mm
Cubic capacity: 4.171
Compression volume: 6.6:1
Maximum output: 100bhp at 3,000rpm

ELECTRICAL SYSTEM
12v battery 75Ah 300w dynamo

TRANSMISSION
Clutch: triple dry-plate
Gearbox: crash gearbox with eight forward and two reverse speeds

STEERING
Angled steering wheel and 'Cletrac' system operating by expanding track brakes mounted on each side of the differential.

SUSPENSION
Front traverse leafspring, two tyres. Rear: three pairs of interleaved road wheels per side suspended by transverse torsion bars, one to each wheel. Front driving sprocket; rear idler wheel.

Above: Another version of the SPW was the SdKfz 251/15 — a specialised vehicle for artillery flash spotting. This one from the 12. SS-Panzer Division Hitlerjugend is being inspected by Generalfeldmarschall Gerd von Rundstedt (saluting with baton), commander of OB West — i.e. the Western Front. On his left is SS-Oberführer (later Brigadeführer) Fritz Witt, divisional commander, and on his right SS-Obergruppenführer 'Sepp' Dietrich, I. SS-Panzer Korps. (Bundesarchiv) *Below:* Allied air supremacy was a vital factor in the success of the Normandy invasion. Blasted and shot up transport lines the roads of north-western France as fighter-bombers range far and wide. Carrouges, August 13, 1944. (US Army)

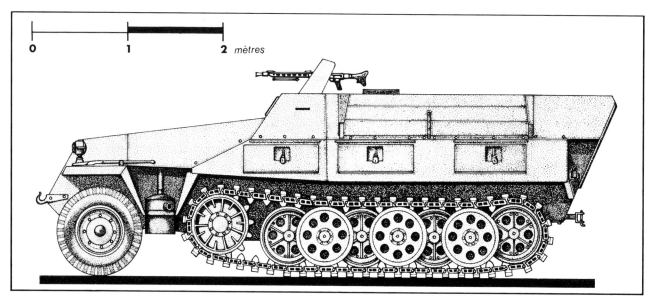

Hanomag type H Kl 6p, the vehicle underwent preliminary trials at the end of 1938 and, under the ordnance number SdKfz 251, was issued to the Heer in the spring of 1939.

Limited numbers saw action in Poland, and by the spring of 1942 (when all panzer divisions were supposedly equipped with SPW battalions) the m.SPW and its smaller counterpart, the le.SPW (le for 'leichter' — light; SdKfz 250), had become invaluable in relation to the continuing effectiveness of the Wehrmacht.

Four basic models were produced: the Ausf A in 1939, Ausf B between 1939 and 1940, Ausf C from 1940 to 1942 and Ausf D from 1943. The all-welded Ausf D, which was designed with the latest mass production methods in mind, had cleaner lines at the front and rear, no air intakes alongside the bonnet, and side lockers incorporated into the super-

structure. During 1944, some 16,000 chassis were built by Skoda, Adler, Auto-Union and other sub-contractors. Given its versatility and the fact that it was in constant demand, the m.SPW nevertheless had its shortcomings. Never-ending modifications of detail brought about a spare parts problem, it was underpowered, and steering across country was tricky because of the driver's limited field of vision.

In a typical 1944 panzer division the bulk of the reconnaissance and engineer battalions and one of the two panzergrenadier regiments were equipped with SPWs — although in reality a regiment could count itself fortunate to have more than one battalion riding in armoured personnel carriers. There were ten in the nominal establishment of a 1944 panzer regiment: five per battalion, comprising three engineer vehicles and two ambulances. Each of the heavy tank

battalions in Normandy had, in theory, eleven.

Of the two versions allocated to a panzer regiment, the Pionier-panzerwagen (SdKfz 251/7) had its upper sides cut away and replaced with wood flaps so that bridging ramps could be carried, and it was also used for transporting inflatable assault craft or demolition equipment and explosives. Armament was provided by two MG 42 machine guns: one mounted behind a shield at the front, the other demountable on a pivot at the rear. The Krankenpanzerwagen (SdKfz 151/8) contained supports for two stretchers, with room for four wounded sitting down. Without stretcher cases, there was room to seat eight wounded. The vehicle was, of course, unarmed and bore large red crosses in white circles on either side.

SdKfz 251/7 carried small assault bridge.

OTHER ARMOURED VEHICLES

Hotchkiss tanks operated in Normandy by Panzer Ersatz und Ausbildings Abteilung 100 and Panzer Abteilung 206.

Production of the PzKpfw III, which had formed the spearhead of the panzer formations in North Africa and Russia, had been halted in August 1943. Command and recovery versions were on the strength of panzer regiments and armoured reconnaissance units in June 1944, and an OP spotter version (Beobachtungspanzer) continued in service with the panzer artillery.

In Normandy there were three PzKpfw III Ausf L or M armed with the L/60 5cm gun in the headquarters company of Panzer Regiment 16 and three in the HQ company of II. Abteilung, plus three in the HQ company of Panzer Regiment 22 and one in I. Abteilung. Another was on the strength of the HQ company of I.

Above: The crew of a Hotchkiss chassis mounting a 7.5cm PaK 40 L/46 is inspected by Generalfeldmarschall Erwin Rommel (extreme left) prior to the invasion. This is a rare vehicle as only 20 or so had been converted. (Bundesarchiv)

Abteilung of SS-Panzer Regiment 9. Among those in the general reserve units, there was one in 2. Kompanie of Panzer Ersatz und Ausbildungs Abteilung 100.

There was usually a command version — Befehlspanzerwagen or Befehlspanzer — of the PzKpfw III, IV, V and VI which differed in its radio equipment with a consequent reduction in the number of rounds it could carry. Variants of the Panther and Tiger were the SdKfz 267 which had the standard Fu 5 wireless/intercom and Fu 8 set which could operate on the main divisional network, and the SdKfz 268 with Fu 5 and Fu 7 sets for ground-air co-ordination, the loader acting as second wireless operator. Two extra aerials were added, one with sprigs. Instead of the normal stowage of 75 rounds a Befehlspanther could accommodate 64; its quota of small arms ammunition increasing to 4,800 rounds for the Ausf A and 5,100 for the Ausf G.

The re-use of captured material was regarded as standard procedure although not necessarily for front line service. After the fall of France in 1940, large numbers of French tanks were taken into German service. From mid-1941, many of these, after some modifications, were issued to German units, being used in Finland, Russia and the Balkans against the partisans. A considerable number of these captured tanks were converted to self-propelled armoured mounts for anti-tank guns of various calibres (Panzerjägers) and for 10.5cm and 15cm field howitzers (Geschützenwagen). These conversions were issued to Panzerjäger and Pan-

About the size of the Bren gun carrier, the Ladungsträger (SdKfz 301) could either be driven by a single crewman or moved under remote-control. The vehicle could transport a 500kg demolition charge up to a pillbox or other target, release it and then back off before the explosive was detonated. A battalion attached to 2. Panzer Division and a company attached to Panzer Lehr Division were so equipped in Normandy. This example has sighting slits in the armour plate around the driving compartment. (IWM)

The Goliath (SdKfz 302) was solely remote-controlled with a 60kg charge. (US Army)

zerartillerie battalions of various panzer divisions. Other vehicles with their turrets removed, were issued as Artillerie Schlepper (artillery tractors) and Munitionsschlepper (ammunition carriers).

Ex-French tanks in Normandy with Panzer Ersatz und Ausbildungs Abteilung 100 and Panzer Abteilung 206, included the Char B-I bis in German service as the PzKpfw B-2 740(f), some of which had been converted to flamethrowers — Flammwagen auf Panzerkampfwagen B-2(f), the Somua S-35 or PzKpfw 35-S 739(f); Renault R-35 or PzKpfw 35-R 731(f) and Hotchkiss H-38 and H-39 or PzKpfw 38-H 735(f).

Besides captured French tanks issued to the panzer regiments, a number of captured French chassis were converted for tank destroyer roles in 1943. Some were fitted with obsolete 37mm or 47mm anti-tank guns, but more numerous were the conversions mounting the potent 75mm PaK. Among these, small numbers had been produced on Hotchkiss and FCM chassis, the Marder I being a somewhat larger series based on the Lorraine tracked carriers. Some 105mm light field howitzers were also mounted on such chassis. These conversions were issued to various panzerjäger and panzerartillerie battalions. In Normandy the 21. Panzer Division was still equipped with numerous Hotchkiss and Somua AFVs and had no less than 45 Lorraine conversions on June 6.

A battalion of Ladungsträgers, Panzer Abteilung (Fkl) 301, was attached to 2. Panzer Division. There was also a

Renault R-35 chassis with a Czechoslovakian 47mm anti-tank gun in German service . . . or rather, late of the German army. (US Army)

company of them, Panzer Kompanie (Fkl) 316, with Panzer Lehr Division. These assault/demolition units were equipped with the SdKfz 301 Ladungsträger B IV and StuG IIIs. Each such company had a theoretical strength of ten StuG IIIs and thirty-six B IVs. The Ladungsträger B IV was a lightly armoured tracked vehicle designed to carry a 500kg demolition charge up to two miles, to a specific target, where the

charge was dropped, the vehicle backed off and the explosives detonated. The B IV could be remotely controlled by radio for the final phase of such an operation, the driver bailing out before the target was reached. Designed and developed by the firm of Borgward, A B and C models of the B IV were produced during 1942-1944. It was also used for disinfection and could be fitted to take photographs.

With some 170 such conversions carried out, this vehicle was a more common sight on the roads of north-west France in the summer of 1944. This was a 'shotgun' marriage between a French prime mover and a German anti-tank gun, the full designation of the offspring being: SdKfz 135, 7.5cm PaK 40/1 auf Lorraine Schlepper (f)! (US Army)

UNIFORMS

'Panzer . . . Maarsch!' One can almost hear the words as the 'Spiess' of an unidentified company in II. Abteilung, Panzer Regiment 3, gives the command to move forward. His function of company sergeant major is indicated by the double rings on his sleeves. He wears the black panzer uniform with a 1940-style forage cap. Below the Hoheitsabzeichen hangs the silver Spanish Cross awarded for service between 1936 and 1939 with the Condor Legion. (Bundesarchiv)

THE HEER

By the summer of 1944, like practically everything else, uniforms were being kept in use until they wore out. Replacement was therefore haphazard and, even within the same unit, the succession of clothing that was issued at varying times included not only differing items of German manufacture but also captured stocks of uniforms and material and supplies adapted or incorporated to meet the needs of the Wehrmacht and Waffen-SS.

As well as the shortages and erratic distribution, uniform practice was made more diverse by changes in regulations concerning insignia and dress and by the introduction of replacement items for standard issue. Nor were regulations always consistently followed — often due to the practical problems involved or to unavailability, but also through personal preference or the policies of individual units in adapting to the situation or in making the most of it to dress differently from what was laid down.

The black panzer uniform which was introduced in November 1934 for tank troops and armoured car reconnaissance units was both practical and evocative of the old Imperial Cavalry. The cut of the cross-over style tunic, with its lack of buttons and pockets, was designed to make getting in and out of an armoured vehicle and moving about inside easier, as were the trousers which tapered at the

Left: A subaltern inspects the destructive power of German anti-tank shells on an M-10 tank destroyer. He is wearing the old style soft-peaked cap worn by officers prior to 1938 but which remained popular after the introduction of the Schirmmütz. The Deutches Kreuz, of which some 30,000 were awarded during WWII, is worn on the right breast of a tanker's battledress blouse over denim trousers. The arm badge signifies the destruction of a tank by an individual weapon. *Right:* Earphones and throat microphone. Note the sliding bracket for the MG34. (Bundesarchiv)

The commander of a Jagdpanther in the schwere Panzerjäger Abteilung 654. Panzerjäger crews were issued with a green uniform cut to exactly the same pattern as the famous black 'panzer' uniform although in this photograph he is wearing the camouflaged version. (Bundesarchiv)

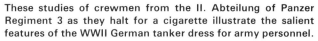

These studies of crewmen from the II. Abteilung of Panzer Regiment 3 as they halt for a cigarette illustrate the salient features of the WWII German tanker dress for army personnel.

Above left: The Oberfeldwebel on the left wears the standard panzer uniform designed for ease of wear inside the cramped interior of a tank. The omission of buttons and pockets gave a close fit and avoided snagging, while the trousers could be closed above the high boots. The tanker on the right is wearing a field-grey jacket over the black uniform. (Bundesarchiv)

Above right: These two Panzerschützen are wearing the protective clothing that was adopted in 1941 for the crews of armoured reconnaissance vehicles and later worn by tank crews. The man on the left is wearing the Einheitsfeldmütze and the other the 1940-style forage cap. The only badges worn are the national emblem on the chest and the shoulder straps although the latter had officially been withdrawn by 1944. (Bundesarchiv)

Left: Normally the black uniform was covered (or replaced in summer) by denim overalls, especially during maintenance periods. Although these pictures were taken during a training session in the plains of Picardy, the fact that three of these crewmen are wearing the old-style side cap would seem to infer that the men are not recruits. Only the Leutnant seated on the turret schützen is wearing the correct 1944 headgear. Both he and the Feldwebel crouching on the left wear jackboots which had not been issued to tank crews since January 1941. After that date recruits were issued a second pair of lace-up boots. This is an interesting shot as it shows the rails on which the skirts were hung, it being necessary to remove one on the left-hand side to refuel a PzKpfw IV. The inscription '4L' on the panel stands for 'Vier links' i.e. fourth on the left. (Bundesarchiv)

ankles and could be pulled together with drawstrings to fit closely over high marching boots. The death's-head emblem and the colour recalled the old Prussian Leibhusaren, and being black was less likely to show up oily marks and stains. Identical for all ranks and intended as service dress, the black panzer uniform soon became so popular that it was worn as parade dress and by personnel in panzer units who were not in tanks. Consequently, on February 2, 1940, a directive was issued stating that troops in anti-aircraft units, and in repair, communications, supply and support units, including armoured half-track crews in panzer divisions, should wear the ordinary standard regulation field-grey uniform.

Up to 1940 shoulder straps were sewn down and the collar was edged with the pink Waffenfarbe (arm-of-service colour) of the Panzertruppe. The silver wire or silver-grey braid of an NCO's field-grey uniform was omitted. By 1944 only officers were issued with field-grey in addition to the black uniform.

Dark grey wool-knit shirts were without breast pockets until June 23, 1943. A black tie was compulsory for walking out and had to be worn in Germany outside military establishments. Although regulations were sometimes ignored, shoulder straps were not supposed to be worn on shirts; only sleeve rank patches which were introduced on August 22, 1942.

A reed green denim outfit, cut to the same style as the black panzer uniform for the armoured car crews of reconnaissance units was adopted on May 5, 1941, and by 1944 was being worn equally among tank crews and assault gun crews, etc. Similar clothing designed for tank crews appeared in 1942, having a patch pocket on the left breast with another above the knee. The national emblem (Hoheitsabzeichen) was in silver-grey on a field-grey patch used for the standard field-grey uniform. Buttons were dished. Shoulder straps were still to be seen (in black as well as green) in place of regulation rank patches.

The denim uniform, which lacked breast pockets or flaps on the side pockets, was also sometimes issued, as was a 1942-45 version of identical cut to the 1933 cloth uniform, having six buttons down the front which fastened at the throat and four unpleated pockets. Tank crews were more often supplied with these, or with the variety of denim outfits, rather than the denim uniform designed especially for them which was a rare sight within the ranks in 1944. The variety of denim clothing that was issued to tank crews was worn as either working (maintenance) or service dress, or both — either on top of the black panzer uniform, instead of it, or combined with it.

Until the appearance in 1938 of the officer's side cap, the peaked field cap was worn. This was the old style field cap inherited in 1934 from the Reichsheer,

The tanker on the left has tucked his blouse into his trousers, revealing the unevenly placed pockets. His headphones have been stuffed into the right-hand pocket with one of the leads tucked into his belt. This is the standard officer's belt of the pre-1943 pattern. After that date the style was changed from brown leather 50mm wide to black leather 45mm in width. The regulation battledress has no shoulder straps. His hat still has the V-shaped braiding with the colour of the arm of service which should have been removed in 1942. The field-glasses are painted yellow as was customary by 1944. The Oberleutnant on the right wears tropical uniform and is without doubt a veteran of the 21. Panzer Division which was decimated in Tunisia and reformed in France in 1943. (Bundesarchiv)

having a smaller profile than the later Schirmmütze, a soft leather peak and no stiffening in the crown, and pink piping around the crown seam and the top and bottom of its bluish dark green band. Officers who possessed one on December 6, 1938 received the right in July 1942 to continue wearing it until the end of the war; and it was sufficiently popular that many newly-promoted officers sought to acquire one in preference to the forage cap.

The forage cap, or side cap — a black version of the standard field-grey service dress side cap — was introduced on March 27, 1940, for all ranks; the officer's cap being identified by silver piping around the seam of the crown and the dip at the front of the turn-up, and having a silver wire national emblem and an inverted chevron piped in pink en-

closing the Reich cockade. The chevron was ordered to be removed from September 8, 1942, but was still to be seen in the years that followed.

For issue in 1942 to NCOs and other ranks, the Feldmütze was akin to an Alpine Troops' ski hat but without a peak. Its turn-up fastened at the front by two small buttons and could be pulled down in cold weather.

Mid-1943 saw the introduction of the Einheitsfeldmütze with a wide, stiffened cloth peak which was intended to replace the side cap throughout the Wehrmacht. Sometimes it had matching plastic buttons at the front instead of metal; the officer's version having silver piping around the crown.

Steel helmets were officially discontinued for tank crews on November 8, 1943.

The Waffen-SS tank crews' dress kindly modelled by the young men of SS-Panzer Regiment 12. This radio operator from the 6. Kompanie is wearing a non-standard black leather uniform liberated from Italian naval stores. (Bundesarchiv)

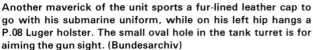

Another maverick of the unit sports a fur-lined leather cap to go with his submarine uniform, while on his left hip hangs a P.08 Luger holster. The small oval hole in the tank turret is for aiming the gun sight. (Bundesarchiv)

This cherub-faced SS-Unterscharführer of II. Abteilung of SS-Panzer Regiment 12 still wears the badges of the LSSAH: shoulder straps with the initials LAH in a pre-1940 style, and an embroidered cuff title. (Bundesarchiv)

WAFFEN-SS

The army black panzer uniform was adopted by the Waffen-SS in 1938 for the crews of armoured car reconnaissance units and was issued to tank crews at the end of 1941. Later the cut of the tunic differed from the Heer uniform in that the lapels continued the same width as the collar, and the front closure was vertical instead of slanting. The national emblem was worn on the upper left sleeve.

An officer's collar was normally edged with silver cord piping but, as in the Heer, an NCO's did not have silver braid. Similarly, Waffen-SS officers also often possessed a field-grey uniform whereas NCOs and other ranks had only a denim outfit apart from the black panzer uniform, which was readily worn by panzer troops other than those actually in tanks.

Among all arms of the Waffen-SS, the traditional brown shirt was superseded on August 15, 1943, by a grey-green wool-knit shirt with breast pockets, (a black tie remaining regulation service dress) although it was sometimes fashionable for tank crews to wear non military issue black shirts. As in the Heer, only sleeve rank patches (which were not adopted in the Waffen-SS until February 15, 1943) were supposed to be worn, but shoulder straps were often worn instead.

The shape of the black Waffen-SS side cap issued on November 1, 1940, which had a continuous turn-up and no dip at the front, was identical to the one worn by the Luftwaffe and Kriegsmarine.

A group from 12. SS-Panzer Division, most probably from the SS-Panzer Aufklärungs Abteilung 12 — the division's reconnaissance unit — not strictly speaking tank crewmen. The man on the left is wearing a jacket made from Italian camouflage material and the one on the right what appears to be the standard camo blouse of 1939-44. One of the others wears the green overalls of armoured car crews with all badges showing, while the other sports a leather naval jacket. Three of them wear army-type belts as the round SS officer's belt buckle had a habit of coming undone.

Officer's cap had silver piping around the edge of the turn-up and woven silver-wire badges.

The first version of the replacement for the forage cap, the cloth-peaked Einheitsfeldmütze (standard service cap) of mid-1943, had two metal buttons securing the front of the turn-up, like that issued to the Heer, with the national emblem worn to the left of the fastening. The second, with only one plastic button, was not issued to officers, whose Einheitsfeldmütze had the usual silver piping and badges woven in silver-wire.

The Schmirmmütze (peaked cap) was also worn as field dress by some officers — sometimes with the silver chinstrap cords removed as a counterpart of the old style field cap. Piping was the regulation white for all arms of the Waffen-SS but panzer pink piping was sometimes to be seen.

Reed green denim clothing, cut in the same style as the black panzer uniform, was introduced for the crews of armoured car reconnaisance units on September 1, 1941, and (as in the Heer) subsequently for tank crews.

On January 15, 1943, Waffen-SS tank crews began to receive a reversible one-piece outfit made of camouflage material; the 'spring' side being basically a shade of purple variegated with dark and light greens on a pink ochre base. This had six buttons from collar to crotch and buttoned-flap breast and 'trouser' pockets. Originally loops and buttons were affixed for shoulder straps until stylised rank patches were ordered to be worn as on shirts. The first ones had the national emblem sewn on to the sleeve during manufacture (the

sleeve emblem being officially stipulated for wear only on the black uniform).

A two-piece camouflage outfit, not reversible, appeared in January 1944. Cut along the same lines as the black panzer uniform, its colouring was predominantly a blend of brown dappled with a light shade of russet and light and dark green.

From June 1, 1942 a reversible camouflage material cap with a peak was produced (for all ranks) but apparently remained in short supply. It was intended to be worn without badges, but on December 1, 1942, the national emblem and death's-head were adopted, woven in brown or green, though non-metal badges remained a rarity.

Some of the canvas material, from which the camouflage garments worn in Normandy were manufactured, came from Italy and it was while the LSSAH was stationed in the north of Italy, from August to December 1943, that the division acquired a considerable amount of Italian military clothing, which included black leather tunics and trousers that had been intended for submarine crews and had originally been handed over to the Italian Navy by the Kriegsmarine. These outfits were often only made of artificial leather, but others were the real thing; they were worn by some of the tank crews in SS-Panzer

Regiments 1 and 12 of the LSSAH and Hitlerjugend Divisions and in schwere SS-Panzer Abteilung 101: all of I. Panzer Korps.

Opposite: **A scene which must have been repeated thousands of times by all armies — briefing by the battalion commander. The unit has been positively identified as schwere SS-Panzer Abteilung 101 of which SS-Obersturmführer Michael Wittmann was commander of 2. Kompanie — the officer in the Kriegsmarine leather coat (obtained via the Italian Navy) on the left. Wittmann wears the normal denim trousers and Schirmmütz cap. On his left stands SS-Obersturmbannführer von Westernhagen, the Abteilung commander, who wears the 1943 camouflage suit with a 1940-type officer's forage cap with aluminium thread piping. On the right, two other company commanders, and the third is possibly SS-Obersturmführer Jürgen Wessel, 1. Zug (platoon leader) in 2. Kompanie, wearing a motorcyclist's grey-green waterproofs — much prized article of clothing but difficult to obtain. His cap is again the 1940 model, while the fourth officer wears the 1942 linen camouflage type. Altogether quite a mixed bunch! The number of the Tiger Ausf E would be in red outlined in white. (Bundesarchiv)**

kept in theory by the company commander. In practice, it would appear that this total was kept on the mean side, indicated by the small number of the higher category badges that were awarded.

Designed by Ernst Peekhaus, the badge was intended to represent an oval oak wreath which was surmounted by a Wehrmacht eagle, beneath which was shown a PzKpfw IV, which at the time of the introduction of the badge was the most powerful German tank then in mass production. The ordinary badge was usually moulded in a mixture of copper, zinc and nickel, in imitation of real silver, but it was often produced in even more inferior metal alloys. The badges in the higher categories had a panel in the lower part which specified the number of actions involved (25, 50, 75 or 100); the crown and the eagle were the colour of old silver, and the tank was grey coloured for the second and third categories. The badges for the fourth and fifth categories were graced with a tank which had a longer gun (PzKpfw III with a 50mm gun). The crown and National Emblem were the colour of old gold, and the tank was coloured grey or silver. This badge was worn on the left side of the chest, only the highest category being worn.

The Panzerkampfabzeichen

German tank crews in the Army or in the Waffen-SS were rewarded for their efforts with the Panzerkampfabzeichen. Created initially only for tank crews on December 20, 1939, this silvered badge was first known as the Panzerkampfwagenabzeichen (the tank badge). It only received its permanent title on June 1, 1940, during the Battle of France, when a bronze badge was created for lorried infantry and for riflemen riding on motorcycles within the panzer divisions.

At first, the silver badge was reserved only for tank crews who had taken part in three consecutive actions on three different days. However in December 1942 the award of this badge was extended to motorcyclists within tank units who had taken part in three days' fighting with the tanks under enemy fire, and to soldiers in recovery units who had

carried out their task in the front-line, but still on three different days.

On July 2, 1943, this badge was divided into five categories: the badge itself for the first category and higher grades for 25, 50, 75 and 100 actions. It was still a case of the number of actions involved in, and of different days during which these actions took place. These days counted with effect from July 1, 1943. However, if a tank crew member was so badly wounded that he was unable to qualify for a higher category, the required number of actions could be reduced according to a previously fixed scale. Furthermore, the amount of time spent at the front without interruption could be taken into account (fifteen months spent continuously in the front line were counted as equivalent to twenty-five actions).

The tally of days in action was to be

In Flanders fields, between Ostend and Bruges, young Panzerschützen make music to entertain their comrades of the II. Abteilung of SS-Panzer Regiment 12. The Feldwebel on guitar wears what appears to be a roll-neck sweater under his field-grey uniform topped by his leather coat. (Bundesarchiv)

The Panzerlied

Written on June 28, 1933 by Leutnant Wiehle during a journey to Königsbrück, to the tune of *Weit über die Klippen* (Far away over the clifftops), the *Panzerleid* was also known as *Luiskalied* (Louiska's Song), although more usually sung within training units than on the field of battle. There are some slight variations to the published text.

1.

Whether there is a storm or whether it snows, whether the sun is smiling at us, the day is hot or the night is icy cold; our faces are covered with dust but we are happy, our tank grinds on into the windy storm.

2.

With thundering motors, as fast as lightning, protected from the enemy in our tank. In front of our comrades, in battle we are alone, so we strike deep into the enemy's lines.

3.

When before us an enemy army appears, we go at full speed to meet it. What is our life worth then for the Army of the Reich? To die for Germany is the greatest honour for us .

4.

Our enemy tries to stop us with obstacles and mines, we laugh and go round them. Guns in front threaten us, hidden in the yellow sand; we look for ways that nobody else has found.

5.

And some day if our good fortune abandons us and we do not return once more to our homeland; the bullet of death hits us, destiny has called out to us, then our tank will become an honourable grave.

21. Panzerlied
Ob's stürmt oder schneit

1. Ob's stürmt o - der schneit, ob die Son - ne uns lacht, der Tag glü-hend heiß o - der eis - kalt die Nacht, be - staubt sind die Ge - sich-ter, doch froh ist un-ser Sinn, ist un-ser Sinn, es braust un-ser Pan - zer im Sturm-wind da - hin.

2. Mit donnernden Motoren geschwind wie der Blitz, dem Feinde entgegen im Panzer geschützt. Voraus den Kameraden, im Kampf steh'n wir allein, steh'n wir allein, so stoßen wir tief in die feindlichen Reihn.

3. Wenn vor uns ein feindliches Heer dann erscheint, wird Vollgas gegeben und ran an den Feind. Was gilt denn unser Leben für unsres Reiches Heer? Für Deutschland zu sterben ist uns höchste Ehr.

4. Mit Sperren und Minen hält der Gegner uns auf, wir lachen darüber und fahren nicht drauf. Und drohen vor uns Geschütze, versteckt im gelben Sand, im gelben Sand, wir suchen uns Wege, die keiner sonst fand.

5. Und läßt uns im Stich einst das treulose Glück und kehren wir nicht mehr zur Heimat zurück; trifft uns die Todeskugel, ruft uns das Schicksal ab, ja Schicksal ab, dann wird uns der Panzer ein ehernes Grab.

PANZER REGIMENTS

SS-Oberstgruppenführer Paul Hausser, centre, commander of 7. Armee since June 30 (following the death of Generaloberst Friedrich Dollman from a heart attack). (Bundesarchiv)

On D-Day there were nominally nine divisions and one panzergrenadier division in the OB West sector. In northern France — the Heeresgruppe B sector with the 7. Armee and 15. Armee — there were two SS panzer divisions, 1. SS-Panzer Division and 12. SS-Panzer Division, their armoured regiments being SS-Panzer Regiment 1 and SS-Panzer Regiment 12. The four army panzer divisions in the sector were Panzer Lehr Division (Panzer Lehr Regiment); 2. Panzer Division (Panzer Regiment 3); 116. Panzer Division (Panzer Regiment 16) and 21. Panzer Division (Panzer Regiment 22).

In the southern area of France — Armeegruppe G — with the 1. Armee and 19. Armee there were the 2. SS-Panzer Division (SS-Panzer Regiment 2) and 17. SS-Panzergrenadier Division (SS-Panzer Abteilung 17) and two army panzer divisions: 9. Panzer Division (Panzer Regiment 33) and 11. Panzer Division (Panzer Regiment 15). All but the latter saw service in Normandy and are covered in the following chapters plus the 9. SS-Panzer Division and 10. SS-Panzer Division transferred from the East.

However it must be pointed out that many, if not the majority, of these panzer divisions were either forming (i.e. 12.SS, 17.SS and 116.) or refitting (such as 1.SS and 2.SS) and were not top line divisions ready and able to be used against Allied forces. It has already been explained that no units were up to the strength of the Panzer Regiment '44' model, and transportation difficulties, with railways, bridges and roads under constant fighter-bomber attack, meant that the equipment actually possessed by a regiment seldom reached the front without loss.

Generalfeldmarschall Günther von Kluge, centre, replaced von Rundstedt as commander OB West on July 7. With him are SS-Oberstgruppenführer Josef (Sepp) Dietrich left, commander I. SS-Panzer Korps, and General der Panzertruppen Heinrich Eberbach, since July 6 commander of Panzergruppe West.

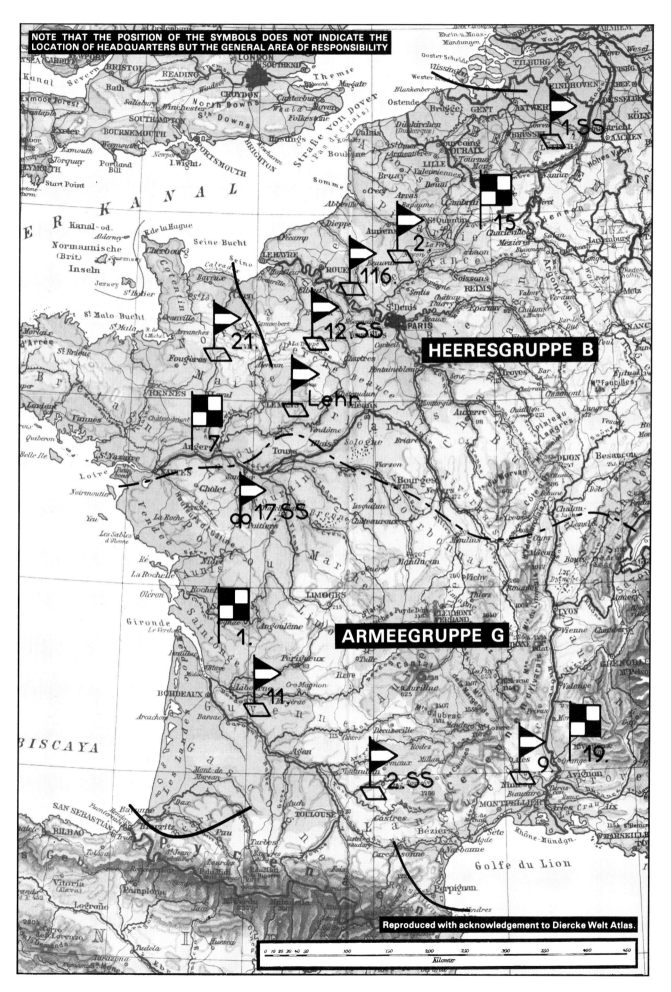

NOTE THAT THE POSITION OF THE SYMBOLS DOES NOT INDICATE THE LOCATION OF HEADQUARTERS BUT THE GENERAL AREA OF RESPONSIBILITY

1. SS

15

2

116

21.

12. SS

Lehr

HEERESGRUPPE B

7

17. SS

1.

ARMEEGRUPPE G

11

9

19.

2. SS

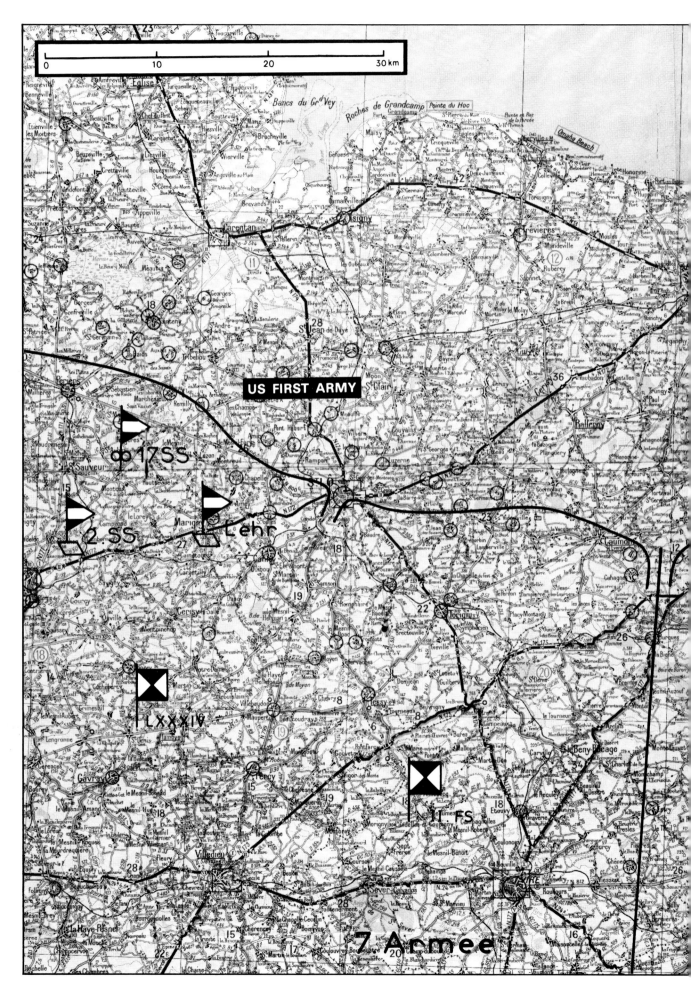

US FIRST ARMY

17 SS

2 SS

Lehr

LXXXIV

II FS

7 Armee

74

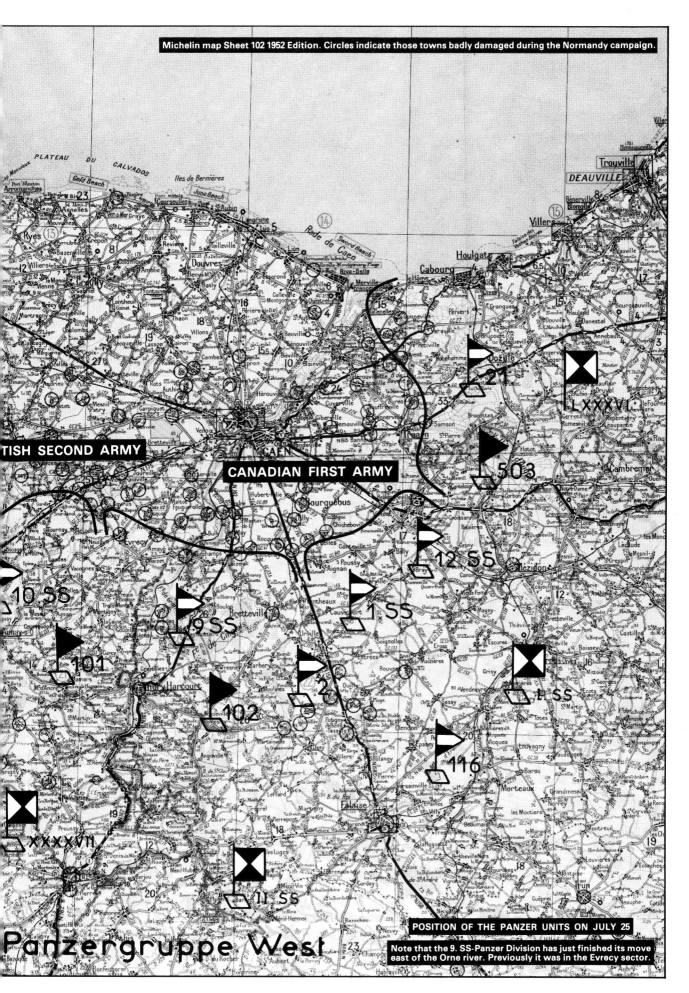

Michelin map Sheet 102 1952 Edition. Circles indicate those towns badly damaged during the Normandy campaign.

BRITISH SECOND ARMY

CANADIAN FIRST ARMY

LXXXVI

1.503

10 SS

101

9 SS

102

1 SS

12 SS

1.SS

2

116

XXXXVII

11 SS

Panzergruppe West

POSITION OF THE PANZER UNITS ON JULY 25

Note that the 9. SS-Panzer Division has just finished its move east of the Orne river. Previously it was in the Evrecy sector.

75

THE HEER

PANZER LEHR REGIMENT

Near Lingèvres, June 1944. Kompanie 2 of the Panther battalion of Panzer Lehr Regiment before the battle. (R. Viollet)

Rudolf Gerhardt was born on March 26, 1896, at Greiz, Thuringia, now in East Germany. Having taken the equivalent of his A-levels, he enlisted in the 96th Thuringian Infantry Regiment when war broke out in August 1914 and within a month he was sent up the line in southern Poland. An Unteroffizier by November, Gerhardt was awarded the Iron Cross II Class in December, when he was wounded. He was made Leutnant in March 1915 and was wounded a second time. Following a three-month officer training course he was sent to the Western Front in 1916 where he commanded a company at Verdun and later on the Somme. In October 1916 he was wounded for the third time and was awarded the Iron Cross I Class. He rejoined his regiment in January 1917 in Flanders, opposite Ypres, and was wounded for the fourth time whilst on the Somme. In 1918 Gerhardt was appointed battalion adjutant and later adjutant for the regiment.

Having left the army on July 31, 1919, Gerhardt rejoined the German army in October 1934 and was given the rank of Hauptmann. After being assured the command of a Motor Vehicle Instruction Detachment, he was given a Kompanie in the completely new Panzer Regiment 1 which was formed at Erfurt in October 1935. In 1936 Gerhardt's company was sent to Ohrdruf in order to form Panzer Regiment 7, which took up its quarters at Stuttgart-Vaihingen the following year.

In January 1939 Gerhardt was made a battalion commander and took over Panzer Abteilung 66 of the 2. Leichte Division, with which he took part in the Polish campaign. He was wounded for the fifth time, received bars to his two Iron Crosses and was awarded the Gold Wound Badge awarded for five or more injuries. In November he was back with Panzer Regiment 7 (now part of 10. Panzer Division) commanding a battalion which in the summer of 1940 reached Lyon, having reached Calais from Sedan, and south through the Weygand Line.

In the attack on Russia in 1941, Major Gerhardt was with Panzer Regiment 7 during its advance from the Bug River to Smolensk and the Beresina, and for his part in the fighting for Jelnja he was awarded the Knights Cross to the Iron Cross. In November 1941, as Panzer Regiment 7 was moving towards Moscow, Gerhardt was placed in temporary command. He was promoted to Oberstleutnant in January 1942 and to Oberst in April, when his command was confirmed, That month Panzer Regiment 7 was sent to France, where it was brought up to strength with a view to the forthcoming offensive in the Caucasus but instead was sent to Tunisia via Marseille and Naples. In North Africa it suffered further losses and on March 23, 1943, Gerhardt was wounded for the sixth time since 1914. On his hospital bed in Germany he was awarded the German Cross in Gold.

In September 1943 he was sent to Rome on the staff of Generalfeldmarschall Kesselring, Commander-in-Chief of the Southern Theatre of Operations, to serve as armaments officer.

In the middle of November 1943, Gerhardt was given command of the Panzer Lehr Regiment, then at Fallingbostel in northern Germany. In April 1945, with a division put together from depot personnel, he took part in the final battles against the Russians on the Oder before being taken prisoner by the Americans on May 6.

Hungary, March 1944. General Walter Krüger, the commander of the LVIII Panzer Korps, is being introduced by Oberst Rudolf Gerhardt (who is hidden by the General) to the officers of the Panzer Lehr Regiment. On the left of the row is Major Prince Wilhelm von Schönburg-Waldenburg, who was killed in Normandy while storming Point 103 just west of Cristot on June 11 at the head of the II. Abteilung. He is buried in a private grave at Parfouru-sur-Odon. (He won his Knights Cross for the capture of Thermopylae Pass in Greece in 1941.) Next to him is Hauptmann Föllmer (commanding 7. Kompanie in II. Abteilung) then Hauptmann von Kühlmann-Stumm. The latter commanded 1. Kompanie in I. Abteilung of Panzer Regiment 6 which was attached to the division and acting as I. Abteilung in Panzer Lehr Regiment. (The officer saluting, also from Panzer Regiment 6, is unidentified). (ECP Armées)

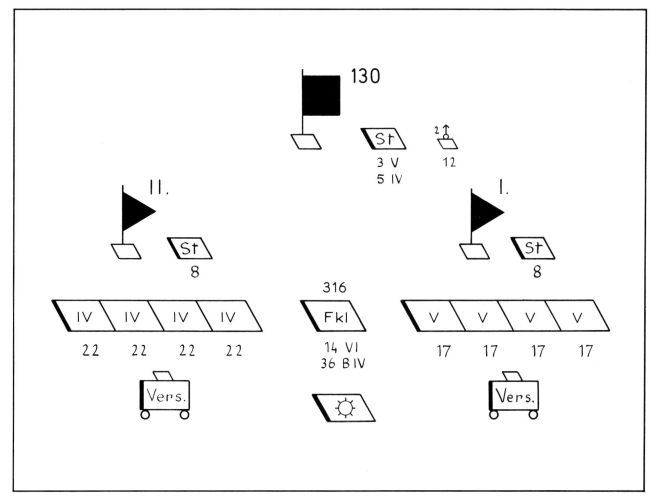

The theoretical organisation of Panzer Lehr Regiment in June 1944. The Panther battalion was not the true I. Abteilung of the regiment (which was not yet available) but the I. Abteilung of Panzer Regiment 6 which was attached to fill the deficiency from January 22 to October 1, 1944. The Panzer Lehr Division was one of the very few to have its panzer units more or less at full strength in June 1944. Its panzer regiment had 97 PzKpfw IVs and 86 Panthers. The attached Panzer Kompanie (Fkl) 316 had 6 Tigers (of which, however, only 3 were combat ready) and 9 StuGs instead of its theoretical 14 Tigers, but had its full complement of 36 remote-controlled vehicles — SdKfz 301 B IV

— and probably some Goliaths too. The Panzerjäger Abteilung 130 had its 31 assault guns among them one company equipped with the new Jagdpanzer IV. By July 1 the regiment only had 36 PzKfw IVs, 32 Panthers and 28 StuGs available. Panzer Kompanie (Fkl) 316 with its Tigers and remote-controlled vehicles had disappeared from the order of battle: either it had been annihilated in the fighting or, more probably, it had been assigned to another unit. Its commander, Oberleutnant Meinhardt, had been killed on June 20. On August 1, the number of PzKfw IVs and Panthers available had sunk to 15 and 12 respectively.

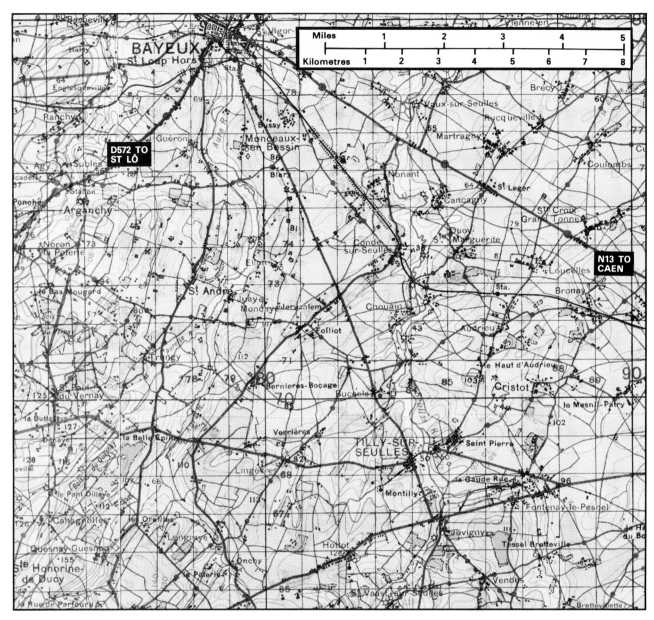

The Panzer Lehr Regiment ('Lehr' meaning 'instruction' or more precisely 'demonstration') came into being in 1938 at the Armoured Training School, Wünsdorf, near Berlin.

Units took part in the Polish campaign of September 1939 with 3. Panzer Division and in France the following summer. In the autumn of 1940 the regiment comprised:

I. Abteilung: 1. to 4. Kompanie (tanks)

II. Abteilung: 5. to 8. Kompanie (motorised infantry)

III. Abteilung: 9. to 12. Kompanie (anti-tank)

During the summer of 1941 the regiment was dispersed between several units to take part in the campaign against Russia. On December 30, 1943, orders were issued from OKH which transferred to France the training regiments of Panzertruppenschule I (Bergen) and Panzertruppenschule II (Krampnitz) with its HQ to form the basis of the Panzer Lehr Division, which was destined to become one of the most powerful panzer divisions in the German Army.

Concentrated in eastern France at Nancy, Verdun and Lunéville, the division was placed under Generalmajor Fritz Bayerlein, who had been Rommel's chief-of-staff in North Africa. Its tank regiment was equipped in Berlin; regimental headquarters stemming from the HQ of Panzertruppenschule II, and the regiment's II. Abteilung from the training school's I. Abteilung. The inclusion of a company of Königstigers was envisaged, and pressure was brought to bear for the repair company to be brought up to strength. If equipment was somewhat slow in arriving, intensive working up was begun under Oberst Gerhardt after the first training exercise on February 5, 1944.

On March 6, 1944 the division received orders to take part in Operation Margarethe which was intended to prevent Hungary from breaking off its alliance with Germany. The division played its part in the swift occupation of Hungary culminating with a show of force in the capital Budapest. Thereafter it made the most of its stay in Hungary by pursuing its training programme and even staged manoeuvres in the Carpathian mountains on March 27.

On April 2, units were given their divisional designations, and thus the panzer regiment became officially Panzer Lehr Regiment 130. Orders for the division to transfer to France were received on April 29 and the move took place between May 1 and May 6. Seventy trains were required, and the division reassembled between Chartres and Le Mans in the vicinity of Illiers and Nogent-le-Rotrou.

TO THE FRONT

At 2.30 a.m. on the night of June 6 the Panther battalion (to which the regiment's company of radio-controlled demolition vehicles had been attached) was being loaded onto railway wagons. Some of the trains had already set off for Poland, when all of them were suddenly recalled. Having been told to stand by, no orders to move were given to the remainder of the regiment. By midday the men who had been killing time standing around their tanks were beginning to grumble at the lack of action. It was only at 5.00 p.m. that General Dollmann, the commander of 7. Armee, gave orders for them to get under way, the Panzer Lehr Division having become part of his command, but by then twelve hours had been lost.

The division took five different routes to Normandy. The vehicles were covered with branches but no form of camouflage could conceal the clouds of dust that rose from the columns, and it was in an atmosphere of impending attack that the Panzer Lehr Regiment moved forward. A little before nightfall the first air raid warning came. The crews scoured the sky to the north. Suddenly fighter-bombers swept down over the thickets and hedges. A Flak-vierling 38 opened up and there was an explosion somewhere ahead. The column got under way again and passed a 'Jabo' that had been brought down, its fuel tanks blazing and ammunition exploding. A Kübelwagen had been hit and, two men killed, plus the Flak gunner.

Towards midnight there was a halt for the tanks to refuel and to give the engines a chance to cool. After an hour's break the ritual word of command was given: 'Panzer Marsch!' and the column pressed forward into the night. At 5.00 a.m. however, when the column stopped for another breather, there were still another fifty kilometres to be covered to reach the sector of the front which the regiment had been allotted. To wait for the cover of darkness would have meant a further day's delay so about half an hour later the tanks moved off once more. Several times Allied fighter-bombers swarmed down . . . and vehicles went up in flames . . . and by 6.30 p.m. that evening the division's losses during its move from south of Chartres to Normandy were alarming. The Panzer Lehr Regiment itself had lost five tanks.

THE FIRST ENGAGEMENT

Panzer Lehr Division was to move into position with its right flank up against 12. SS-Panzer Division. The orders for the Panzer Lehr Regiment on June 8 were that 5. and 6. Kompanies from II. Abteilung were to reinforce one of the division's two panzergrenadier regiments (the 901) in an attack in the Norrey-en-Bessin area, mid-way between Caen and Bayeux just south of the N13. Other units from II. Abteilung were to support the other (the 902) in an attack further west in the Brouay sector where elements of the 3rd Canadian Infantry Division had infiltrated.

The attacks went in that night. Losses were heavy as it was difficult to distinguish friend from foe. In the close fighting some Canadian tanks were destroyed by panzergrenadiers and Brouay was finally cleared.

At 7.05 p.m. the division had been given a new objective for the following day: Bayeux. Regrouping took place during the night. Since packs of British tanks were already on the D6 from

A PzKpfw IV, or rather what is left of it, from Panzer Lehr Regiment near Audrieu. During the British attack of June 10, which was supported by large-calibre naval guns, a shell must have scored a direct hit. Even the Tommies seem amazed yet the type can still be identified as an Ausf H by the small engine on the rear of the body. Photographed by Sergeant Midgeley on June 13. (IWM)

Bayeux to Tilly-sur-Seulles, the attack would have to be made to the west of this road. On the right flank an attack that had been launched by 12. SS-Panzer Division Hitlerjugend in the direction of Bretteville-l'Orgueilleuse with an armoured reconnaissance group and a company of tanks had come up against fierce opposition and had been recalled.

OBJECTIVE BAYEUX

Bayerlein led the attack on June 9 at the head of his reconnaissance group and by mid-morning he was at Ellon and

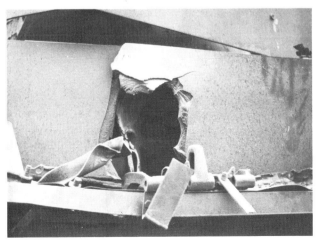

Another Ausf H casualty of the June 10 battle on the Panzer Lehr Division front. This tank from the 5th company received a six-pounder shell in its side, the resulting explosion blowing off the upper front of the armour plate. (IWM)

an hour later at Arganchy — both just due south of Bayeux. The tanks followed on with the panzergrenadiers, but their movements had been spotted and British warships began sending over shells along their line of approach. Through the dense plumes of smoke and dust thrown up by the massive explosions the tanks pressed on regardless and, towards midday, II. Abteilung, commanded by Oberstleutnant Prinz Wilhelm von Schönburg-Waldenburg, were in sight of the church tower at Ellon.

At the outskirts of the village the panzergrenadiers from 901 regiment moved up quickly behind the tanks; then troops belonging to the British 49th Infantry Division opened fire from within Ellon itself. The PzKpfw IVs advanced on a broad front. The leading British tank loomed in front of tank 602. The first anti-tank round aimed at the British tank tore off its track; the second brewed it up. A group of soldiers made a dash for tank 604 but were cut down by its machine guns: three grenades exploded harmlessly against the frontal armour.

The British artillery fire now turned to Ellon itself. Shells from all calibres of guns and heavy mortars now fell on houses and tanks alike. Steel splinters tore off the side skirts, hammered on the turrets and scarred the armour-plate. Nevertheless it did not stop 7. and 8. Kompanies from pushing on to the northern edge of Ellon with 5. and 6. Kompanies remaining in support in the village itself. By now the first fatalities had occurred — some of them comrades of Oberstleutnant von Schönburg-Waldenburg from Panzer Regiment 31 who had been with him in 1. Kompanie when he had been awarded his Knights Cross in May 1941.

Bayeux — almost unscathed — was now only five kilometres away and an excellent start line had already been chosen when the order arrived from I. SS-Panzer Korps to break off the attack and fall back to the division at Tilly. This order did not suit the tank crews at all, for on the horizon the spires of the cathedral of Nôtre Dame were clearly visible, but heavy Canadian reinforcements had managed to insert themselves between the regiment and 12. SS-Panzer Division Hitlerjugend and had penetrated the area around Tilly, Audrieu and Cristot. Grenadiers of I. Batallion, Panzergrenadier Lehr Regiment 901 stayed to cover Ellon, supported by 5. and 6. Kompanies of Panzer Lehr Regiment, whilst 7. and 8. Kompanies undertook the attack against the Canadians.

It was about 2.00 p.m. on June 11 when Hauptmann Reche, commanding 8. Kompanie, received the order from his battalion commander to get ready to attack from Fontenay-le-Pesnel, to the east of Tilly, to throw back the troops that had infiltrated and — once more — to try to break through to the coast.

The tanks did not set out until dusk and soon reached Audrieu and Chouain. Hauptmann Reche, however, had been the victim of a very bad attack of dysentry for several days and, at this critical stage, had to be sent back to hospital by the battalion medical officer. In his place, Oberleutnant Walter, who had been a schoolmaster in civilian life, took over the Kompanie, which was very much composed of veterans.

One-and-a-half kilometres ahead there were two thick woods on either side of the road which meant that they would have to pass through a dangerous bottleneck just 300 metres wide. On the left flank Leutnant Stöhr's tank 801 was moving forward, its turret pointing towards 10 o'clock. There was open ground as far as the bottleneck and the Canadian forward positions were soon reached although they were found to have been vacated as the tanks approached. When the leaders entered the narrow passage between the woods, the fanned-out formation was compressed into one great traffic jam. At this point, having withheld its fire, the Allied artillery opened up in force. The tanks in the rear were bunched too closely together, consequently those in front could not fall back and were forced to keep going.

Von Schönburg-Waldenburg was in the lead and with his command tank he made for Point 103 at full speed to get a better view of the situation. It was 4.00 p.m. Hidden 200 metres away on the other side of the crest, however, was an anti-tank gun. Its shell cut through the turret killing von Schönburg-Waldenburg outright and badly wounding the crew. At once, Hauptmann Ritgen assumed command and, in the face of what amounted to a suicidal advance into a curtain of defensive fire, decided to recall the tanks. Tank 801 covered the withdrawal and gave cover to those that had been immobilised and which were trying to be recovered under fire.

In these preliminary battles, Panzer Lehr Regiment had been fighting at half-strength. By now the I. Abteilung (Panthers) of Major Markowski was ready to support the grenadiers.

A Panther Ausf A from Panzer Lehr beside the road to Tilly-sur-Seulles. Although we were unable to pinpoint the exact location it would appear to have been destroyed about June 15. Tilly was captured by British troops on June 19 and this photograph was taken by Sergeant Midgeley the same day. The complete rear end has been on fire, burning off the anti-magnetic coating. (IWM)

THE BATTLE FOR TILLY

The British and Canadians, having been confronted by the resistance of the Hitlerjugend Division in front of Caen, shifted their main effort further west to the area around Tilly-sur-Seulles, with the object of outflanking and encircling the German positions in and around Caen by striking across the Odon and from east of the Orne.

Bayerlein was given orders that the line Verrières-Tilly-Cristot was to be held whatever the cost. The Allies were already to the north of Tilly; for the moment, it was no longer a question of making for the sea but of conducting a defensive battle, and the division took up new positions in an arc seventeen kilometres wide that went through St Germain d'Ectot, Torteval, la Belle Epine, Bernières, Verrières, the north of Tilly and Cristot.

On June 10 the British attack had been launched with a massive concentration of fire from naval guns. North of Tilly, the situation had become serious and Bayerlein's ordnance officier, Alexander Hartdegen, brought up four Panthers and two 88s. Three Allied tanks attempting to climb a slope were turned into blazing hulks by the 88s. Allied naval artillery, however, was making the high ground which was held by the Germans untenable and Bayerlein gave the order to withdraw.

The following day Bayerlein learned via the German strongpoint at Douvres-

Above: The first attack on Lingèvres went in on June 11 with the PzKpfw IVs of II. Abteilung soon joined by Panthers. These two lying at the sides of the D13 at the western end of the village belonged to the I. Abteilung of Panzer Regiment 6, then attached as I. Abteilung to Panzer Regiment 130. *Below:* The scenery has changed little at Lingèvres in the ensuing forty years — the pylon has been replaced where the Panther snapped it off. (IWM)

la-Delivrande, just inland from Luc-sur-Mer and still in German hands, that the British and Canadians were sending large armoured formations in his direction: up to eighty tanks having been counted going by in one hour alone.

Bayerlein positioned his troops with the infantry forward and his tanks in reserve to the rear with the heavy artillery.

In 8. Kompanie Leutenant Stöhr's platoon was in support of Hauptmann Philipps and his panzergrenadiers from

Opposite the church Panther 225, an Ausf A, lies wrecked beside the war memorial which still bears its battle scars today. (IWM)

the Panzergrenadier Lehr Regiment 901. For the umpteenth time, Stöhr counterattacked with his four tanks, moving forward through the grounds of the château at Fontenay-le-Pesnel, to engage units of the British 7th Armoured Division. Tilly was cleared of the enemy once again and the panzergrenadiers took up defensive positions in the cellars of the ruined houses.

West of Tilly a brigade from the British 50th (Northumbrian) Infantry Division supported by tanks from the 7th Armoured got through near Verrières. With a surge, the British reconnaissance armour came out from a wood to the north of the village and made towards Lingèvres. As I. Bataillon of Panzergrenadier Lehr Regiment 902 faced being surrounded, 6. and 7. Kompanies of Panzer Lehr Regiment, which until then had been held in reserve, were thrown into the battle.

The countryside dominated by the massive stone tower of the church at Lingèvres was divided up by hedges formed from age-old thorn bushes, and beneath the spread of some apple trees lurked Leutnant Ernst's PzKpfw IV, code named 'Zitrone' (Lemon). Ernst was a platoon leader in 6. Kompanie and he set out as soon as the alert was given.

'We reached Lingèvres,' Ernst wrote later, 'and straightaway joined in the counter-attack. In the narrow village streets the noise of the tracks and engines of our tanks was deafening. Our tracks screeched as we turned just in front of the church, where we came across the hulk of a British signals tank that had been knocked out. Along a stony track, we headed for a small wood about 300 metres away.

'"Battle Stations! Close hatches!" came the order from Hauptmann Ritgen. Inside "Zitrone" there was tension in the air. Now that the hatches were closed, the noise of the engine and tracks was muffled. All that could be seen of the outside world through the vision ports of the cupola was a narrow strip of hedges, fields and the edge of a wood. Ahead of "Zitrone" three other tanks were moving in single file up the narrow track. They turned off westwards along the edge of the wood and into a field. The wood, although very leafy, was really nothing more than a very thick copse composed of undergrowth, hedges and apple trees that had been allowed to grow wild. Tanks would only get entangled in it.

'Suddenly, the gun-layers heard the tank commanders shout: "Take aim, enemy tank at 11 o'clock — fire!"'

Ernst ordered his tank to the right and, on turning towards the small wood, he could see three tanks fifty metres away and a Churchill on fire. Behind the Churchill the outlines of the other British tanks wavered in the thick smoke as they made use of it to withdraw and disappear behind a hedge. Within a few more metres it was obvious to Leutnant Ernst that they were British — and in that instant a Cromwell on the right opened up.

'I shouted to my gun-layer: "Feuer!" and our round grazed the top of the Cromwell's cupola and flew past it' recounted Ernst. 'The enemy disappeared behind the hedge; then we came under fire from the other side. "To the left!", I shouted, and the PzKpfw IV heaved round with a jolt. The shape of the enemy tank grew larger in the gunsight. The recoil jarred the tank backwards as the round flew towards the thicket. It sounded like a direct hit. Smoke rose up into the sky. Nothing further moved. Evidently they must have been as surprised as we were, and had got out of the tank on impact and thus escaped being killed.'

Throughout June 12 and 13 the fighting for this small wood went on. They were short, sharp encounters. Whilst the shells from naval guns crossed the sky heading for Tilly or Lingèvres, the German tanks stalked their opposite numbers along the hedgerows. In these point-blank duels all that counted was accuracy and speed of shooting. Losses mounted in a battle of attrition between tanks which ended

The two Panthers on page 83 lie either side of the D13 to Balleroy which runs downhill on the right.

with the Allies capturing the wood and the panzergrenadiers of Panzergrenadier Regiment Lehr 902 holding on to the track which led to the church.

Leutnant Ernst's tank and another had been pulled back for a rest up the road from Lingèvres. The two crews had almost finished preparing a wholesome country breakfast (usually of eggs and fried potatoes) when a tremendous artillery and naval bombardment opened up on the village. Hardly had the food been dished out when over the earphones crackled a request for immediate assistance from 'Kirsche' (Cherry), unable to move and surrounded by infantry.

The meal had to stay in their mess tins. Blankets, washing kit and crew all disappeared inside the tank and the engine was started up. During the previous two days they had been called upon a number of times to perform a similar task, and soon after passing the knocked-out British signals tank they came up to the immobilised 'Kirsche'. Along the hedge they could make out the British troops by their round steel helmets. There was an exchange of shots and machine gun fire. Ernst and some of his crew opened their hatches and came out of the tank, although exposed to enemy fire, to try to tow out the damaged tank whilst the second PzKpfw IV which had accompanied them gave covering

fire — which it kept up despite having been hit at point-blank range.

Ernst again takes up the story: 'With the help of the crew from the damaged tank we managed to fix a tow. At that very moment, a soldier with both arms torn off by a shell appeared in front of me, moaning incomprehensibly in all the din that was going on. We hauled him up on to our tank to get him away to safety and then made our first attempt at towing the other panzer away. Slowly but surely we moved a few metres while the cable tautened. The fire from the British tanks positioned in the little wood was getting more drastic by the minute; we had to get a move on. It was one of those moments when, with no hope of success, there was nothing else to do except get on with it. A young radio operator lent a hand. Shell bursts were hitting the hedge next to us. It seemed unbelievable that it did not occur to the enemy opposite to aim higher, but I expect it must all have taken place in the space of a few seconds. Inside of me a voice was saying: "It's not going to work," but I somehow managed to keep cool and was more concerned at the time with getting the tank to move exactly right — to the nearest millimetre — than with how lucky I was.'

On the British side, Driver R. S. Bullen described what it was like to be on the opposing force:

'My regiment, the Herts Yeomanry, was a three-battery, self-propelled, 25-pounder field gun unit. Each battery consisted of eight Sextons (25-pdr gun mounted on Sherman chassis) and four Shermans with main armament removed and substituted by a dummy gun barrel, this to enable the gun turret to contain a plotting table and various other items for pin-point bombardment. In addition to these vehicles there were various Bren carriers, armoured cars and, of course, numerous trucks — the idea being that Bren carriers would go forward with the infantry and bring down artillery support where needed and the Shermans would do likewise with armoured units. In our case, our main armament was the No. 19 wireless set and, but for the insistence of the wireless operator to carry a 'walkie talkie', Lingèvres might have taken a little longer to eliminate.

'At dusk on June 13, our Commander, Major Kenneth Swann gathered the crew of 'X' tank and told us that we were to join a squadron of 4/7 Dragoon Guards immediately. We moved off and before complete darkness fell had met up with our "big boy friends" . . . a term used largely when units were in company with armour.

'While the skipper was away at Commanders' briefing, we prepared a cold meal. Fires were not allowed but the cans of self-heating soup were a blessing,

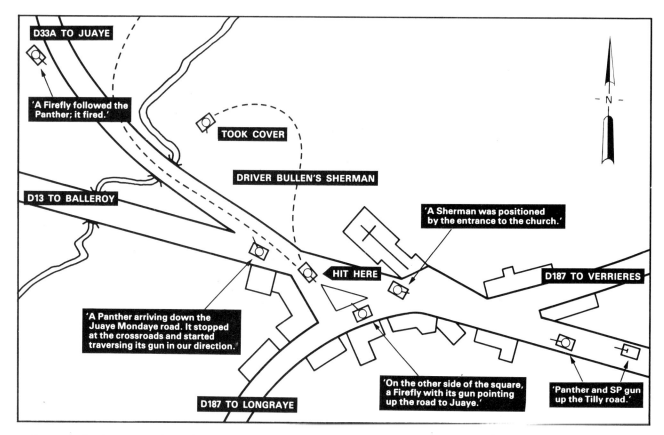

'A Firefly followed the Panther; it fired.'

TOOK COVER

DRIVER BULLEN'S SHERMAN

D33A TO JUAYE

D13 TO BALLEROY

'A Sherman was positioned by the entrance to the church.'

D187 TO VERRIERES

HIT HERE

'A Panther arriving down the Juaye Mondaye road. It stopped at the crossroads and started traversing its gun in our direction.'

'On the other side of the square, a Firefly with its gun pointing up the road to Juaye.'

'Panther and SP gun up the Tilly road.'

D187 TO LONGRAYE

as they proved to be on several occasions. While we ate our meal, the skipper gave us crew briefing. Although every detail was covered, it simply meant that at first light several flights of rocket-firing Typhoons would loosen up the enemy, who were holding Lingèvres. While the Typhoons were attacking the armour would advance, giving close support to the Somerset Light Infantry, to capture and hold the village.

The main road at Lingèvres was of secondary standard only, both in terms of width and surface. The village square is bisected by the main road and again by a single track road leading from Longraye to Verrières. Another, even smaller track, led off the Longraye road to Juaye Mondaye, scene of a vicious infantry engagement two or three days previously.

'"Stand to" at first light on the 14th was no different from previous ones. It was possible to discern black from grey but not men from shrubs and trees and the tanks in "league" could have been mistaken for buildings. As the sky lightened and turned to sunrise, it was apparent that the previous day's hot and sunny weather was to continue.

'Breakfast, maintenance, checking of guns, ammunition, the wireless nets and dozens of other personal and tank daily checks were done almost in silence. Probably everyone shared the same thought: "I wonder if . . ."

'Around 8 o'clock we heard the RAF arrive and minutes later the familiar sound of rockets came to us. "Mount . . . start up . . . driver advance . . ." and we were off. We went up a slight rise in the ground, through a hedge and had

our first sight of Lingèvres. From the angle we were at, it appeared to be a fairly large village, complete with a church and a few outlying farms, situated about half way up a small hill. One or two small fires were burning but it wasn't possible to say where as we were still about 2,000 yards away. We did, however, have a good view of the Typhoons going in. My own thought was that we would only have the sweeping up to do.

'We were now advancing across a large field of corn in company with eight other Shermans in a rough line abreast, with each tank well separated from the next one. As a driver I was getting many changes of direction, unnecessarily I thought, until I realised we were advancing through our own infantry who were invisible to me through my periscope. The corn was almost eye level!

'About 500 yards from the village I saw a Dragoon tank hit way over to our right. Suddenly one to our left stopped and the crew baled out. That, too, was hit. Then, quite suddenly, all hell let loose. Small arms and machine gun fire was exchanged across the cornfield. The main armament of tanks fired at targets I couldn't see and the wireless sets which I could hear in the background were constantly receiving and sending messages. I can remember one in particular: "Mike target . . . Mike target . . . Mike target . . ." followed by a map reference. This was from my own Commander and seconds later a barrage of shellfire burst upon the village. It seemed to go on for an hour or more. In reality it was only a few minutes.

'We were now at the end of the cornfield facing a typical Norman hedge. My instructions came over the intercom: "Go through and turn left." This was unusual. We had seen tanks defeated by such rows of hedges before and, of course, the thin armour of the belly of the tank was exposed. I engaged low gear and went through, made a left turn and continued ahead. I can remember seeing a car, motorcycle and machine gun crew all knocked out. We were in a very narrow road and about a hundred yards ahead was the church where some infantry chaps of ours were digging in.

'As we got closer I could see more infantry setting up machine gun positions. Then I turned into the village square and found far more destruction. The church, houses and shops had obviously been caught in the Typhoon raid. A few dead German and British soldiers were scattered about. A Sherman was positioned by the entrance to the church and, on the other side of what I call a square but was in fact just a road junction, a Firefly stood with its gun pointing up the road to Juaye Mondaye.

'I was told to stop by a Sherman and wait, engine running. The Commander called a greeting and waved. In answer to a request from our skipper he pointed to the Firefly. Our Commander ran across the road, climbed on the Firefly and pointed to something out of my vision. I didn't have a chance to wonder what he was pointing at. Our own wireless operator shouted into the intercom: "Driver reverse, right-hand down and go like ****!" I didn't hear the last word — I was already going!

'The tank lurched, a building to our right collapsed, followed by a loud explosion and pieces of flaked enamel came flying around inside the driving compartment of the tank. For a minute I couldn't gather my thoughts. I remember saying to the co-driver: "Christ!" His reply was something to the effect that his wireless had gone "diss".

'When the Major rejoined us he gave me directions and guided us across a small field behind the church, we broke through a low hedge and parked in the corner of a field. We found a stream running down one side of the hedge with a culvert about three feet deep in the corner. Taking cover there were about a dozen of the Somersets, most of them wounded. We gathered what might have been useful — grenades, Stens, a Browning, first-aid box and a No. 18 wireless, which the operator extracted from the bowels of a Sherman — and joined the infantry. From our new position we had a good view of the crossroads and saw that our friendly Sherman had been knocked out. We couldn't see the Firefly. Apart from spasmodic small arms fire and the occasional thump of a tank gun, it was reasonably quiet.

'We learned from the skipper that he had seen an SP gun that required the attention of the Firefly's 17-pounder. While he was directing the fire he spotted a Panther up the Tilly road bringing its gun to bear in our direction. He shouted to our operator to "move". The shell, an HE, took us on the right-hand side while we were in reverse. It ricochetted off and exploded in the shop we were going behind for cover. When we examined the damage sustained outwardly there was not too much to see. The shell had left some score marks about a foot long and about an inch deep. The side of the tank was slightly concave for about two feet. Inwardly, the

'From our new position we had a good view of the crossroads and saw that our friendly Sherman had been knocked out.' (IWM)

'We found a stream with a culvert.'

front set was out of commission, as was the forward Browning. Flakes of white enamel covered the driving compartment.

'The infantry officer and our own quickly exchanged views on the situation, which wasn't very comforting. Our tanks had come up against a strong armoured force of panzergrenadiers and several of the 4/7 Dragoon Shermans had been knocked out. Our own infantry had lost a great many men and those remaining were engaged in house to house fighting. About half-a-dozen tanks on the enemy side were knocked out, along with some SPs, but two or three were still roaming about. This was particularly disturbing as we had previously seen shots from the Shermans bouncing off the enemy armour.

'After about half an hour in the one position, our officer took the No. 18 set and went off to the village to see what was happening. The ground was higher

there. Judging by the artillery barrage that arrived shortly after, he must have found things a little sticky as he was bringing shellfire down on or very close to his own map reference. He arrived back shortly afterwards and said he had seen a Panther arriving down the Juaye Mondaye road in our direction. A few minutes later it arrived and stopped about twenty yards from our position. Only a hedge separated us. We were relieved when it moved off again but our relief was short lived. It stopped at the crossroads and started traversing its gun in our direction. Whether it was going to fire at us with its co-ax or finish off our Sherman we didn't know. Fortunately a Firefly of the 4/7 Dragoons, which looked as if it had been following the Panther, stopped where the German tank had originally halted. It fired two quick shots of AP at three hundred yards. The Panther had no chance with two 17 pounders up its stern!'

An Ausf A from Panzer Lehr knocked out near Hottot during the night of June 15/16 when the I. Abteilung tried to retake the village. The Panther has been hit right on the angle of the turret, the explosion inside forcing open the body on the opposite side above the tracks. (IWM)

During the fighting for the village Leutnant Ernst's tank was damaged as the result of a strike by a phosphorous shell and Ernst himself was slightly burned. Two other vehicles were hit and he and his crew tried to rescue the men from the flames:

'That last journey from Lingèvres is something I shall never forget', he recalled. 'On top of the tank, sitting or crouching down, were wounded men, most of whom had been badly burned, and as we picked up speed to get away from the artillery they were crying out with pain because of the heat from our exhausts. We were sent to a field hospital which had been set up in a fine château and ended up in a gothic hall lit by a few flickering candles. On the wall, I remember, was a portrait of a Renaissance lady. Outside the war rumbled on but here everything was absolutely still. Most of the wounded had been given injections and were lying there quietly. The doctors and nurses talked softly but I was close enough to overhear what they were saying about the wounded man beside me: "I can't inject him; his skin is completely burnt". They were talking about a tank man called Schmielewski who lay motionless and silent — and who died that night.'

Whilst the British 49th and 50th Divisions kept up the pressure on Tilly-sur-Seulles and Lingèvres, the Panzer Lehr Division escaped a serious threat which might have ended in the collapse of the whole German front. On June 13, whilst it was being held down frontally by the British 50th Division, a strong detachment of the British 7th Armoured Division moved rapidly into a broad gap and penetrated as far as Villers-Bocage. Only luck could prevent the collapse of the front line and the success of a huge gamble that was being tried on by Montgomery — and that luck came in the intervention of SS-Obersturmführer Michael Wittmann and the Tigers from schwere SS-Panzer Abteilung 101.

The Panzer Lehr Division sent reinforcements to help out Wittmann's few tanks which had wiped out an advance party of the British 22nd Armoured Brigade and 8th Hussars; and a few hours later forward elements of von Lüttwitz's 2. Panzer Division, coming up from the south, made certain of things. The British 7th Armoured Division pulled back to Livry, having left behind 255 men, 27 tanks and numerous half-tracks and other vehicles.

During the evening of June 15 Lingèvres and la Belle Epine were finally taken by the British, who managed to advance along a wide front on the Tilly-Balleroy road (the D13) which was defended by infantry from Panzergrenadier Lehr Regiment 902 which was under the command of Oberstleutnant Willi Welsch.

Welsch's Bataillon had been almost surrounded, and Bayerlein issued orders

Another type A from the regiment photographed by Sergeant Midgeley on June 14 north-west of Tilly near Bernières. The criss-cross pattern of the Zimmerit coating was often used on Panthers. The armoured car crew are from the 11th Hussars. (IWM)

This PzKpfw IV from the II. Abteilung was recovered intact by the British 27th Armoured Brigade after it had been captured during the fighting at the Château de la Londe where it was used as a pillbox. Although not visible here, its number is 612. The driving wheel and turret design identify this as an Ausf H. Photographed by Sergeant Mapham on July 3. (IWM)

that I. Abteilung was to relieve the situation by retaking Hottot. Major Markowski's Panthers were already on stand by when the orders came through, and he moved off with twenty-two of them, carrying panzergrenadiers from 1. and 2. Kompanies on top.

After they had cleared a slight depression — with Markowski's tank leading — Hottot lay ahead, and the shells from their own artillery started to come flying across and onto the village. From the cellars came fierce defensive fire. 'Feuer frei!' yelled Markowski into his throat microphone, and the Panthers aimed for the muzzle flashes of the opposing guns. A Cromwell fired at Markowski's Panther but missed. His response was immediate and the Cromwell blew up ten metres away. After Markowski's second kill all the Panthers joined in, and the British withdrew. Approaching the village from both sides, the Panthers charged towards it, skirting the buildings that had come crashing down. The panzergrenadiers cleaned up the British positions one by one, but before the village was cleared and back in German hands, Markowski's Panther was hit killing the radio operator and wounding the gun-layer and had to be abandoned.

Two hours later Bayerlein recalled all the tanks at Hottot to Tilly-sur-Seulles where all hell had been let loose. For two hours the panzergrenadiers held out in the cellars amidst the ruins of what remained of the town against concerted attacks from the British 49th and 50th Divisions. Tanks from I. Abteilung were

sent in to support them and, when II. Abteilung went in, Gerhardt had committed his last reserves. Yet once more an attack on Tilly was held off . . .

The previous day (June 14), Obergefreiter Hoffmann and Unteroffizier Nürnberger, both from 8. Kompanie, were returning from leave when they found that they could get no further than the area around Carpiquet because of the fighting in the vicinity of the airfield. The 12. SS-Panzer Division would have happily co-opted them, but the two men managed to slip away that evening and found a sign that pointed in the direction of II. Abteilung. They managed to locate 8. Kompanie in a small wood, but even before they were out of their uniforms and into their tank overalls, Allied naval guns had forced them to take cover. Hoffmann ultimately ended up with Unteroffizier Westphal (who had a reputation for being an old hand at destroying tanks). Westphal's tank was one of four from 8. Kompanie that spent the whole of the following two days laying in wait under cover — the other tanks being commanded by Unteroffiziers Schultz and Pausch and, over on the right, Hauptmann Felmer. Two kilometres to the rear the rest were in reserve with 6. and 7. Kompanies.

At dawn on June 17 the area underwent a heavy artillery barrage in

preparation for an attack which those up front waited for all day. Back in the rear the shelling took Leutnant Stöhr (tank 801) by surprise. Panzeroberschütze Heinz Loewe was savouring the thought of a good open air breakfast when it was scattered from the frying pan and he had to throw himself under his tank to take cover. The barrage continued for the best part of two hours. Later, at noon, when a dispatch rider appeared on his motor-cycle, one of the crew of tank 801 went off to get some food from the other side of the road. Just as he was coming back with the mess tins the bombardment started up afresh. With naval shells landing only twenty-five metres away, lunch went the same way as breakfast and all that could be salvaged were the cigarettes. Bombing followed on, right up till nightfall . . .

Next day the Allied guns opened up once more at dawn, but again there was still no sign of a British attack through the morning mist. Finally it was launched in a neighbouring sector and Westphal's tank was called up to provide support. Although this attack was repulsed the Allies managed to capture Cristot, where grenadiers lay buried beneath the ruins of the village, and by 7.45 p.m., when the first British tanks got into Tilly, the front line had been redrawn south of the village. By June 20,

Although there is no positive proof that this Maultier belonged to the Panzer Lehr Regiment, it makes a nice comparison in Monts-en-Bessin, the village where Generalleutnant Fritz Bayerlein, divisional commander, had his HQ. The Maultier was a 4½-tonne Mercedes-Benz truck with the rear axle assembly replaced by tracked suspension and used as a cargo carrier. (IWM)

out of some 190 tanks that had made up Panzer Lehr Regiment on June 6, there were only 66 runners left.

On June 26 the British and Canadians launched a great offensive against the Odon and Point 112 preceded by an artillery bombardment that lasted three hours, and on June 27 the British 11th Armoured Division had established a bridgehead across the river. Around Tilly, Panzer Lehr Division faced three British divisions. Then on June 29 orders came through for the division to leave the area around Tilly on July 2 for the area south-east of Carentan, where there was comparatively little armour to confront any major American attack. When relieved by an infantry division,

part of Panzer Lehr Division was to remain where it was, however, and this included one third of Panzer Lehr Regiment's tanks.

THE MOVE WESTWARD

During the evening of July 2 Bayerlein took stock of the situation with his officers at his headquarters in Monts-en-Bessin. By now only about sixty tanks remained servicable and eighty-four had been destroyed or so badly mauled that it would take time for them to be put back into action. However the main concern was the lack of spare engines and gearboxes needed to repair both Panthers and PzKpfw IVs.

The division moved out in columns during the night of July 3, heading west. In the darkness the tank commanders had no idea of whether they were heading in the right direction and frequently had to get down and go forward on foot to reconnoitre the way ahead; yet being unable to see where they were going was perhaps preferable to being shot up by fighter-bombers. Next morning, however, Bayerlein issued an order to every unit in the division that the move was to continue. No damaged vehicles were to be taken in tow as this would slow down the advance. In the event of an air attack every available weapon was to be used; even tank guns. To make the most of overcast weather, the columns were to press on without wasting any time.

The tank crews were half asleep from exhaustion when they were jolted into action by the sound of their own guns. Quickly splitting up, II. Abteilung moved along both sides of the road in order not to present too compact a target from the air as the rockets hissed down. With hatches closed and machine guns trained upwards, the first bursts were loosed off at the aircraft overhead. Cannon shells and rockets ripped into the road all around but miraculously only one tank was hit, sustaining a hole in its gun barrel, which did not prevent it from continuing. Soon afterwards it started to rain and under the cover of a leaden sky the tanks reached St Lô that evening without having sustained a single loss.

Regrouping was completed by July 7. The following day a counter-attack was planned to begin along the Vire river. The aim was to push as far north as possible to block the American advance, cut this in two, and press forward to the Vire-Taute canal, destroying the forces to the south of it. The Allies, however, were already aware of this plan from an intercepted message sent to Bayerlein via the German transmitter at Calais.

THE ATTACK ON THE VIRE-TAUTE CANAL

At about 5.30 a.m. on July 8 II. Abteilung of the Panzer Lehr Regiment made for Pont-Hébert to capture the village which was to be its start line. To trace the progress of 8. Kompanie, its advance on Pont-Hébert was swift. Defensive fire from anti-tank guns and machine gun nests grew as the tanks got nearer but no damage was caused by heavy artillery and mortar fire coming in from the right. After this had been silenced, the panzers entered the village and took up positions for the night.

At first light, American tanks broke through the defence line that had been established around the village and began to advance along the main street. Brief duels — tank against tank — ensued, in which one German crew member recalled that: 'the loader and gun-layer were working with clockwork precision.

Our commander was giving out orders and we moved forward, turning this way and that. An American tank was hit, our round going straight through his armour. Flames shot up from the hatches and the crew baled out. The men were on fire, running, and rolling themselves over and over on the ground. Our commander was calling out for us to go on. Other tanks were advancing with us. Three, four, five American tanks were brought to a standstill; our tank, though, had been hit, and again over the earphones you could hear the shouts of: "We've been hit! Out, everybody!" We lost seven tanks and a lot of our crewmen were dead or wounded, but the American thrust had been stopped in its tracks!'

The previous day, (July 7) the Americans had launched the 9th and 20th Infantry Divisions, and then the 3rd Armored, as part of their attempts to gain ground further south. The latter was brought to a halt on July 9 by 2. SS-Panzer Division Das Reich near Point-32, between Pont-Hébert and St. Jean-de-Daye, and that afternoon Das Reich also reached the Chateau de la Mare at Cavigny, to the east, giving the 120th Regiment of the 30th Infantry a drubbing.

The major attack to gain the line of the Vire-Taute canal went in at 5.30 a.m. on July 11. On the right flank an assault group comprising Panzergrenadier Lehr Regiment 902 commanded by Oberstleutnant Welsch, plus twenty Panthers from I. Abteilung, Panzer Lehr Regiment, moved forward against the US 30th Infantry Division. The assault group on the left — comprising Panzergrenadier Lehr Regiment 901,

The close proximity of the charred corpse of one of the crewmen of this Panzer Lehr Regiment Panther does not seem to deter these GIs from examining their prize knocked out at le Désert, about twenty kilometres north of St Lô, most probably during the regiment's counter-attack of July 11. (US Army)

under Major Scholze, reinforced by an anti-tank company and twelve tanks from II. Abteilung — struck against the US 9th Division.

Within the hour they were already three kilometres behind the American front lines. Near the village of le Désert some of the tanks were held in check by powerful American forces; otherwise the rapid advance continued. One clash followed another, with tanks exchanging fire at ranges of between 100 to 150 metres amidst the orchards and sunken lanes, but the division had been too badly depleted around Tilly and was now fighting at perhaps a third of its original strength. Out in front as usual was Leutnant Stöhr, who had joined 8. Kompanie from 7. Kompanie and had been hailed enthusiastically by his former comrades only the day before. A phosphorous shell set his PzKpfw IV alight and he died instantly from a shrapnel wound in the head, whilst the other four of his crew were burned to death.

Towards midday the weather improved and Allied fighter-bombers were soon taking to the air. Panzergrenadier Lehr Regiment 901 was pinned to the ground. The tanks, out ahead on their own, were knocked out one by one: out of the 32 that had started out at dawn only 12 were still battleworthy and the infantry had suffered some 500 killed or wounded. Nevertheless the 12 tanks had reached the canal.

In the respite that was gained, time

was utilised to the full in getting both men and machines back into shape. The 8. Kompanie, with seventeen tanks operational, was one of the units that had suffered the least.

During the night of July 15-16 there was more artillery fire which apparently caused no damage among 8. Kompanie's panzers, and an American attack made under cover of smoke shells failed to break through the divisional front. At dawn, the tanks changed their positions and camouflaged themselves in a wood; then an aircraft engine was heard and a spotter flew over. The first shells began coming down half an hour later. One fell only five metres in front of Unteroffizier Westphal's tank and another burst immediately overhead. The barrage had found its mark. Two more shells hit the same tank, bursting open the hatches. Flames were spreading through the hull; the gun-layer, aimer and radio operator scrambled clear but the driver's hatch was blocked by the gun barrel and Obergefreiter Gerbig could be heard yelling from inside. The tank was well alight by now, though, and the heat beat back all attempts to rescue him, with the added risk of the ammunition likely to go up at any moment. Westphal went out on the recovery of two of 7. Kompanie's tanks and when he got back the smell of burning flesh was still hanging in the air.

The four men, who all had slight burns, set out to rejoin their unit on foot and managed to get a lift on a half-track, but they had to endure a second bout of shelling at a crossroads and only succeeded in reaching 8. Kompanie's makeshift camp by nightfall. First thing on the morning of June 17, Westphal gave a report on the fate of tank 801 to his company sergeant major.

On July 20, the tank crews from 8. Kompanie were distributed amongst the remaining tanks. The gun-layer and radio operator from 801 found themselves together again in 812. This tank had the job of relieving Unteroffizier Schultz, whose tank had been acting as a picket for several days, which meant that the crew had to stay inside the stationary tank, constantly on the alert. The relief took place under artillery fire, and tank 812 was careful not to occupy exactly the same spot as the tank it had come to replace. The crew were gripped with fear, and their commander, Unteroffizier Fontaine, was a novice. They were due to stay put for three days and for a while made an effort to get to know each other, before boredom set in.

On the fourth day, while they were

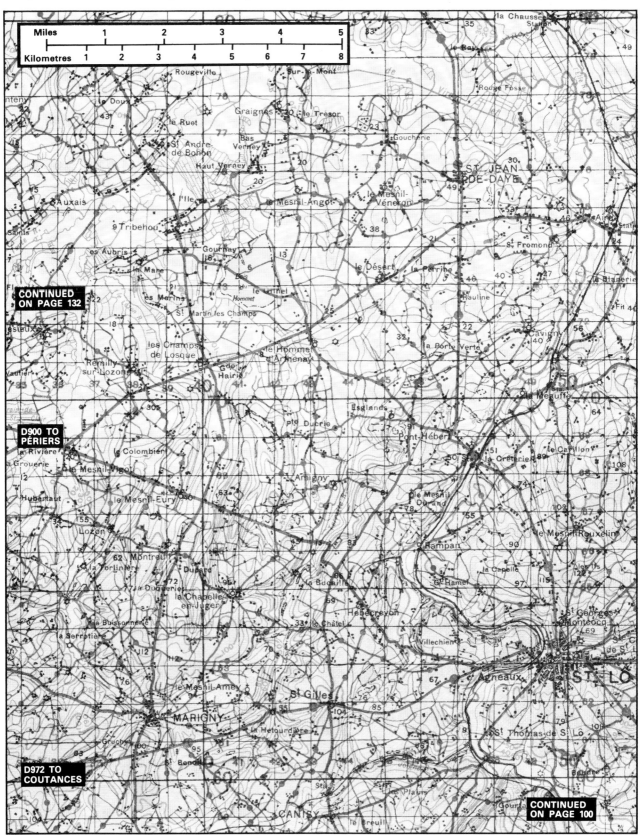

CONTINUED ON PAGE 132

CONTINUED ON PAGE 100

Le Mesnil-Durand — then and now. This PzKpfw IV was knocked out during the attempt of the US 30th Infantry Division to capture the D77 ridge road to the west of the village. The village itself was captured by the 117th Infantry. (US Army)

waiting to be relieved themselves, Unteroffizier Fontaine decided to get out of the tank to check that the branches covering the tank were still in position just at the very moment when two fighter-bombers were circling overhead. By the time he had shouted a warning, the aircraft were already diving down towards them. The roar of their engines drowned the noise of the hatches being shut and the explosions rocked the tank like a boat in a storm, tossing the crew all over the place. The driver could not see a thing. Cannon fire was coming at them now. The tank shuddered into life, shaking off some of the earth that had covered it, and Fontaine raised his hatch in time to see the two fighter-bombers getting ready to make another run. After managing to reach the cover of three houses about 500 metres away, the crew had to clear the top of the tank with spades. Mortar fire forced them to take cover in one of the three tumbledown buildings, then field guns joined in. Other tanks from 8. Kompanie had sought the shelter of this imaginary haven when, suddenly, the gun-layer of tank 812 noticed their radio operator, Rudi Weiss, lying on the ground, his face unrecognisable. Westphal pointed out that the gun-layer was himself bleeding — with blood oozing from his right eye.

On top of the mortar and artillery fire came the bombs, which meant that it was a long time before the wounded could be placed inside the tanks. Weiss died as they reached the divisional first-aid post (all they had been able to do for him was to apply a field dressing) and the gun-layer was evacuated, being in no condition to take any further part in the battle.

The following day, July 24, a fleet of about 2,000 bombers flattened the area held by the Panzer Lehr Division, laying waste a rectangle seven kilometres by three. There were now no more than forty tanks in the line and not one came through unscathed. Some were turned on their sides, others were blown into bomb craters. . . . The seven that were still operational were committed by Oberst Gerhardt against the American offensive that followed, and during that night recovery teams succeeded in getting nine more into running order. A few others came back from the workshops to bolster the numbers.

On July 26, B–17s and Liberators finished off the previous day's work; field artillery then took over, followed by fighter-bombers. The American infantry were then able to move forward.

When the remnants of the Panzer Lehr Division reformed at Canisy, Panzer Lehr Regiment could only put together fourteen tanks, but the repair units worked flat out and another fourteen had rejoined the regiment by July 27 before the US 1st Infantry and 3rd Armored Division's thrust towards Coutances. However the regiment was still short of spare engines and gearboxes

Above: Two PzKpfw IVs knocked out in the village of St Gilles, six kilometres to the south-west of St Lô on the road to Coutances. This photograph was taken on July 25 after the very heavy bombing raid which took place over the positions of the Panzer Lehr Division. Although technically St Gilles lay just south-east of the area that was bombed, one tank appears to have received a direct hit. (US Army) *Below:* It is difficult to conceive the pounding received by the village — all has been rebuilt in modern style.

and of spare parts in general, all of which prevented many tanks being repaired to fight again . . .

Patton's Third Army had broken out, and on August 6 its spearheads were approaching Le Mans. On August 7, in the German counter-attack aimed in the direction of Avranches to cut off the American advance, the Panzer Lehr Division could only throw in what they had left. In 8. Kompanie, a radio operator who had been reported missing managed to find his unit on August 3 and was immediately put into tank 806 commanded by Unteroffizier Schultz. Up to August 10 the tank acted as a

look-out, with the turret permanently manned from 6.00 a.m. onwards. A Sherman succeeded in brewing it up and the crew got away on foot, but they were soon rounded up and led away near Carrouges.

At dawn on August 13 all that remained of Panzer Lehr Division was a battlegroup in position at Habloville, twelve kilometres north-west of Argentan. At the end of the month, after 6,000 men and divisional services had re-assembled near Fontainebleau, the repair units were able to hand over only twenty tanks — amounting to just one company.

Above: Engines of war beside a French lane. A striking shot of two Ausf A Panthers at le Dèsert belonging to Kompanie 1 of the I. Abteilung, Panzer Regiment 6 attached to the Panzer Lehr Regiment. The American caption states that they were knocked out by anti-tank fire by the US 9th Infantry Division yet there is no sign of damage. Is it possible that they were abandoned by their crews and later pushed off the road to clear the way? Note the driver's vision port is still open on the left-hand tank. (US Army) *Below:* Few identifying features remain to pinpoint the precise location.

PANZER REGIMENT 3

Formerly the motorised Reiter Regiment 12, Panzer Regiment 3 was one of the very first tank regiments in the new panzer divisions established in 1935, and as part of 2. Panzer Division it fought in Poland, France, the Balkans and on the centre of the Eastern Front. After the Anschluss the division transferred to Vienna and its recruits then came mainly from Austria. In 1942 the regiment's I. Abteilung was transferred to become III. Abteilung, Panzer Regiment 33 of 9. Panzer Division. I. Abteilung was reconstituted at Sennelager, the panzer breeding ground,

in March 1943 and rejoined Panzer Regiment 3 three months later.

The division left the Eastern Front for northern France in December 1943, where it was stationed in the Amiens area. On June 3, 1944, divisional headquarters was at Courcelles, southwest of the town.

At 2.00 a.m. on June 6 the division was put on the alert — in readiness for the assault that was still expected to be made on the Pas-de-Calais. Then, on June 9 it was despatched to the Argentan-Sées sector in Normandy. Forced to go via Paris since there were no

Above: Although conclusive evidence is not available, this Ausf D Panther, a rare example in the panzer battalions in Normandy, is most probably from Panzer Regiment 3. The location is the Route Nationale 175 at Tourville-sur-Odon, between Villers-Bocage and Caen, which is the area where the regiment's I. Abteilung was operating when seconded to the Hitlerjugend Division in the latter days of June. (The only other possible contender would be SS-Panzer Regiment 12.) The main characteristics of the D-type are the old-style turret and no position for a machine gun in the front glacis. This picture was taken on July 16. (IWM) *Below:* New housing, constructed in the late 1970s, now looks out upon the old.

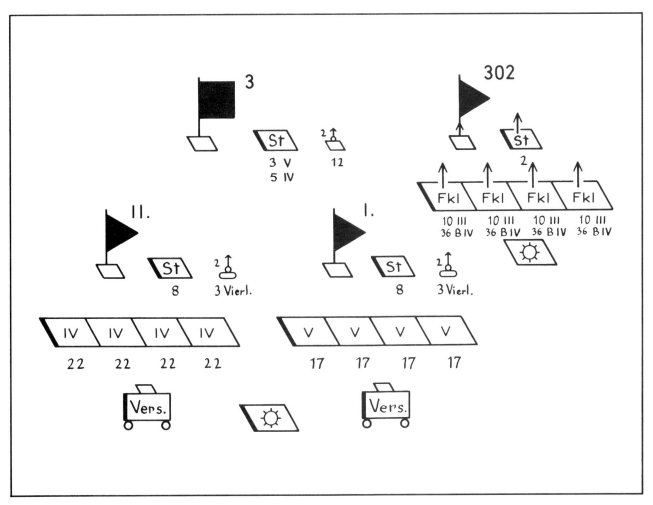

The theoretical organisation of Panzer Regiment 3 in June 1944. Exceptionally 2. Panzer Division was nearly at full strength on June 1. Its Panzer Regiment 3, commanded by Oberst Köhn, had 94 PzKpfw IVs and 67 Panthers, and was well equipped with Flak having 5 SdKfz 7/1 and 12 Flakpanzer 38(t). The Panzerjäger Abteilung 38 of the division was equipped with 21 assault guns, amongst them a handful of Jagdpanzer IV.

The Panzer Abteilung (Fkl) 302 had been attached to the division since March 20, 1944 but its precise strength on June 1 is not known having approximately 20 StuGs and less than a 100 remote-controlled vehicles. By July 1 the regiment was down to 85 PzKpfw IVs and 21 Panthers and Panzer Abteilung (Fkl) 302 has been reduced to a single company. One month later it was reduced to just 32 PzKpfw IVs and 6 Panthers.

bridges left standing over the Seine downstream from Paris and — like many other units making for Normandy — unable for the most part to travel by rail because of the bombing of the main railway centres, the division had to take two different routes; Panzer Regiment 3 taking the right-hand one through Poix, Beauvais, Paris, Versailles, Dreux, l'Aigle and Argentan.

On June 12, divisional headquarters was set up at Lignou, just to the south of Briouze on the N24 bis between Flers and Argentan, whilst units moved northwards to take up positions on the left of the Panzer Lehr Division, where the panzergrenadiers went into action — without tank support — against the British around Villers-Bocage during the afternoon of the 13th.

Divisional headquarters had been moved to Brémoy, between Vire and Villers-Bocage, where it was then learned that the armour, including Panzer Regiment 3's tanks, was only just being unloaded east of Paris and was going to have to continue the journey in stages by road as fast as possible. The

first panzers only managed to arrive on June 18. Although they had been held up by fighter-bombers, the havoc created by these attacks had been much less than anticipated. Nevertheless at the end of this forced march large numbers had to go into the field workshops to be put into proper running order again.

An early improvisation was made by the service company of the divisional reconnaissance group which came across an almost intact Sherman in Villers-Bocage: by removing the turret it became a valuable recovery vehicle.

At about this time, as the recently arrived tanks were rejoining the regiment one by one, 2. Panzer Division was getting ready to take Caumont-l'Eventé, on the left, where its flank was being seriously threatened. On June 25 and 26, however, the British broke through east of Tilly-sur-Seulles along the front held by the Panzer Lehr.

The Hitlerjugend Division counter-attacked on the right, for which I. Abteilung of Panzer Regiment 3 was loaned in support, and in the fighting on June 27 its Panthers succeeded in

destroying 14 tanks. Next day its score leapt to 53 tanks and 15 anti-tank guns, but none of this made any difference to the outcome, and nor was the division able to re-take Caumont-l'Eventé minus half its tanks.

By July 1, the tally for I. Abteilung had reached an impressive 89 tanks, 19 anti-tank guns and 13 Bren gun carriers. Its own losses came to 20: the equivalent of a company. Yet, as everywhere, the shortage of spare parts was critical: a point made forcibly in General von Lüttwitz's monthly divisional report, as the panzers survival was dependent on obtaining them.

On July 16, I. Abteilung was again used as reinforcements — on the left with the Panzer Lehr Division, in a Kampfgruppe led by the regiment's commanding officer, Oberst Köhn, and formed to go in against units that had broken through to the right of Villers-Bocage. In the event the Kampfgruppe was unable to exploit its success and the colonel was among those killed, I. Abteilung losing a number of tanks.

Between July 21 and 24, 2. Panzer

Division was relieved by an infantry division and regrouped to the east of Thury-Harcourt, but II. Abteilung remained behind as a mobile reserve.

From July 24 to 27, divisional units were sent into action separately to the south of Caen with other divisions, and a Kampfgruppe made up around 2. Panzer Division's anti-tank battalion with a company of Panthers from I. Abteilung was sent in by I. Panzer Korps against St Martin-de-Fontenay,

A Panther Ausf G, almost completely burned out, pictured near Villy-Bocage (just north-west of Villers-Bocage) by Sergeant Mapham on August 4. It is a strong possibility that it is from the I. Abteilung of Panzer Regiment 3 and had been knocked out between July 16 and 20. REs are still sweeping the field although a mine-free path is marked with white tape.

about five kilometres south of the city. After some initial success, the Kampfgruppe's advance got bogged down south of the village, and the troops had to undergo both artillery fire and attacks by fighter-bombers. To the left the

Panthers came in for particular attention and also had to fight it out with anti-tank guns hidden within the ruined houses. A point was reached when the attack had to be called off, although a few Allied tanks had been destroyed.

Left: August 3 and an American patrol passes one of Panzer Regiment 3's PzKpfw IVs in the ruins of Pontfarcy. (US Army) Above: We took our comparison from the garden of René Douin's house 'Le Bas du Bourg'.

Later it was pushed off the road into the garden. The truck is going towards Vire — to the right lies Tessy. (US Army)

On July 29, 2. Panzer Division was fighting on a different front, to the south of St. Lô. Its objective was to go all out westwards to link up with units of the Panzer Lehr and 2. SS-Panzer Division. A Kampfgruppe which contained twenty of the regiment's tanks succeeded in reaching the crossroads at la Denisière on the road between St Lô and Villebaudon. Adopting hedgehog formation, they managed to knock out twenty-five American tanks and, cut off from the division except for radio contact, fought on throughout July 30 to August 1; about seven tanks forcing their way through back to Moyon, about two-and-a-half kilometres east after the rest of the Kampfgruppe had been wiped out.

As preparations were completed for the counter-offensive at Mortain, Panzer Regiment 3 had only sixty operational tanks. The offensive was to begin at midnight on August 6, the plan being to move forward without preliminary artillery fire in a surprise attack. One of the regiment's battalions would go in on the division's right; other units on the left.

The right wing advanced as far as le-Mesnil-Tôve and le-Mesnil-Adelée, north-west of Mortain; the left were halted in front of le Valle. Allied fighter-bombers swooped over the columns unceasingly. Le-Mesnil-Tôve had to be abandoned in the face of a counter-attack by infantry and tanks and, near the village, Major Schneider-Kostalski became the second commanding officer of Panzer Regiment 3 to be killed in less than a month.

On August 13, 2. Panzer Division was again withdrawn, in order to regroup east of Carrouges in the Ecouves Forest, south of Argentan, for an attack that was never to take place. At that time, the regiment could still line up twenty-five to thirty tanks.

On August 17 the division was east of the Orne, and at 7.00 p.m. on the 19th orders came through for it to leave the Falaise pocket via St Lambert-sur-Dives. It was not until 4.00 a.m. the following day that the units began to pull out; the few remaining tanks of Panzer Regiment 3 and troops of Panzergrenadier Regiment 2 reaching St Lambert in good order about six hours later.

Regrouping took place north-east of Bernay between August 21 and 23 and on August 28 the division managed to get across the Seine. Panzer Regiment 3 had just five tanks left, but losses among the service and HQ companies had been even more extensive. Altogether, 2. Panzer Division numbered barely 1,200 men.

Panzer Regiment 3 might well be termed the roving regiment, being switched from one side of Normandy to the other in July and August. This was their battle-ground south of St Lô. We found photographs of their armour in both Tessy and Pontfarcy.

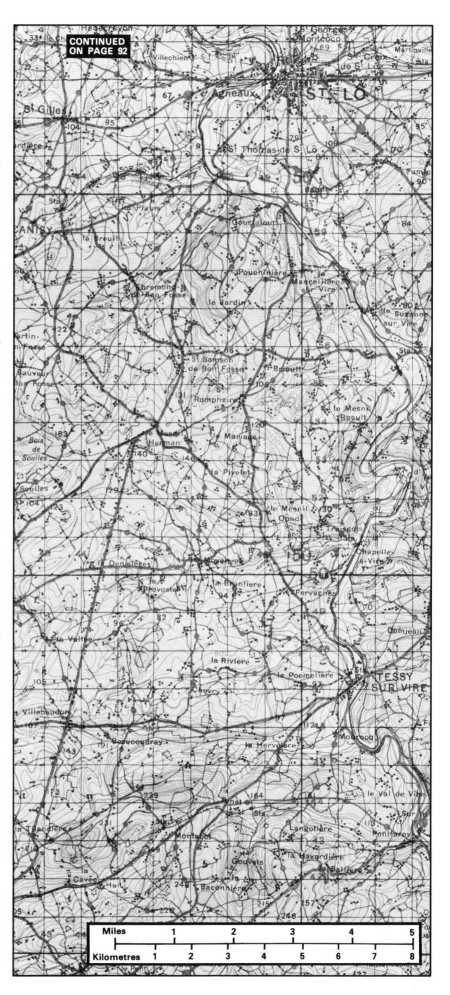

CONTINUED ON PAGE 92

Above: **We searched in vain for this shot of a knocked out Flakpanzer 38(t) of the command company of Panzer Regiment 3 captioned by the American photographer as having been** taken in Torigny-sur-Vire. (US Army) *Below:* **No wonder we could not find it — our comparison was taken in Tessy-sur-Vire, twelve kilometres to the south-west!**

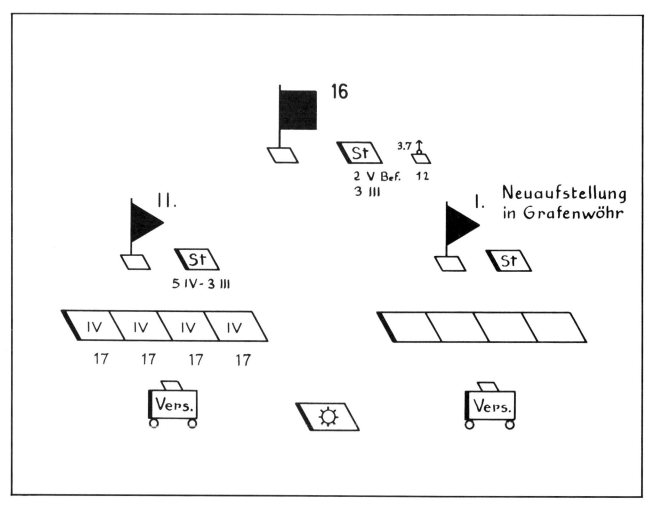

16

St
2 V Bef. 12
3 III

3.7

II.

St
5 IV - 3 III

I. Neuaufstellung
in Grafenwöhr

St

IV IV IV IV
17 17 17 17

Vers.

Vers.

PANZER REGIMENT 16

The 116. Panzer Division was formed in France in March 1944 from the remnants of 16. Panzer Grenadier Division which had been decimated on the Eastern Front. As part of the new division, Panzer Regiment 16 was created on May 27, 1944. The regiment's headquarters was made up from that of Panzer Regiment 69; its I. Abteilung was formerly the Panzer Abteilung 116 of the 16. Panzer Grenadier Division and its II. Abteilung came from Reserve Panzer Abteilung 1 of the 179. Reserve Panzer Division.

In the spring of 1944, I. Abteilung had been sent to Grafenwöhr, Bavaria, to join up with Panzer Brigade 111. It was replaced by I. Abteilung of Panzer Regiment 24 although it did not arrive

The theoretical organisation of Panzer Regiment 16 in June 1944. During that month and throughout the summer, the 116. Panzer Division fought without the I. Abteilung of its Panzer Regiment 16 as the battalion was at Grafenwöhr equipping with Panthers. The II. Abteilung had only 58 PzKpfw IVs available, amongst them four obsolete Ausf C (with the short gun barrel), with 10 PzKpfw IIIs making up the shortage. Most of these were Ausf Js mounting the long 50mm gun and these were assigned to the staff companies of both the regiment and II. Abteilung. The 7. Kompanie had an assorted collection of 12 PzKpfw, IVs both Ausf H and J, 4 Ausf Cs and an old PzKpfw III Ausf H. Panzerjäger Abteilung 228 had 6 of the potent Jagdpanzer IVs. By July 1, the divisional strength was more or less unchanged with the addition of another 10 PzKpfw IVs bringing the total on hand to 68. *Left:* Camouflaged Jagdpanzer IV on the strength of Panzerjäger Abteilung 228, 116. Panzer Division.

until the autumn thus not participating in the Normandy battles. The regiment was initially under the command of Oberstleutnant von Trotha, later Major Rüder who was succeeded in turn by Oberst Bayer on August 26. II. Abteilung was under the command of Major Graf von Brühl.

On D-Day, 116. Panzer Division was east of Rouen, with divisional headquarters at Bernouville, but was not brought into action until after the American break-out in the Cotentin,

though some units may have been committed beforehand. It was intended that the division would be used against the American flank around St Lô, but it was sent instead towards Mortain for the offensive aimed at Avranches.

By August 12 there were only fifteen tanks left in Panzer Regiment 16, then between Argentan and Sées. In getting out of the Falaise pocket the division managed to escape without too many losses and it crossed the Seine either side of Rouen.

Above: Lovely photograph — if that word can be used to describe such a picture — which epitomises the 'after the battle' scene. Taken on August 20, just as the gap in the Allied lines east of Falaise was being closed, this Panther Ausf A was abandoned by one of the fleeing German units and probably once belonged to Panzer Regiment 16. (US Army) *Below:* Argentan on a quiet Sunday morning in April 1983. The bells of the rebuilt church of St Germain (on the left just out of the picture) peal out their message.

PANZER REGIMENT 22

A rare photograph from the defenders' standpoint pictured at the tip of the division's task along the Orne river: Lion-sur-Mer. (Bundesarchiv)

Part of the Afrika Korps, 21. Panzer Division had been formed in the summer of 1941 from 5. Leichte Division. After the division was captured in Tunisia, a new 21. Panzer Division was reformed in France (at Rennes) on July 15, 1943. It was given Panzer Regiment 100 which was formed in January 1943 at Versailles from Panzer Abteilung 223, Panzer Kompanie Paris, the Panzer Kompanie from LXXXI Armee Korps and the Panzer Kompanie of LXXXII Armee Korps. Equipped with a motley collection of captured French tanks, it was then far from being an elite unit. The division remained in France, retaining its French tanks right up to the summer of 1944, by which time Panzer Regiment 100 had become Panzer Regiment 22.

Of the panzer divisions in Normandy, 21. Panzer Division had been stationed there the longest. In general, it was in pretty bad shape with most of its equipment both obsolete and in short supply — and this included practice ammunition. In April 1944 the tanks were allocated only five rounds each per month. Divisional headquarters in the spring of 1944 was at St Pierre-sur-Dives, thirty kilometres south-east of Caen, most of the units being deployed between Caen and Falaise. Oberst von Oppeln-Bronikowski had his regimental headquarters at Falaise.

During the night of June 5/6, Panzer Regiment 22 was put on official standby at about midnight, but Oberst von Oppeln-Bronikowski had no need to alert I. Abteilung as its commanding officer, Hauptmann von Gottberg, happened to overhear him on the telephone with the divisional commander and Gottberg himself put his battalion at readiness.

So long had the regiment been in the area that the personnel had become accustomed to local delicacies. Fancy going shopping for your Camembert cheese in a tank. 'Hedi' is an old-type PzKpfw IV Ausf B or C, and is seen outside the grocery shop in St Martin de Fresnay, south-east of St Pierre-sur-Dives and not that far from the village of Camembert itself. (Bundesarchiv)

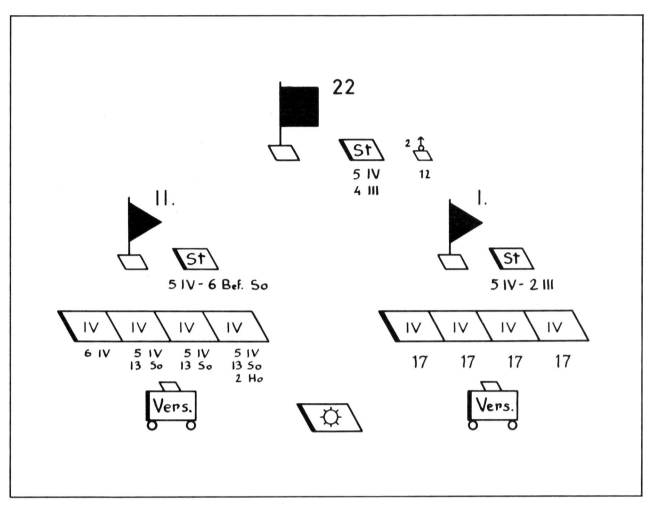

The theoretical organisation of Panzer Regiment 22 in June 1944 when the panzer units of 21. Panzer Division recorded an assorted collection of armour on their books, much of it obsolete. Between its Panzer Regiment 22, Sturmgeschütz Abteilung 200 and Panzer Artillerie Regiment 155, the division had 98 PzKpfw IVs, of which 6 were old Ausf Gs, 6 PzKpfw IIIs, 23 Somuas, 43 assault guns on Hotchkiss chassis' and 45 Lorraine conversions. Four weeks later only 61 PzKpfw IVs and 32 assault guns remained available although none of the Lorraines had been lost. On August 1 the PzKpfw IVs were down to 42.

A Panzer Regiment 22 PzKpfw IV in the Caen sector. This is a type H or J and it is interesting to see that Zimmerit has been applied to the turret schürzen during a second partial application of the compound. (Bundesarchiv)

On the flat plain north-east of Caen, not far from Lebisey, the regiment met its match. Although dug in 'desert style', tank 134 (an Ausf H) received a direct hit on the front of the turret which penetrated the 50mm armour. (IWM)

Meanwhile, II. Abteilung, Panzer Regiment 22 was making its way east to take part in a night exercise. From the distant drone of aircraft and flashes in the sky, it was apparent that something was happening along the coast, although this was nothing out of the ordinary. Then at 2.00 a.m. precisely, when they were about ten kilometres east of Falaise, a dispatch rider caught them up: the tanks turned back for their bases and went onto the alert. At 4.00 a.m. the order came through for their few practice rounds to be replaced with live ammunition, and from then on — for five hours — the crews waited for the order to start engines.

At divisional headquarters, the GOC, General Feuchtinger, was in a quandary. General Richter, commanding 716. Infanterie Division to which 21. Panzer Division was attached for tactical purposes, had duly ordered him at 1.20 a.m. to move forward against the enemy parachutists east of the Orne. Feuchtinger, though, was as dependent upon the OKW for orders as a reserve unit and did not dare intervene since his instructions were that he was not to move without sanction from higher command.

From II. Abteilung, at about 6.00 a.m., Major Vierzig dispatched one of his officers to Falaise, who on his return from regimental headquarters announced nothing less than the news that the long-expected invasion was in progress.

It was 6.30 a.m. when Feuchtinger resolved to take action. Dispatch riders were sent racing off to all the villages where I. Abteilung's tanks were warmed up and waiting. At the command 'Abstand dreissig Meter' — keeping thirty metres apart — the tanks crunched along the roads again. The order to move out reached II. Abteilung at 9.00 a.m. The regiment's task was to destroy the paratroopers east of the Orne.

I. Abteilung set off towards the north-east at a steady pace, with II. Abteilung following on. The blazing city of Caen was behind them and 4. Kompanie (I. Abteilung) had caught sight of the first few isolated parachutists when, without a shot having been fired, the tanks were abruptly recalled. The 4. Kompanie alone remained to the north of Caen, while the others made their way back towards the city. Maintaining radio silence, 5. Kompanie took the lead this time in II. Abteilung and Major Vierzig brought up the rear. Alongside I. Abteilung, von Oppeln-Bronikowski urged the tanks to press on through the bombed streets of Caen, contact having been lost with Vierzig's unit as the tanks had to go via Colombelles, losing a lot of time in so doing.

By early afternoon I. Abteilung was in position to the north of the city — clearly visible from where Major Vierzig was stationed on the banks of the Orne at Lebisey. Still observing strict radio silence, Vierzig deployed to the left of them and, after he had gone across to von Gottberg, the two men made their way to a hill where von Oppeln had set up his advance HQ, and where they had noticed the presence of General Marcks of LXXXIV Korps. (It was Marcks who had been responsible for their turn-around.)

The division's objective was to get to the coast. Troops from Panzergrenadier Regiment 902 had succeeded in getting through at about 8.00 p.m. Inland, the PzKpfw IVs were met by fire from firmly established anti-tank guns in front of Biéville and Périers; before the regiment had fired its first shot the leading PzKpfw IV went up in flames and very quickly the tanks came to a halt. Yet to have pulled back would have meant abandoning the panzergrenadiers who had reached Lion-sur-Mer. Von Oppeln, the cavalry officer, had no option but to order the tanks to dig in. In their turn, they were thus able to repulse the British 27th Brigade — but the toll for the first

Nearby, another Mk IV from the II. Abteilung also received a direct hit on its turret. This shell appears to have struck from the opposite side, smashing the 30mm armour beside the hatch and blowing off the skirt. (IWM)

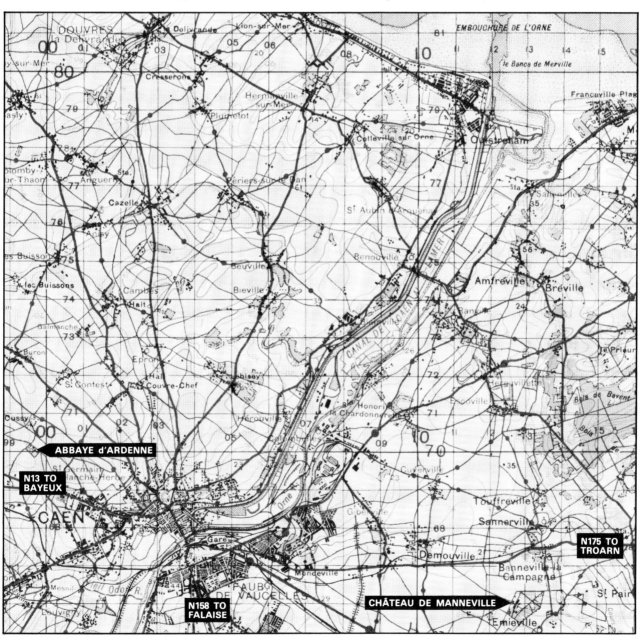

day had been high: sixteen tanks lost, about half of them belonging to I. Abteilung around Périers.

On the right, 4. Kompanie was getting on with hunting down parachutists. Moving in on Hérouvillette, they arrived as darkness came down only to find that they had been firing on their own positions. That night the crews slept inside their tanks.

Next day, following their mistaken attack on the panzergrenadiers, 4. Kompanie was to attack with them this time . . . from the direction of Ranville where it was believed that the 6th Airborne Division had set up its HQ. The panzergrenadiers were in armoured personnel carriers. Then, as the tanks swung round towards Longueval, they received their baptism of fire beneath the guns of the Allied ships offshore, which was to have a catastrophic effect on the younger crew members and keep them awake for nights on end. Opposite them, nevertheless, among the British 3rd Division the PzKpfw IVs had caused quite a commotion within the ranks . . . not for the last time had they been mistaken for Tigers.

That day, the rest of Panzer Regiment 22 was to take part in the offensive that was intended to cut off the British left from the Canadians but, even as the tanks waited in position, it was for an offensive that was never to take place. . . .

On the right of the Orne the British once again came up against 4. Kompanie on June 13, destroying four of its tanks. With its numbers down to eight, morale was starting to crumble. Thereafter integrated into Kampfgruppe

Lück, the Kompanie took part in its last offensive action as part of the battle group on June 16 against the hamlet of St Honorine. With the grenadiers pinned down by naval artillery, the PzKpfw IVs went on alone and took on the Shermans. They had to pull back quickly, however, losing another PzKpfw IV.

The 4. Kompanie remained in the area until June 27, when it was transferred to Verson, on the other side of Caen, where it went into an attack against Mouen with a few of the Panthers of 1. Abteilung, SS-Panzer Regiment 12. At about 5.00 p.m. it was heavily involved against tanks and anti-tank guns between Mouen and Cheux. Tank 413 lost one of its tracks. The commander in 421 had his head blown off while standing in the cupola; the driver being so horrified that he put the steering out of action by slamming the tank into reverse. Tank 422 had its turret jammed and pulled back into a sunken lane to try to repair it. Tank 425 first lost the use of its engine, then its gun; isolated in the midst of the opposing infantry, it was soon set on fire. No. 412, the company commander's tank, brewed up. . . .

The 21. Panzer Division remained in position to the north of Caen until it was pulled out, much depleted, in the second week of July to the south and south-east

of Caen from where it could be quickly brought back into the line. On July 11 divisional headquarters was moved from St André-sur-Orne where it had been located from the outset. Newly arrived on the right of Panzer Regiment 22, and attached to it tactically, were the Tigers of schwere Panzer Abteilung 503 — the only heavy tank batallion with Königstigers in Normandy.

On July 18, during the bombing that preceded Operation Goodwood, some of the regiment's units were caught in the southern part of the target zone, 4. Kompanie being among them. Hatches clanged shut when the Allied formations droned over and, as the bombs came whistling down, reportedly there were a few young crew members who committed suicide. Others went out of their minds as the fearful saturation bombing went on all around them. Tanks were left blazing or buried and Tigers were tossed upside down almost as if they were made of matchwood.

East of Caen, in the villages surrounding the Pont L'Evèque road, PzKpfw IVs battled alongside Tigers and a large part of the regiment fought at Cagny on the N13. Four more of the regiment's tanks were lost. . . . Inexorably the regiment was sucked with the division into the Falaise pocket, where they were to experience a common fate.

Armed with the old-type 24 calibre 75mm gun, this Ausf B or C of Panzer Regiment 22 was photographed on August 26 by Sergeant Wilkes. This model featured narrow 36cm tracks with the turret hatch opening in two directions. No Zimmerit has been applied and camouflage appears to be wide olive green bands. Rather crude was the sliding shutter in the front plate: in the absence of a fixed machine gun this was provided to allow shots to be fired from inside, most probably using a semi-automatic pistol! (IWM)

While in the company of schwere Panzer Abteilung 503 in the vicinity of the Château de Manneville, some ten kilometres east of Caen, part of Panzer Regiment 22 was caught in the Allied saturation bombing on July 18. (IWM)

With local help, we were able to pinpoint the spot where this Ausf H came to grief — along this tree line at Emiéville a few hundred metres from the château. Although restored to pasture, the field still shows evidence of the bombing.

OBERST HERMANN VON OPPELN-BRONIKOWSKI

Hermann von Oppeln-Bronikowski was born on January 2, 1899, in Berlin. The son of a regular army officer, he entered the cadet school at Berlin-Lichterfelde, and at the outbreak of war in 1914 was a Leutnant in Uhlan Regiment 10 at Torgau. During the war he served in the infantry, becoming a platoon leader in the Infanterie Regiment 118. After the Armistice, he joined the Kavallerie Regiment 10 in the Reichsheer, to which he was to belong for twenty years.

Von Oppeln-Bronikowski was an accomplished horseman and a first-class riding instructor. He taught first at the Ohrdruf Infantry School and then, in 1933, at the Cavalry School in Hannover. In 1936 he won a Gold Medal at the Berlin Olympics.

In 1939 he commanded a reconnaissance unit, Aufklärungs Abteilung 24, in Poland, where he won the 1939 Clasp to his 1914 Iron Cross I Class. In 1940, after the campaign in France, he was transferred to the staff of the inspectorate of mobile troops (cavalry and armoured). He took part in Operation Barbarossa in 1941 with Panzer Regiment 35 (4. Panzer Division), being given command of the regiment in succession to Oberst Eberbach (later 5. Panzer Armee and 7. Armee commander in Normandy) in January 1942.

On January 1, 1943, von Oppeln-Bronikowski was awarded the Knights Cross to the Iron Cross for his success at the head of Panzer Regiment 204 during the autumn. Shortly afterwards, he was given command of Panzer Regiment 11, (6. Panzer Division). He was wounded at Kursk and on his return from convalescence took over Panzer Regiment 100, belonging to 21. Panzer Division, which, as Panzer Regiment 22, he commanded in Normandy. On July 28, 1944 he was awarded the Oak Leaves to the Knights Cross (the 536th awarded during the Second World War).

In November 1944 he took over 20. Panzer Division and in January 1945 was promoted to Generalmajor. For service on the Eastern Front he received the Swords to the Knights Cross on April 17, 1945 (142nd since the first award to Adolf Galland in June 1941). He was taken prisoner by the Allies on the same day near Plauen.

Released on August 4, 1947, he later took an active part in the development of the Bundeswehr and trained the Canadian horseriding team for the Tokyo Olympics in 1964. He died on September 19, 1966.

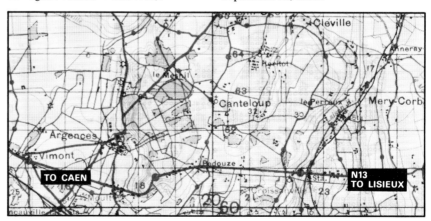

Early in July, Oberst Hermann von Oppeln-Bronikowski visited 'his' Tiger battalion schwere Panzer Abteilung 503 (see page 114) which, for tactical purposes was attached to 21. Panzer Division. The picture was taken on the steps of the battalion HQ, the Château de Canteloup, south-east of Caen near Argences. (Bundesarchiv)

PANZER REGIMENT 33

The threat of Allied fighter-bombers ranging far and wide over northern France was an ever-present hazard to the movement of men, machines and materials. Armour was a prize target — hence the precautions taken by panzer troops. Panzer Regiment 33 of 9. Panzer Division suffered heavily during its march to the front from the south of France where it was based. In the end, it only served in Normandy for little over two weeks at the beginning of August. (Bundesarchiv)

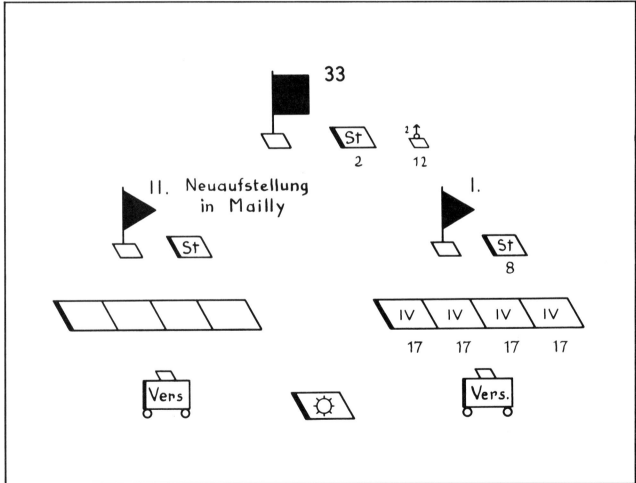

The theoretical organisation of Panzer Regiment 33 as at June 1944. At the beginning of the month, 9. Panzer Division had only one tank battalion in its Panzer Regiment 33 as the II. Abteilung was at Mailly-le-Camp obtaining its Panthers. I. Abteilung then had 71 PzKpfw IVs. The division's Panzerjäger Abteilung 50 had only 5 assault guns available. By July 1 the situation had not improved for the division had not yet moved north and its II. Abteilung was still at Mailly, although it had by now received 39 Panthers. Because of unrecorded losses during the move to Normandy, it is impossible to state with accuracy how many of the 70-odd PzKpfw IVs and 40-odd Panthers actually took part in the campaign.

Formed on February 2, 1940 as part of 9. Panzer Division, Panzer Regiment 33 fought with the division in Holland, France and Greece, and then in Russia from 1941 until the division was transferred to the south of France to refit and re-form with 155. Reserve Panzer Division near Nîmes in April 1944.

The regimental depot was located at Vienna. When the regiment was formed, the tank instruction battalion became its I. Abteilung and Panzer Abteilung 33 its II. In 1943 Panzer Regiment 33 was strengthened by a third battalion, ex-I. Abteilung, Panzer Regiment 3. In 1943 the regiment's II. Abteilung became Panzer Abteilung 51 and its III. Abteilung schwere Panzer Abteilung 506. In January 1944 Panzer Abteilung 51 reverted to the II. Abteilung Panzer Regiment 33.

After the division's arrival in the area of Avignon in the south of France, its refit was not properly completed until the end of July; and on July 27 it was warned to be ready to move and sent up north, where 7. Armee was hoping to deploy it between Alençon and Domfront, and wanted it to take part in the Mortain offensive. On its journey north, having to pass through areas where the Resistance was very active, the division was plagued by attacks from them and by Allied aircraft. At this stage, Panzer Regiment 33 still only had its I. Abteilung operational with PzKpfw IVs.

From August 6, 9. Panzer Division was mixed in with other units on a line from Domfront to Mayenne, and from the 10th was involved increasingly in the bitter fighting south of Alençon. On August 15 II. Abteilung of Panzer Regiment 33 was pulled out — it was to fight on the lower Seine — and the division ended up south-east of Paris.

Left: Allied air supremacy spelt death and destruction to any German forces caught out in the open during the summer of 1944. This convoy of the 9. Panzer Division has been spotted on a vulnerable stretch of road between Mailly-le-Camp and Normandy and raked from one end to the other. *Above:* Grenadiers have taken cover under a tree — the Kubelwagen is an army vehicle although the gentleman on the left belongs to the Waffen-SS. (Bundesarchiv)

Some way ahead of the burning trucks, this Panther of the division's armoured regiment (Panzer Regiment 33) has halted in a perilous position, the crew most probably looking back to the rising column of smoke. This Ausf G is of recent manufacture as evidenced by the rear mounting for the gun cleaning rod canister. The spare track wheel on the turret serves also to strengthen its protection — this is one of the old 16-bolt wheels like those on the Ausf D which proved too weak in service. (Bundesarchiv)

SCHWERE PANZER ABTEILUNG 503

Schwere Panzer Abteilung 503 was formed in May 1942 around a nucleus of men from Panzer Regiments 5 and 6. Initially, it could not be fully equipped with the new Tiger and was brought up to strength with the PzKpfw III Ausf N with its 24-calibre 7.5cm gun.

In December 1942 the Abteilung arrived on the southern part of the Eastern Front, finally receiving its missing Tigers in April 1943. In July it took part in Operation Zitadelle near Kursk, and by September the losses it had inflicted on the Russians amounted to 501 tanks, 388 anti-tank guns, 79 artillery pieces, plus 8 aircraft. After a full seventeen months on the Eastern Front, the Abteilung was pulled back in the spring of 1944 to Lemberg, on the border with Poland, before being sent to Ohrdruf, Thuringia, to refit.

Its new tanks only materialised between June 11 and June 17 — when 1. Kompanie had the distinction of being equipped with the Königstiger, which had not long entered service. The new commanding officer was Hauptmann Fromme whose illustrious predecessor, Count Clemens von Kageneck, was awarded the Oak Leaves to his Knights Cross of the Iron Cross on June 26. The 1. Kompanie was commanded by Oberleutnant Oemler, 2. Kompanie by Hauptmann Baron von Eichel-Streiber, and 3. Kompanie by Hauptmann Scherf. In command of the Stabskompanie (Headquarters Company) was Hauptmann Wiegand.

During June, two visits were made by Guderian to schwere Panzer Abteilung 503 on the training grounds at Ohrdruf and twice the Abteilung was ordered to leave for Normandy before it actually departed for France at the end of the month. The eight convoys that transported the unit reached Paris in five days and arrived at Dreux on July 2. From there, the Tigers covered the further 200 kilometres to the front,

Two Porsche-turreted Königstigers from the 1. Kompanie, schwere (heavy) Panzer Abteilung 503, parked under cover in the leafy lane which runs from the D43 to the Château de Canteloup (see page 110) and through the grounds of the house. The battalion was stationed in this sector during the first two weeks of July 1944. British PoWs bring up food containers for the crews. (Bundesarchiv)

How are the mighty fallen! Young French girls cycle down the gravelled track. Although the trees on the left have since been felled, the stumps still remain.

Hauptmann Walter Scherf pictured in Russia in 1944 shortly after the award of his Ritterkreuz (February 23). During the journey from the Eastern Front, the battalion commander, Hauptmann Rolf Fromme, was wounded so Scherf took over for the first two weeks of July. He then commanded 3. Kompanie which was withdrawn from the front towards the end of the month for re-equipping with Ausf B Tigers. (ECP Armées)

Night move by the unit. A spotlight illuminates the scene so evidently the crews do not fear an attack from ground or air. This probably dates the photograph as early July in a village east of Caen. Logically Tank 301 should have belonged to Hauptmann Scherf (3. Kompanie commander, tank 1) but in point of fact his was number 300 — a typical example of the disregard sometimes shown to the standard numbering system. (Bundesarchiv)

entering the little village of Rupierre, between Troarn and Moult, after a four-stage journey by night.

Fifteen kilometres to the west, on July 7, Caen underwent the final bombardment that preceded the Allied capture of the city. By now the Abteilung was at full strength and its tanks were deployed to take up various positions from time to time.

The alert came at 5.00 a.m. on July 11. Tactically, schwere Panzer Abteilung 503 was attached to Panzer Regiment 22, belonging to 21. Panzer Division which was responsible for the whole area from Hérouvillette, north-east of Caen, down to the south of the city; and from divisional headquarters young Leutnant Baron von Rosen (who had once been Fromme's orderly officer and was now a platoon leader) learned that the British had broken through at Colombelles, just across the Orne. The unit commanders were in favour of a counter-attack and, half an hour later, 3. Kompanie was heading westwards.

Three kilometres from their objective, as the Tigers approached Cuverville in the direction of Colombelles, they came under fire from some British tanks. Leutnant Koppe took his section off to the right while Feldwebel Sachs's No. 1 Platoon went to the left and von Rosen's 3. Platoon kept to the road. As one platoon opened fire, the other advanced. With the dust and smoke getting thicker between the houses, the British infantry pulled out. The Tigers were no more than 200 metres outside the hamlet and their crews could see the Shermans brewing up; others were turning back, and two of them ran into one another, their crews coming forward with their hands up. Altogether, twelve Shermans were accounted for.

Luftwaffe personnel are most probably from 16. Luftwaffen Division. (Bundesarchiv)

Another illustration of the lack of time to change numbers by the hard-pressed German tank battalions in Normandy is shown by Tiger 313. In theory it should have been the third tank in the first section or platoon of the third company whereas, in reality, it was the tank of Feldwebel Sachs who, as section leader, should have carried number 311. The fifty-odd ton Tiger was tossed over when it was caught in the fierce bombing of July 18 which preceeded Operation Goodwood while in the grounds of the Château de Manneville (the same attack which hit the Mk IVs of Panzer Regiment 22 — see page 109). Two of Sachs's crewmen were killed and others were unconscious. It took several hours to open up the rear escape hatch in the turret (that of the loader) and free the survivors. This picture clearly shows the interleaved new type of steel-tyred rubber road wheels which were fitted to the last 350 PzKpfw IV Ausf Es constructed. (IWM)

Awaiting their infantry, the Tigers sought cover and von Rosen got down to have a look at the knocked-out Shermans. From the papers inside one of them, the tanks belonged to the Royal Armoured Corps. Then there was a faint buzz of an aircraft somewhere overhead, and soon afterwards a naval bombardment started up from the guns offshore which ranged onto the hamlet. When the shelling had stopped, Hauptmann Scherf went over to their commanding officer, who had just arrived from hospital. Fromme was very keen to recover the two Shermans that had been in collision but which were still in running order. So, while the rest of the Tigers returned to the rear, von Rosen took two experienced drivers with him and tried to get the Shermans going. They managed to do so but not without coming under rocket and machine gun fire from Allied fighters on the way back.

Before the success of this encounter had time to fade, however, the German positions east of Caen were subjected to carpet bombing by some 2,100 aircraft from 5.00 a.m. on July 18 over a period of four hours. Against this kind of attack

Thirty-nine years later we visited the same wood in the château grounds and found bomb craters still very much in evidence. This section of woodland is currently being thinned out and will be replanted.

no tank was immune: von Rosen's tank was seriously damaged (ultimately it was repaired), but that of Unterfeldwebel Westerhausen was burnt out with the crew inside, and Feldwebel Sachs's Tiger was turned upside down.

After the battering was over von Rosen was unconscious but when he came round he tried to stagger back to the Abteilung HQ. The château where the HQ had been installed lay in ruins, though Hauptmann Fromme had escaped unharmed. Von Rosen made a start on trying to recover those tanks that could be repaired and, as he was returning to his own tank within the grounds, he could hear noises coming from inside Sachs's overturned tank. It took no less than three hours to prise open the loader's hatch at the rear of the turret, which was the only opening still accessible, and to get three of the crew out, the other two having been killed.

That afternoon Fromme had to send eight of his Tigers into the front line which had now reached the very edge of the château grounds. Feldwebel Schönrock's tank was brewed up by an anti-tank round and others caught fire as a result of the bombing earlier. By evening, 3. Kompanie consisted of just one operational tank.

Meanwhile, 1. and 2. Kompanies had pulled back ten kilometres during the day to repulse the British who had got as far as Cagny, six kilometres south-east of Caen on the N13. According to Wehrmacht records forty Allied tanks were destroyed in this sector, of which schwere Panzer Abteilung 503 could claim the lion's share.

At the end of July, 1. and 2. Kompanies were apparently still fighting with 21. Panzer Division around Bretteville-sur-Laize, fifteen kilometres south of Caen. A photograph exists of a knocked-out Königstiger twenty-five miles west of Bretteville-sur-Laize, and one was abandoned near Vimoutiers as the gap was closing east of Falaise. (Incidentally, the Abteilung monthly report for July makes particular mention of the fact that the men were complaining of eating badly at this time.)

Another shot in the same sequence, taken by Sergeant Coverley on July 25-26, shows a second knocked out Tiger. (IWM)

A third, photographed after the war by M. Bequer, shows its prize crew: Annick and Colette. The name painted on the front of the Tiger, which appears to be 'BARAT', is that of the scrapyard which had purchased it after the war.

One of the more peaceful pursuits at the château today is breeding race horses.

Above: Plessis-Grimoult lies at the foot of Mont Pinçon to the south of Aunay-sur-Odon. Here another of schwere Panzer Abteilung 503's Tigers came to grief, providing an interesting specimen for these British tankers. It was not uncommon for panzer crews to leave the towing cable attached when in action. A violent explosion has lifted the turret from its seating and torn off the track guards, tools and spare tracks. (IWM) *Below:* All repaired today . . . except for that weather-vane!

Very interesting photo from Canadian archives showing a King Tiger abandoned while being towed by a Bergepanther — one of only two such recovery vehicles on the strength of the 1. Kompanie of schwere Panzer Abteilung 503. The picture was taken near Vimoutiers on August 22, i.e. around the end of the Normandy campaign. The Tiger retreating eastwards has been set on fire partially burning the ladder, possibly carried by the crew to reach the turret easier. (Public Archives of Canada)

Shortly after the earlier battles of July for the high ground south-west of Cagny, 3. Kompanie had been withdrawn and sent to Mailly-le-Camp, east of Paris, to be equipped with Königstigers. With its new tanks, the Kompanie entrained on August 11 on the first stage of the journey via Paris. Next day, when the train was between Sézanne and Esternay, still about eighty kilometres from the capital, it was pounced on by five Thunderbolts. One of the ammunition trucks containing 8.8cm shells was set on fire although it failed to explode. Von Rosen's tank was also set alight and lay where it had been blown upside down beside the line. Unterfeldwebel Werheim and Oberfeldwebel Bormann were killed and a number of men wounded.

The rest of 3. Kompanie reached Paris, but not Normandy, and von Rosen only met up with his unit at Beauvais. Most of the Abteilung's tanks ended up on the wrong side of the Seine (probably around la Bouille, near Rouen), as there were no ferries available to take the weight of a 57-tonne Tiger or 68-tonne Königstiger. The 3. Kompanie — by then the sole operational unit of schwere Panzer Abteilung 503 — lost the last of its Königstigers near Amiens.

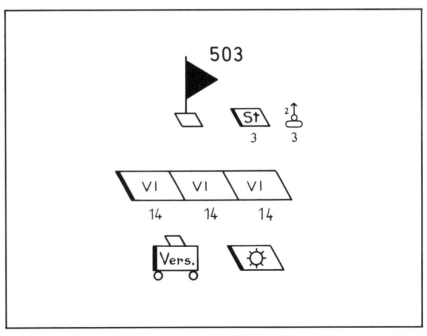

The theoretical organisation of schwere Panzer Abteilung 503 in June 1944. No precise information has survived as to the number of Tigers on strength on June 1 but we know that the battalion had only 24 Tigers available (as opposed to the 45 'on paper') on March 1. Some 13 were recorded on August 1 together with 3 SdKfz 10/4 20mm Flak half-tracks.

The normal method of transportation for tanks was by flat-bed railway wagons — under normal circumstances this was quicker and of course it saved on track wear. The Panther (this is an Ausf G of Panzer Regiment 33) could just be carried 'as is' but both the Tiger and King Tiger had to have narrower transit tracks fitted. Evidence of Allied air interdiction is apparent although there seems no immediate danger as the crew carry out their ablutions. (Bundesarchiv)

MISCELLANEOUS ARMY PANZER UNITS

Although a battalion of Panzer Regiment Grossdeutschland — the elite of the Heer — was in the West in the summer of 1944, records are unclear as to its part in the Normandy campaign. On June 1, the I. Abteilung of the regiment was in France, re-equipping with Panthers, and on July 1 it appears that the unit was assigned to OB West. If the battalion was engaged in the fighting it was most probably whilst subordinated to another division for a short period only as by September it was on the Eastern Front with 6. Panzer Division.

SCHWERE PANZERJÄGER ABTEILUNG 654

The schwere Panzerjäger Abteilung 654 was being equipped with the new Jagdpanther at Mailly-le-Camp when the invasion was launched. On July 1 the battalion commander, Hauptmann Noak, reported that only twenty-five Jagdpanthers were available and that his 1. Kompanie was still at Mailly le Camp without their tank destroyers. Of the other two companies, it seems that only 2. Kompanie, with a dozen Jagdpanthers, was present in Normandy.

Fighting on the left flank of the 7. Armee, the Jagdpanthers faced British

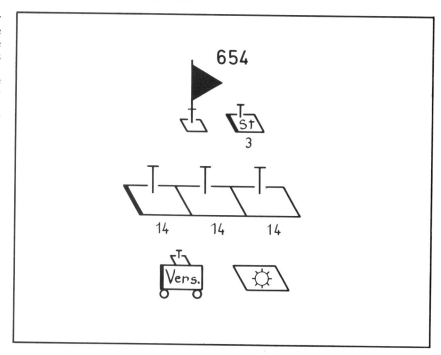

troops and, in spite of their small number, they succeeded in making their presence felt. On July 30 the 15th Scottish Division, supported by the 6th Guards Tank Brigade, broke through south of Caumont l'Eventé, where the front was weakly held by the 326. Infanterie Division, and made a ten kilometre drive to secure Point 309 controlling the N175 road. A squadron of Churchills was detailed to cover the left flank from the slope of Point 226. All

Two Jagdpanthers (of the dozen or so which saw service in Normandy) of 2. Kompanie, schwere Panzerjäger Abteilung 654 pass through Bourgtheroulde. Together with the Tigers of schwere Panzer Abteilung 503 they are retreating north towards the Seine crossing at Elbeuf. See also pages 192-197. (Bundesarchiv)

remained quiet for a while but suddenly tanks started to explode in flames, one after another. Two Jagdpanthers pulled out of cover onto the crest covered by a third from where, within seconds, they had destroyed some more Churchills. The crews had actually broken cover without realising that three tank squadrons were facing them and the sight of the two other Churchill squadrons soon prompted them to move back, receiving some hits from the British armour before disappearing beyond the crest. The whole action had lasted less than two minutes yet it had cost the Guards eleven Churchills and reduced one of the squadrons to four vehicles. Two of the Jagdpanthers were later found abandoned on the reverse slope with some track damage but the third escaped unscathed.

PANZER ERSATZ UND AUSBILDUNGS ABTEILUNG 100

The Abteilung was formed in April 1941 as a panzer recruitment and training unit at Schwetzingen in the Rhineland, within Wehrkreis (Military District) XII. A year later it was posted to Satory camp, near Versailles, where it came under the Kommandant Gross Paris (Greater Paris Command). Much of the troops' time was spent guarding the railways around Paris and the Metro against increasing acts of sabotage, and a detachment was even sent to Vercors in south-east France near Grenoble to counter the activities of the Maquis. Most of the Abteilung's officers were convalescing from wounds; its NCOs were experienced soldiers but men who had been away too long from active service. The tanks with which the unit was equipped for its role of training and replacement (Ersatz und Ausbildungs) were ex-French Army — some of which ran on coal gas or were without turrets — adequate for learning the rudiments but leaving their crews in need of further training when they came to handle armour in actual service.

Hardly an operational unit, the Abteilung was sent to Normandy at the beginning of May 1944 and was stationed west of Carentan, with its HQ at the Château de Francquetot and companies spread out in the area between Baupte, Carentan and Ste Mère-Eglise. In command was Major Bardlenschlager, who was tactically responsible to the 91. Infanterie Division which covered the central part of the Cotentin.

There was not much question of training; all the crews being set to work

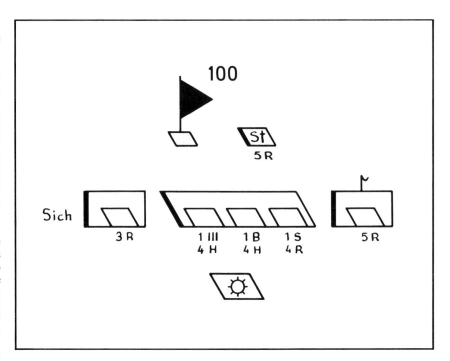

The theoretical organisation of Panzer Ersatz und Ausbildungs Abteilung 100. As a tank training and replacement battalion (Ersatz und Ausbildungs Abteilung) it had simply to make do with whatever outdated tanks it could be spared, making it appear a pretty strange-looking outfit. Besides 8 Hotchkiss, one Somua and one Renault B-1 bis, it was supposed to have a PzKpfw III and 17 Renault R-35s. Its precise strength on June 6 is unknown but it is recorded that it had some 15 tanks available.

with forced French labour in planting the fields with a crop of Rommel's asparagus — as the stakes to prevent aircraft from landing were nicknamed.

On the night of June 4 a magnificent fireworks display took place in the sky over Carentan and thousands of rounds of tracer climbed up into the darkness amidst all the din. When it started up

again the following night — June 5 — Oberleutnant Weber, in charge of 1. Kompanie, reassured his men: 'Zirkus! Nicht für uns bestimmt.' It was only a circus display; nothing that they need worry about.

Early the following morning the men were taken aback by the sight of parachutes hanging from the trees and

The Somua S-35 equipped several of the odd units in Normandy including Panzer Ersatz und Ausbildungs Abteilung 100.

of the wreckage of Allied gliders in the fields. Anxiously they spied out the land, but there was not a soul to be seen. Just as they did every morning, a party went out to fetch the milk . . . their bodies were found later. Later still it was learned that Oberleutnant Weber had also been killed.

The Abteilung only went over to battle readiness at 9.00 a.m. No instructions came over the wireless, and it was the dispatch riders who finally found out what was happening. Major Bardlen-schlager set off from the Château de Francquetot for 91. Infanterie Division headquarters at Houtteville a kilometre or so away . . . and was never seen again.

At about 8.00 p.m. the Abteilung's adjutant brought 1. and 2. Kompanies together at Baupte to form a road block across the N803 to Carentan. During the night the outdated tanks opened fire on anything suspected as being infantry. At the slightest sound of an engine, though, they broke off and made for cover. In the morning No. 1 Platoon of 1. Kompanie was sent off towards St Lô and No. 2 towards Carentan . . .

In the end, Panzer Ersatz und Ausbildungs Abteilung 100 was reduced to the strength of an anti-tank company, with the panzerfaust its heaviest weapon and bicycles in place of armour! On July 7, the unit was disbanded by OB West having disappeared in the turmoil of the Normandy battle.

PANZER ABTEILUNG 206

Another panzer unit, equipped with captured French tanks, was Panzer Abteilung 206, which was formed as a reserve formation of 7. Armee at Satory camp, south-west of Versailles, in November 1941.

The drawing shows the theoretical

structure of Panzer Abteilung 206 in mid-January 1944. The battalion was equipped with a motley collection of captured French tanks:

Fourteen 'H' identifies fourteen PzKpfw 38-H 735(f), which was the French Hotchkiss H-35, H-38 and H-39.

Four 'S' identifies four PzKpfw 35-S 739(f) — the French Somua S-35. These tanks were issued mainly to platoon and company commanders.

Five 'B' identifies five PzKpfw B-2 740(f), the French Renault B-1 bis, some of which had been converted into flame-thrower tanks.

Two 'Schulfahrgestell H' identifies two Hotchkiss tanks converted as driver training vehicles.

The 'T' identifies three anti-tank guns, probably 75mm PaK.

On June 1 the Abteilung had the

A considerable number of the Char B-1 bis, the main French battle tank in 1940, were captured and pressed into German service under various guises; training vehicles, conversion to flame throwers, and the issue to second line units such as Panzer Abteilung 206. (Bundesarchiv)

following tanks available: 16 Hotchkiss, 2 Somua, 4 Renault B-1 bis, and 2 Renault R-35 (called PzKpfw 35-R 731(f) by the Germans), not provided for in the theoretical establishment, identified by 'R' on the organisation chart.

On D-Day Panzer Abteilung 206 was at the northernmost tip of the Contentin peninsular at Cap de la Hague, with its battalion headquarters at Beaumont, eight kilometres to the south-east and the Abteilung was completely wiped out in the Cherbourg peninsula.

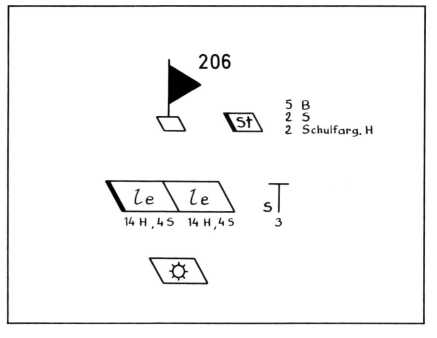

WAFFEN-SS

The temptation of a parade along the Champs-Elysées was too much to resist for SS-Panzer Regiment 1 (belonging to 1. SS-Panzer Division) during their journey to the front. In actual fact they may well be 'commuting' from the Gare du Nord to the Gare St Lazare! Nonetheless the crowds were notably absent. Picture taken at the beginning of July. (Bundesarchiv)

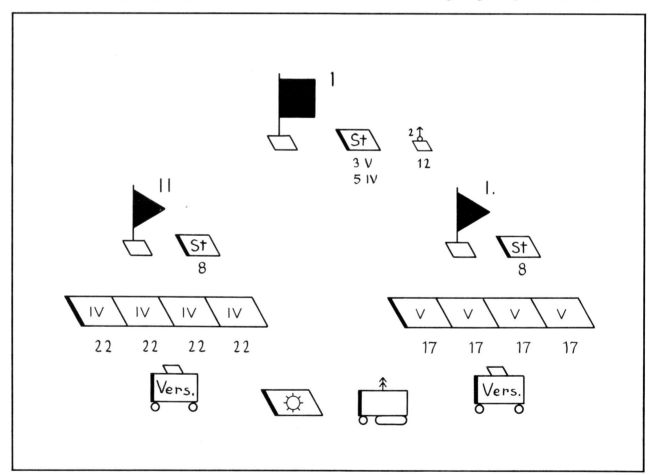

Theoretical organisation of SS-Panzer Regiment 1 in June 1944. On June 1 the regiment (commander SS-Obersturmbannführer Peiper) had 42 PzKpfw IVs in its II. Abteilung (commanded by SS-Sturmbannführer Kling) and 38 Panthers in its I. Abteilung (commander SS-Hauptsturmführer Pötschke). A company of engineers, 9. Kompanie, formed part of the panzer regiment. The SS-Sturmgeschütz Abteilung 1 of SS-Sturmbannführer Heimann was almost at full strength having 44 StuGs (theoretically 45). By July 1, 1. SS-Panzer Division was left with 30 PzKpfw IVs, 25 Panthers and 31 StuGs. Four weeks later these figures were 61, 40 and 23 respectively. No doubt the division's maintenance units had worked hard to repair damaged tanks but, in spite of shattered railways, it is obvious that the division had received an allocation of new tanks.

SS-PANZER REGIMENT 1

From a motorised regiment which took part in the campaigns in Poland and the West, the Leibstandarte had grown to divisional strength by early 1941 and was officially designated SS-Division Adolf Hitler at the end of the Balkans campaign. Further expansion took place before its advance into Russia. The division was transferred to northern France in the summer of 1942 and reformed as a panzergrenadier division. A panzer division in all but name, its tank regiment was formed towards the end of the year from the nucleus of its tank battalion, established in January 1942. SS-Panzer Regiment LSSAH received Tigers in December and Panthers in the first half of 1943.

In March 1943 the Leibstandarte took part in the German counter-offensive for the recapture of Kharkov in Operation Zitadelle before being sent to northern Italy in August where it undertook occupation duties and was involved in anti-partisan operations. On October 22, 1943 it became 1. SS-Panzer Division Liebstandarte SS Adolf Hitler and its panzer regiment was renamed SS-Panzer Regiment 1. After returning to the Eastern Front in the autumn and suffering heavy losses in the south, it was transferred to Belgium for rest and refitting in the spring of 1944.

The Liebstandarte did not leave the Beverlo area for Normandy until the

Another part of the regiment en route by rail. Here a stop appears to have been made to cut branches for camouflage. Note that the Panthers are spread out, not all together, to minimise the risk of all being wiped out if shot up. A normal freight train could carry about twenty such tanks. In between are the battalion's service vehicles — the divisional symbol of the LSSAH being visible under a magnifying glass on the rearmost truck. (Ullstein)

middle of June. Regrouping took place initially south of Caen between Thury-Harcourt and Bretteville-sur-Laize; then to the south-west, north of Potigny, on the N158 between Caen and Falaise; and then further north between Bretteville-sur-Laize and Caen.

By July 1 SS-Panzer Regiment 1 had still not been assembled together and the greater part of the division was not in the line before July 9 although some units were rapidly brought into action early on. From July 12 to July 17 divisional headquarters was located at Fresney-le-Puceux, just to the north-west of Bretteville.

Having first been sent closer to Caen, between Eterville and Mondeville, the division was moved east towards Cagny at the time of Operation Goodwood — a few units being caught up in the bombing that preceded the offensive on July 18.

I. Abteilung was in action in the vicinity of Bourguébus. No more than about forty-six tanks were available and they suffered heavy losses — but the Allies had lost a hundred and could advance no further.

On July 20, near Verrières, three kilometres west of Bourguébus on the other side of the main road from Caen to Falaise, SS-Panzer Regiment 1 was able to assemble seventy Panthers and PzKpfw IVs. After the Canadian attack on Verrières ridge, the Allied offensive marked time.

The 'black panther'. Inspired by the unofficial insignia, this Panther Ausf A also has LSSAH etched in the Zimmerit on the turret. R 02 identifies it as belonging to SS-Hauptsturmführer Gruhle, adjutant to SS-Obersturmbannführer Peiper who would have used Panther R 01. (Bundesarchiv)

The division continued the fight between the two main roads N158 Caen-Falaise and N13 Caen-Lisieux and took part in a counter-attack at Tilly-la-Campagne on July 25.

On August 3 the division was withdrawn from the Caen sector and transferred south-west towards Avranches, sustaining particularly heavy losses from air attacks on the way. The offensive at Mortain began at dawn on August 7 with the LSSAH Division on the right, though its armoured columns were pinned to the ground by Allied air power. By August 12 SS-Panzer Regiment 1 (then at Carrouges) possessed only 30 tanks; the following day the total was down to 19 (14 PzKpfw IVs and 5 Panthers). Three days later 1. SS-Panzer Division was forced to pull back and it regrouped on August 18 and 19 on the River Dives. Reduced to a Kampfgruppe, it broke out on the afternoon of August 20 from the Gouffern Forest and managed to extricate itself through the St Lambert-sur-Dive corridor.

Above: This drowned Sturmgeschütz 40 Ausf G belonged to SS-Sturmgeschütz Abteilung 1. It fell or was pushed from the bridge at Putanges (south of Falaise) into the fast flowing Orne river. (IWM) Right: Fishing for smaller fry.

Sergeant Laing may well have pictured one of the regiment's PzKpfw IVs in this picture taken near Cagny on July 19. (IWM)

SS-OBERSTURMBANNFÜHRER JOCHEN PEIPER

Peiper was born on January 30, 1915, in Berlin. The son of an army officer, he was attracted to a military career and joined up in the Leibstandarte SS Adolf Hitler, where he was well thought of and was sent to the SS officer training school at Brunswick, passing out as an SS-Untersturmführer. Like Max Wünsche, who rose to command SS-Panzer Regiment 12, Peiper was just the kind of man the SS aimed to produce, which led to him being posted to Himmler's staff as an adjutant in 1938.

Peiper commanded 10. Kompanie of the LSSAH in Poland in September 1939 and in the West during the summer of 1940, being awarded the Iron Cross I and II Class. In Russia, in 1941, he was in command of III. Abteilung of the newly motorised division's SS-Panzer Grenadier Regiment 2.

For his part in the recapture of Kharkov Peiper was awarded the Knight's Cross to the Iron Cross on March 9, 1943. By then he was battalion commander and, having also made a name for himself at Kursk during the summer, in November Peiper succeeded SS-Obersturmbannführer Schönberger as commanding officer of SS-Panzer Regiment 1, which he remained throughout the rest of the war. On January 27, 1944, after his tanks had cut a swathe through four Russian divisions that winter, he received the Oak Leaves to his Knight's Cross. On January 11, 1945 he added the Swords to the award as a result of his performance in the Ardennes the previous month, the 119th officer to be so honoured.

After the war Peiper achieved notoriety as a result of the 'Malmedy Massacre' war crimes trial where the American Army tried, with dubious efficiency, to find and convict those responsible for the deaths of American PoWs in the Ardennes.

Peiper was murdered at his home in Traves in eastern France in the early hours of July 14, 1976, in circumstances which have never satisfactorily been resolved. His mild features and appearance of being a well brought up young man belied a considerable reputation for toughness. Every move that he undertook had the prospect of success — even those that looked hopeless from the start — for, like Michael Wittmann, his decisions were based on a sound grasp of military principles.

SS-PANZER REGIMENT 2

SS-Panzer Regiment 2 formed part of 2. SS-Panzer Division Das Reich. The division originated from the three motorised infantry regiments of the SS-Verfügungstruppe ('SS Special Forces' — literally 'Special Disposal Troops'): Standarte 1 Deutschland, 2 Germania and 3 Der Führer, which fought in Poland in 1939 and were formed into the motorised SS-Verfügungs Division on April 1, 1940, fighting in the Low Countries and France and becoming SS-Division Reich in December 1940. Less Germania, which was detached to help form what later became 5. SS-Division Wiking, it took part in the Balkans operations prior to the invasion of Russia.

The division was brought back to Normandy from Russia in June 1942 to reorganise and re-equip. It also received a panzer battalion — SS-Panzer Abteilung Das Reich and was designated SS-Panzer Grenadier Division Das Reich in November 1942. It returned to Russia early in 1943 where it fought at Kharkov and on the Dnieper. In October 1943 it became 2. SS-Panzer Division Das Reich when its panzer battalion expanded into SS-Panzer Regiment 2. The division returned to France in April 1944 and, stationed in south-west France near

Toulouse, with divisional headquarters at Montauban, it was ordered to move up to Normandy shortly after D-Day. Travelling through a stronghold of the Maquis, the division took six days to cover the first ninety miles to Brive-la-Gaillard, and from there the armour made a detour by rail via Perigueux, Angoulême and Poitiers whilst the rest of the division continued by road via Limoges. The battles against the Maquis en route were harsh and 99 people were executed at Tulle (east of Brive) on June 9, another 642 at Oradour-sur-Glane (north-west of Limoges) on June 10, and another 50 on June 11 at Mussidan, south-west of Perigueux.

The division assembled south of St Lô towards the end of June and beginning of July. A Kampfgruppe was sent across to fight on the left flank of the Odon salient, in the vicinity of Noyers Bocage, but the bulk of the division entered the line to the north-east of Périers around July 10.

From St Sébastien-de-Raids, two kilometres outside Périers, I. Abteilung under SS-Sturmbannführer Enseling moved forward in an attack launched towards Sainteny six kilometres to the north-east. In the lead was 4. Kompanie, led by SS-Unterscharführer Ernst

Two PzKpfw IVs, Ausf J, of SS-Panzer Regiment 2 identified by the yellow 'Kampfrune' painted on the rear of the tanks. The tank numbers on the turret skirts identify them as being from its 6th Company. The location is St Fromond which lies just east of the N174 from Carentan to St Lô. The American unit in this area was the 117th Infantry of the 30th Infantry Division and as the photo is dated July 9 it shows a very early encounter by the SS-Panzer Division 2. (US Army)

Barkmann, who had been with the unit from the time the regiment's first Panthers had been delivered a year previously.

From Barkmann's own account, he destroyed his first Sherman on July 8. His Kompanie had come under artillery fire and they had been forced to get out of their tanks and take cover underneath them. At the time the Abteilung was pitted against the US 3rd Armored Division attempting to force a way through. Next day they were in action again and on July 12 Barkmann knocked out two more Sherman's and immobilised his fourth. Fighting in the bocage of Normandy, however, was quite a different matter than on the steppes of Russia; here there was no question of attacking other than in platoons or companies — and tanks were expected to advance without supporting infantry.

Then there was a lull. Barkmann recalled that checking the way his tank was camouflaged was by now almost a reflex action among German tank crews in Normandy, for whom covering a tank with foliage had become a normal part of its maintenance . . . and survival. The following morning he was slowly surveying the area where the Americans were supposed to be through his field-glasses when, suddenly, from behind a hedge, he spotted a movement.

'Turret to 11 o'clock . . . anti-tank round . . . range 400 metres. . . .'

First came a clattering noise; then, from behind the hedge, the rounded hull of a Sherman heaved into view . . . and behind it, five more. The first panzergranate hit the leading tank in the hull. Smoke appeared from its open turret hatch. The other Shermans had come to a halt. A second round from the Panther knocked off one of the leading tank's tracks. The hedge behind which it had sought shelter had a hole in it as large as a man. The damaged Sherman was returning fire . . . a third round hit its turret. The four tanks that were left opened fire with their machine guns which merely tore jagged holes in the Panther's Zimmerit. One of them was unwise enough to show its side. A fourth round went right through it. Three of the crew got out, searching for a fold in the ground as they ran.

Ten minutes later a panzergrenadier came dashing up to Barkmann's tank: 'The Americans are behind you; they've got anti-tank guns!'

The Panther moved off towards a small wood, went through it, and caught the American spearhead by surprise.

'HE round. 400 metres. . . .'

The first round took off the top of a tree; the second hit a group of American infantry. The wireless operator had taken off his earphones and, as the Panther came up behind the American troops, he was firing the bow MG34.

All of a sudden, there was a flash ahead of them and an anti-tank round skidded off the turret. Barkmann's gunlayer hit the anti-tank gun with his second shot. Another anti-tank round banged into the turret and fire broke out.

'Ausbooten!' The men tumbled outside, but the gun-layer was not among them. Barkmann got him out through the top hatch before they tackled the fire. Thereafter they managed to get the tank back to the repair company.

Next day, July 14, Barkmann was involved in relieving four of his Kompanie's tanks which had become surrounded. His own tank was not yet repaired, and when he slid into the turret of a replacement he found it was still stained with the blood of the previous commander. In the company of three other tanks his Panther accounted for three more Shermans.

Towards midday the regiment's commanding officer, SS-Obersturm-

A view taken at St Fromond two days later on what appears to be the same stretch of road enables us to hazard a comparison as to the possible location. (US Army):

bannführer Tychsen came up to Barkmann's tank. Tychsen, a big man with blond hair, ice-cold eyes and a chin that was heavily scarred, pointed a finger towards the horizon: 'Away you go, Barkmann. In that house over there they've got our wounded, and we're going to get them back.' Three panzers set off at full tilt across the 800 metres to the house and in one swoop rescued the wounded.

The same day, Barkmann's Panther took the full force of an artillery shell. HE shell bursts from 105 or 155mm guns caused few real problems for the larger tanks though a direct hit on the side could cripple the tracks. That is precisely what happened this time although back at the repair company Barkmann was able to take out his own 424 which was ready again.

On July 25 SS-Panzer Regiment 2 was pulled back to St Aubin-du-Perron, three kilometres south of the N800 from Périers to St Lô. By this time the front line was beginning to look something like the blade of a saw — with the dug-in tanks as its teeth.

As the American break-out got into gear, on July 26 SS-Panzer Regiment 2 was thrown into the gap left by the decimated Panzer Lehr Division. Despite intense air activity, the tanks managed to reach the sector without loss. Several that had fallen back on St Sauveur-Lendelin, six kilometres south of Périers, were sent south-east to Marigny, where they went in against the Americans during the same afternoon.

This time the carburettor on Barkmann's tank gave up and stranded the tank out in the open. There was no time

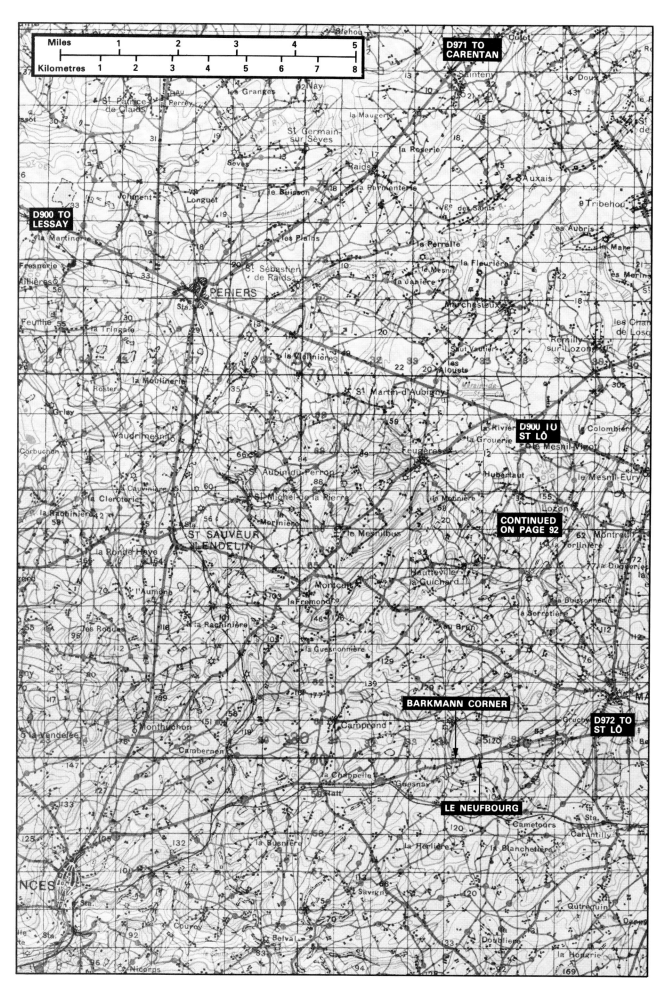

Miles
Kilometres

D971 TO
CARENTAN

D900 TO
LESSAY

D900 TO
ST LÔ

CONTINUED
ON PAGE 92

BARKMANN CORNER

D972 TO
ST LÔ

LE NEUFBOURG

PERIERS

St Sauveur Lendelin

to tow it under cover, and a repair unit was doing its utmost to fix the trouble when four fighter-bombers dived down. As the engine hatches were open, there was nothing to stop their cannon-shells from smashing into the cooling system and the oil sump, which resulted in the engine catching fire. This they managed to extinguish, and the repair crew and tank mechanics worked right through the night so that by dawn on July 27 the Panther was finally back in running order.

As Barkmann set out to rejoin his Kompanie at its latest position, SS-Hauptscharführer Heinze and a motor transport NCO, Corth, were clinging to the roof of the tank and taking a look at their new surroundings. Coming out of the village of le Lorey, to the north of the St Lô-Coutances road, they pulled up alongside some infantry and rear area troops who were running in the opposite direction. The answer to the men's shouts from on top of the tank came from a Feldwebel: the Americans were on their way from St. Lô — in fact, from where the regiment's tanks were supposed to have been — and even as the two NCOs looked hard at one another they could make out the sounds of fighting. Heinze and Corth went forward on foot to investigate. Shots were heard and they came running back, one of them having been hit in the shoulder and arm. The Americans were indeed on the main road from St Lô. Barkmann decided to go as far as the crossroads.

At battle stations, the Panther moved along between a row of hedges which screened it on both sides, and stopped at the crossroads under the thick spread of an oak tree. Armoured vehicles with white stars on them were coming along

'Barkmann Corner' at the junction of the Lorey road and the N172, between Coutances and St Lô, which has unfortunately since been widened destroying its originality. After the battle the crew managed to get their damaged Panther back up the hill (to the right) to the little hamlet of le Neufbourg.

from the left. The gun-layer, Poggendorf, estimated that they were 200 metres away. Carefully, he adjusted his sight to the base of the olive-green silhouette that stood out magnified in the viewer. The Panther's turret shuddered. Flames leapt up from the leading American vehicle and the others started to back away. The loader, in his shirtsleeves, was by now shoving round after round into the breech; the dull thud of the gun and the clang of spent shell cases adding to the background noise of the ventilator as it drew out the cordite fumes from inside the turret.

Further along, smoke from burning petrol tankers sullied the sky with black oily scrolls, and jeeps and half-tracks lay twisted and torn under the fire of the 7.5cm gun. Barkmann scanned the whole area around him continuously. To the left of the road two Shermans were coming up. It took two shots to brew up the first, although the second managed to get two hits on the Panther before it too fell victim. Beneath clouds of black smoke, the crossroads were no longer visible yet still more vehicles kept coming.

It had to end somehow. Fighter-bombers were now cratering the ground all around. One bomb landed five metres away and nearly turned the tank over, another rocked it on the left and damaged the running wheels, and cannon shells bit into the armour plate as the aircraft concentrated on this solitary tank that, singlehanded, was blocking the road. Yet Barkmann hung

SS-Unterscharführer Ernst Barkmann's single-handed exploit will surely go down in the annals of Das Reich. His feat was acknowledged with the award of the Ritterkreuz. His last known whereabouts were when registered as a British PoW on June 9, 1946.

on, continuing to fire at anything that came in sight.

Two Shermans opened fire from a flank, their shells scraping along the sides of the Panther's hull. As the Panther's turret turned relentlessly, the

It would have been nice to claim this picture as being of Barkmann's Panther. It does show the N174; there is a junction on the left leading to le Lorey indicated by the drunken road sign, and the Panther's barrel is pointing in the right direction — east. Alas when we located the spot on the Coutances-St Lô road it proved to be too far to the west . . . by about five kilometres! Nevertheless it is an SS-Panzer Regiment 2 machine and it makes a good comparison photograph so is therefore worthy of inclusion. The American monster is a tank recovery vehicle 'Ausf' M-31. (US Army)

gun-layer responded instinctively. Both Shermans brewed up. Battered and scarred, tank 424 was missing a track torn off by a direct hit, one of the hull welds had been ripped open, and its ammunition was practically exhausted. The driver, who had been wounded in the neck and was moaning with pain and trembling uncontrollably, was struggling to open his hatch and get out — but it had jammed. Throwing aside his earphones, he tried to work his levers to get the tank onto a slant. Barkmann called out to his gun-layer to try to calm him. A shell clanged against the Panther's side. Back in his seat, the driver wrestled to get the tank away. With only one track and a twisted drive sprocket, he somehow managed to get it to reverse — in the meantime the gun-layer had managed to knock out another Sherman.

The two NCOs who had remained behind had totted up Barkmann's kills: the tanks alone came to nine. Crab-like, his Panther crawled back to the little village of le Neufbourg; only then were they able to prise open the jammed hatches with crowbars to release the driver and radio operator.

That day, July 27, ten Panthers belonging to I. Abteilung, SS-Panzer Regiment 12 were to the north of Cambernon, about four kilometres north-east of Coutances. The bulk of SS-Panzer Regiment 2 headed towards Belval, five kilometres further south, and to Courcy below the main St Lô-

Another of the regiment's Panthers, an Ausf A, burns in Sainteny, eight kilometres south-west of Carentan. GIs from the 4th Infantry Division are surrounding the tank although the situation is a little absurd as the tank had already been knocked out when it was set on fire by a deliberate shot with a bazooka. Possibly re-enacted merely for the photograph. SS-Panzer Regiment 2 fought in this area around July 8-10. (US Army)

Coutances road. Eight of the regiment's tanks remained on a line Montcuit-St Sauveur-Lendelin as a rearguard. Four PzKpfw IVs of II. Abteilung, SS-Panzer Regiment 2 were knocked out south of Périers, and by evening a number of tanks had been destroyed due east of Coutances and south-west of St Lô around Quibou, Dangy and Cerisy-la-Salle.

On July 28 two of the Panthers that had remained behind at Cambernon were destroyed by bazookas. Another fifteen of I. Abteilung's Panthers could see that their advance towards Marigny, mid-way between Coutances and St. Lô, had been blocked, and they were handed over to Panzer Lehr by the 7. Armee.

About ten kilometres south of Coutances, SS-Obersturmbannführer

Above: GI Private Ward Watley inspects an SS-Panzer Regiment 2 Panther knocked out by his 22nd Infantry Regiment (4th Infantry Division) on July 16. Like most Allied photographs showing German tanks, the original caption claims it as a 'Tiger' near Sainteny. (US Army) *Below:* Sainteny it may be but it's certainly not a Tiger!

Tychsen was being driven back to regimental headquarters at Trelly, where it had been set up the previous day, when his vehicle ran straight into an American patrol to the north-east of the little hamlet of Cambry at the crossroads with the D7. A burst of machine gun fire sent the vehicle into a hedge and Tychsen was carried away dying. His successor, SS-Sturmbannführer Rudolf Enseling (awarded the Knights Cross on August 23), was promoted from I. Abteilung.

Meanwhile Barkmann — with the Shermans at his heels but still adding them to his tally, which had leapt to fifteen in just two days — had managed to reach Coutances. He got over the River Sienne by a bridge that he came upon by chance, and by the afternoon he was in sight of the sea at Granville although in an air attack the loader had been injured and Barkmann wounded in the calf. Passing through one village that day, his tank and one that he afterwards took in tow had accidentally knocked down two houses; though when the villagers rushed out, it was to fete them with bouquets and bottles of wine as liberators!

There were still several of the regiment's tanks trying to break out on July 29 from Roncey, south-east of Coutances, southwards in the direction of Gavray. The 3. and 4. Kompanies had to leave their Panthers behind as they had no more fuel. No. 2. Kompanie, camouflaged at Hambye, were waiting for nightfall to make their move south-west to Percy, on the road towards Villedieu-les-Poêles, and by 8.00 p.m. that evening the last PzKpfw IV at Trelly had been destroyed.

On July 30 the Americans were at Granville. Encircled, Barkmann's 424

Roncey lies some ten kilometres south-east of Coutances in the area overrun by the American VII Corps offensive west of St Lô on July 25. The town was captured five days later — littered with wrecked German armour. This is the Panzerjäger 38(t) Ausf M (SdKfz 138) armed with the 7.5cm PaK 40 and most probably belonged to SS-Panzerjäger Abteilung 2 of the 2. SS-Panzer Division. (US Army)

managed to break through with a second tank in tow. On August 1 this tank was abandoned and set alight, but, when its ammunition went up, 424 was too close and it caught fire as well. On foot, the crew of 424 did not catch up with their Kompanie until August 5. Although unaware of it at the time, Barkmann's name had been put forward for the Knight's Cross to the Iron Cross which was awarded on August 27.

Ultimately came encirclement in the Falaise pocket and the breakthrough in indescribable confusion. At the end of August, it was again a Panther from the I. Abteilung which knocked out five tanks of the 1st Polish Armoured Division which were firing from Point 262, at the foot of Mont Ormel, which dominates Chambois and St Lambert-sur-Dive from the east through which the retreating Germans were passing.

The power of the Typhoon's rockets graphically illustrated on a PzKpfw IV of 7. Kompanie of SS-Panzer Regiment 2. The RAF 2nd Tactical Air Force were officially credited with fifty tanks destroyed in this operation near Coutances. (IWM)

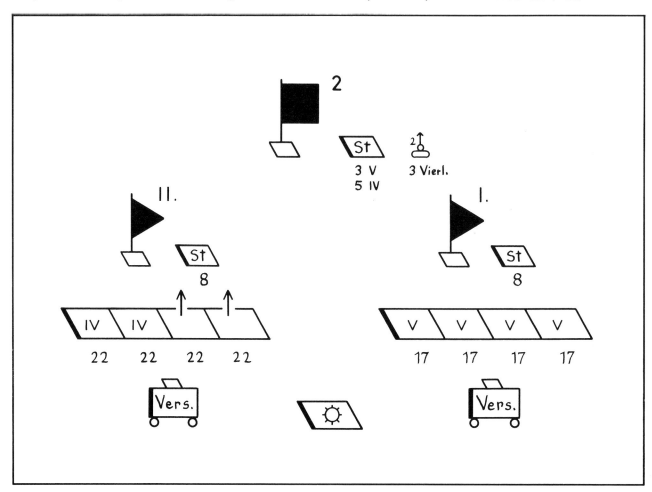

Theoretical organisation chart for SS-Panzer Regiment 2 as at June 1944. On June 1 the 2. SS-Panzer Division had 44 PzKpfw IVs and 25 Panthers in its SS-Panzer Regiment 2. Of the 75 StuGs the division was supposed to possess to equip 5. and 6. Kompanies of its panzer regiment and its SS-Sturmgeschütz Abteilung 2, only 33 were available. SS-Panzer Regiment 2 had 6 SdKfz 7/1 quadruple 20mm Flak half-tracks. On July 1 the 5. and 6. Kompanies were equipped with PzKpfw IVs instead of the StuGs but had only 50 PzKpfw IV and 26 Panthers. The SS-Sturmgeschütz Abteilung 2 then had 36 StuGs.

SS-OBERSTURMBANNFÜHRER CHRISTIAN TYCHSEN

Tychsen was born on February 3, 1910, at Flensburg, Schleswig-Holstein. He joined up in the SS-Verfügungstruppe in 1934 and by 1938 was an SS-Obersturmführer in the signals battalion. After the campaign in the West in 1940, when he was awarded the Iron Cross I and II Class, Tychsen was transferred to the reconnaissance group of what had since become the SS-Division Reich as a company commander and, as such, took part in the offensive against Russia in June 1941.

In 1942 Tychsen was given the command of II. Abteilung of the newly formed divisional SS-Panzer Regiment 2, which he led in Russia during 1943. On March 31 he was awarded the Knight's Cross of the Iron Cross and on December 10 the Oak Leaves to the Knights Cross. By then he was commanding officer of SS-Panzer Regiment 2, which he was with in Normandy when he was killed on July 28, 1944. He was wounded nine times in all, and was known as a brave, coldly efficient and battle-hardened leader. Now buried at Marigny Soldatenfriedhof, west of St Lô, Block 5, Row 24, Grave 1196.

Christian Tychsen was killed at this crossroad near Cambry on July 28. View from the US machine gunners' position.

SS-PANZER REGIMENT 9

SS-Panzer Regiment 9 came into being as part of SS-Panzer Grenadier Division 9 on February 1, 1943 spending the remainder of the year in the Ypres area of Belgium. On October 22, 1943 the division became 9. SS-Panzer Division Hohenstaufen and in mid-March 1944 was transferred to the Eastern Front, where it fought under 4. Panzer Armee in the Tarnopol area, suffering heavy losses. At the beginning of June it was in the northern Ukraine and had been re-equipped with new

vehicles ready to take part in a counter-offensive at Kovel since its attachment to II. SS Panzer Korps the previous month. When the corps was despatched to Normandy it moved west on June 12 in the company of its sister division, the 10. SS-Panzer.

The commander of SS-Panzer Regiment 9 was SS-Obersturmbann-führer Otto Meyer. Born on December 23, 1912 at Moldenit in Schleswig, he was awarded the Knights Cross of the Iron Cross on June 2, 1944 for his

Top: **Panther Ausf G of I. Abteilung, SS-Panzer Regiment 9 knocked out beside the D562 at St André-sur-Orne. This Canadian soldier of the Fusiliers Mont-Royal is examining the tank on August 9 but it was probably destroyed towards the end of July. (Public Archives of Canada)** *Below:* **Our technical advisor, Jean Paul Pallud, checks the location for the comparison — rather a disappointing one as the railings have been removed and the château itself, peeping through the trees, gutted by fire.**

leadership at Tarnopol. He was killed at Duclair on August 30 during the crossing of the Seine.

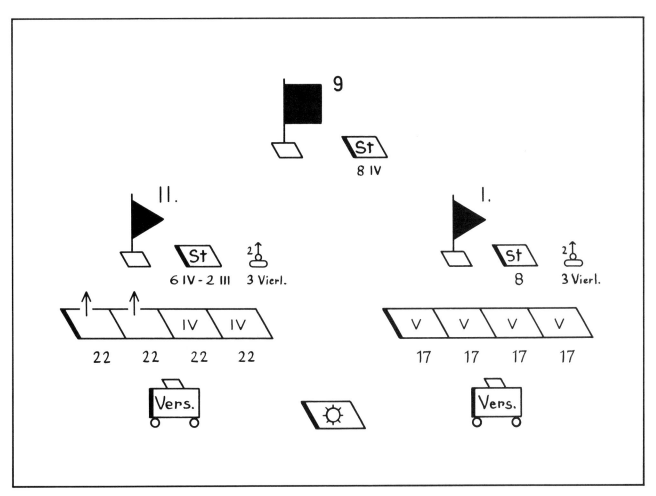

9

St
8 IV

II.

St
6 IV - 2 III   3 Vierl.

IV   IV

22   22   22   22

Vers.

I.

St
8   3 Vierl.

V   V   V   V

17   17   17   17

Vers.

Theoretical organisation table for SS-Panzer Regiment 9 in June 1944. At the beginning of the month the 9. SS-Panzer Division only possesed the II. Abteilung of its panzer regiment as the I. Abteilung, which had just been equipped with Panthers at Mailly-le-Camp, was retained there in Army Group reserve. The division had neither a Sturmgeschütz nor a Panzerjäger Abteilung, i.e. no assault guns as such. On June 1, SS-Panzer Regiment 9 had 41 PzKpfw IVs and 38 StuGs in its II. Abteilung (7. and 8. Kompanies were then equipped with StuGs), and it had 3 Befehlspanzer III and 3 SdKfz 7/1 quadruple 20mm Flak half-tracks. At Mailly-le-Camp, I. Abteilung's strength was 30 Panthers and 3 SdKfz 7/1.

NORMANDY

At the time when 9. SS-Panzer Division was transferred from the East, I. Abteilung of SS-Panzer Regiment 9 was still at Mailly-le-Camp barracks, near Troyes in eastern France, where the tank crews were familiarising themselves with their new Panthers on the training grounds of the Champagne. Joining up with the division en route for Normandy, one of the convoys that was going by rail was shot up by fighter-bombers and a number of its trucks carrying fuel were left blazing. In open country, the Panthers had to be off-loaded and moved clear. Afterwards, they resumed their journey by road, travelling by night and hiding in the daytime, which entailed a wearing 300-kilometre drive.

ON THE RIGHT OF THE ORNE

The division was not able to reform until the end of June south of a line that ran from Falaise to Condé-sur-Noireau, before moving northwards towards the sector that ran through Tournay-sur-Odon and Neuilly-le-Malherbe, between Caen and Villers-Bocage.

The divisional attack was set to go in on the left of the Odon on June 29 with I. and II. Abteilung of SS-Panzer Regiment 9 in support of the infantry, SS-Panzer Grenadier Regiments 20 and 19 respectively. Grainville-sur-Odon was taken. Just as the second group was about to make for Cheux from Noyers-Bocage and the hamlet of Bas-de-Forges, about a hundred Lancasters laid waste their jumping-off positions. . . . In a few days, 7. and 8. Kompanies of SS-Panzer Regiment 9, equipped with assault guns, destroyed 49 tanks while the PzKpfw IVs and Panthers accounted for 13. Against this the regiment had lost 11 PzKpfw IVs, 11 Panthers and 9 assault guns.

On July 12 regimental headquarters was set up at Bully, about four kilometres east of Point 112 between Caen and Evrecy. I. Abteilung established its HQ just north of the village at Feuguerolles-sur-Orne and II. Abteilung at Courvaudon about sixteen kilometres to the south-west. When the British attacked on July 16 between Gavrus and Noyers-Bocage 9. SS-Panzer Division was put on the alert and moved up to go into the line, its tanks following

SS-Obersturmbannführer Otto Meyer (not to be confused with Kurt 'Panzer' Meyer of the 12. SS-Panzer Division) was posthumously awarded the Oak Leaves to his Ritterkreuz on September 30, 1944. He now lies buried in Bourdon Soldatenfriedhof, north-west of Amiens (Block 39, Row 7, Grave 106).

on much later as a start had just been made the previous day on carrying out extensive maintenance work. With 227. Infanterie Division, its grenadiers were to re-take positions that had been lost, supported by SS-Panzer Regiment 9.

The start-line was from Evrecy on the right to Neuilly-le-Malherbe on the left, a front of three kilometres parallel with Gavrus and Noyers-Bocage. No more than twenty tanks could be put together, and these set off to the right of Point 113

north of Evrecy. In full spate the attack came up against the British, who set down a blanket of smoke shells, and the advance pulled back. For two hours Point 113 remained unoccupied. Then the regiment's tanks set off again aiming

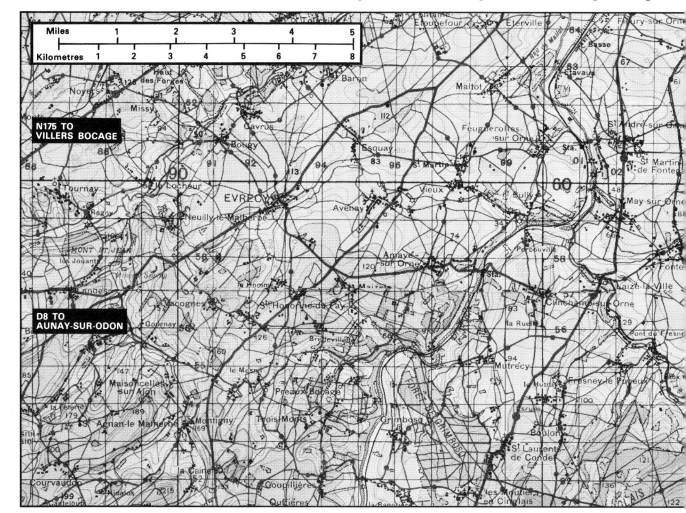

for Bougy. At 2.00 p.m. the village was taken and the panzers kept on going as far as Gavrus where they began moving along the wooded valley of the Orne. I. Abteilung's Panthers, led by SS-Sturmbannführer Bollert, accounted for a number of Shermans and Churchills. The tanks were in the forefront of the attack, but because of the smoke they were limited to firing at point-blank range. Out of the day's tally of 40 Allied tanks (48 according to an amended report), II. Abteilung knocked out 18 around Bougy and I. Abteilung 8 at Point 113. The regiment lost 5 of its tanks and, among the casualties, Bollert was seriously wounded.

By July 17 SS-Panzer Regiment 9 could only muster 25 Panthers, 13 PzKpfw IVs and 15 assault guns, and the division's infantry had been combined into a single regiment.

MAY-SUR-ORNE

A Kampfgruppe was formed on July 18 to re-take the three villages of St Martin, St André and May-sur-Orne, east of the Orne and south of Caen. Along with I. Abteilung's Panthers were elements of 272. Infanterie Division, 10. SS-Panzer Division Frundsberg, and divisional infantry; but at that time the Panthers were still involved at Bougy and could only be brought across sparingly. Three each were to support two companies of the Frundsberg's reconnaissance group; the rest of I. Abteilung were to attack south of May. By the early hours of July 22, when the attack was due to go in, most of the Panthers had failed to materialise except for a few belonging to 2. Kompanie which had the specific task of gaining the high ground north-east of May, where in the early hours SS-Oberscharführer Wehrle's platoon was sent on reconnaissance by the company commander, SS-Hauptsturmführer Seiler.

Together with two other tanks, Wehrle advanced the route his company would have to take. Nothing was known

Opposite left: **Not a hundred metres away lay another Panther, this time an Ausf A belonging to 2. Kompanie. It probably received a hit from a 17-pounder just between the body and turret, popping the 'lid' like a cork. These Mont-Royal Fusiliers have been joined by an American First Sergeant. (Public Archives of Canada)** *Above:* **Today a new estate covers the spot yet the shattered wall of Le Clos du Hamel remains behind the houses.**

about the enemy, and the Panthers continued forward without encountering any opposition until, as it got light, they realised that they were in fact right in the middle of the British positions. Hatches were closed, the guns loaded, and Wehrle decided to give the order to prepare to open fire. Opening up with all their armament, the Panthers caught the British totally unawares, scattering them from their guns and vehicles, and kept on firing until the magazines were practically empty. Having alerted his company commander over the radio as to what was happening, Wehrle hung on and waited for the rest of 2. Kompanie to get there — but they were only then arriving at their start line. For four hours Seiler waited for the rest of I. Abteilung's Panthers, until finally the infantry had to go in against May-sur-Orne without tank support. It was almost midday when I. Abteilung arrived on the scene, or rather the twenty-four Panthers that were all that was left of it. Two of them were sent towards May to help out, but the attack was getting nowhere.

Wehrle rejoined his company commander. The tanks were beginning to move at last. Three from 2. Kompanie were knocked out, broadside, by anti-tank guns; the others were unable to get

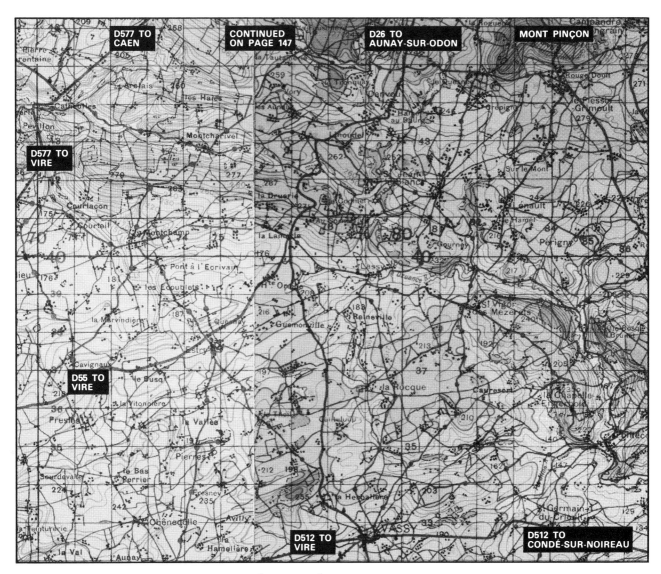

D577 TO CAEN

CONTINUED ON PAGE 147

D26 TO AUNAY-SUR-ODON

MONT PINÇON

D577 TO VIRE

D55 TO VIRE

D512 TO VIRE

D512 TO CONDÉ-SUR-NOIREAU

over a slight hill without presenting themselves as a target. SS-Hauptsturm-führer Seiler called them off and they fell back, this time behind their own smoke-screen. Nine of the Abteilung's Panthers had been knocked out, though most of them were repairable.

On the night of July 25 the division was on a line May-sur-Orne and Fontenay-le-Marmion but, whereas St Martin and St André had been captured, the tanks had come to a standstill to the north of Fontenay at Point 88. SS-Panzer Regiment 9 now had 18 Panthers, 18 PzKpfw IVs and 11 assault guns; augmented three days later to 26 Panthers, 22 PzKpfw IVs and 22 assault guns as others returned from being repaired.

On July 29 II. Abteilung was astride the Caen-Falaise road level with Verrières and Tilly-la-Campagne. I. Abteilung was in reserve eight kilometres to the south at Bretteville-sur-Laize. The regiment's strength had increased further to 29 Panthers, 22 PzKpfw IVs and 27 assault guns. Two days later, I. Abteilung relieved II. and regimental headquarters was set up at the Château d'Outre Laize, near Gouvix, just south of Bretteville-sur-Laize.

CHÊNEDOLLÉ

On August 1, 9. SS-Panzer Division was relieved by the 1. SS (the LSSAH). That night the 31 Panthers, 17 PzKpfw IVs and 28 assault guns of SS-Panzer Regiment 9 set off westwards as part of a Kampfgruppe commanded by the regiment's commanding officer, SS-Obersturmbannführer Otto Meyer, and by daybreak they were on a line from Arclais to Montchauvet and Montchamp, to the west of Mont Pinçon and between Villers-Bocage and Vire.

In the afternoon 2. Kompanie attacked at Montchauvet, where between the village and le Bény-Bocage five Cromwells were knocked out in tank-versus-tank fighting at Point 170. In command was SS-Obersturmbannführer Fröhlich (who had replaced SS-Obersturmbannführer Höhn after he had been killed) and, despite his tanks and assault guns being surrounded by nightfall, he managed to get them out. Further south, three PzKpfw IVs were sent off in support of troops between Montchauvet and Montchamp, whilst other tanks joined the divisional panzergrenadier regiment in its attempt to advance westward.

The following day there was fighting on Point 176 to the west of Montchamp. The bulk of SS-Panzer Regiment 9 moved out from the Pierres-Estry sector against Presles, a couple of kilometres to the west, but the village was taken from the north.

The objective for August 4 was to cut off at the rear the British breakthrough to Chênedollé, a few kilometres to the south. Another thirty-nine Allied tanks were knocked out in the battle before the situation changed: the road that ran north-west of Chênedollé had to be blocked at all costs. The only tanks available were those near Estry that belonged to SS-Obersturmbannführer Meyer: 18 Panthers and 7 PzKpfw IVs plus 7 assault guns. With the British salient now stretching between Sourdeval, Viessoix and Chênedollé, the division had no choice but to go on the defensive.

For the period of August 11 and 12, 9. SS-Panzer Division claimed twenty-two enemy tanks destroyed but on the 12th the units on the western flank pulled back towards the east. After that 9. SS-Panzer Division had to cut its way through as far as Vimoutiers via the bloody bottleneck of Trun.

SS-PANZER REGIMENT 10

Formed on February 1, 1943 in the south of France as SS-Panzer Grenadier Division 10, it was known briefly as 10. SS-Division Karl der Grosse before officially becoming 10. SS-Panzer Division Frundsberg on October 22, 1943. By the end of the year the division was stationed in Normandy but was sent to Russia in March 1944. It fought in the Tarnopol and Lemberg areas, joining the 9. SS-Panzer Division as part of the II. SS-Panzer Korps, returning to Normandy on June 12. I. Abteilung of the division's SS-Panzer Regiment 10

Death of a panzer near Aunay-sur-Odon. A type G Panther (container on rear for cleaning rods). The Germans never seemed to leave their pails behind . . . even in battle! Lieutenant Handford, who took the picture at the end of July, gave the location as Jurques on the line of advance of the 7th Armoured Division and 1st/5th Queens Regiment. The crosses on the rear lockers are somewhat unusual. (IWM)

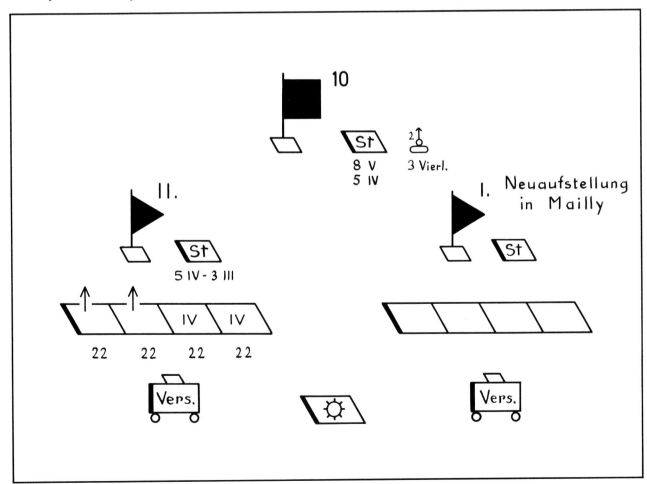

Theoretical organisation of SS-Panzer Regiment 10 in June 1944, when 10. SS-Panzer Division had only one panzer unit, the II. Abteilung of SS-Panzer Regiment 10. The division had no assault gun battalion and the I. Abteilung of its panzer regiment was equipping with Panthers at Mailly-le-Camp. On June 1 the regiment had 32 PzKpfw IVs (5. and 6. Kompanies) and 34 StuGs (7. and 8. Kompanies) in its II. Abteilung. It had 3 Befehlspanzer IIIs and 3 SdKfz 7/1 quadruple 20mm half-tracks.

was then at Mailly-le-Camp, having not yet taken delivery of its Panthers.

II. Abteilung's PzKpfw IVs were loaded onto six trains which left Russia for the West from Sokol and Krystinowpol; the tanks which were loaned out to other units followed on with those that were still in the Carpathians at Sanok. In the first train travelled SS-Sturmbannführer Reinhold, the battalion commander. The further west they went, the slower the journey became. It took them five whole days to reach their assembly point at Saarbrücken. With the trains held up for hours on end in open country, the chances of being attacked by fighter-bombers increased as they moved across France. On June 18 the first train arrived south-west of Paris at Houdan from where the tanks moved on by road through Dreux, Châteauneuf, Digny and le Magne to Longy, where they remained until June 25.

The I. Abteiling was at Mailly-le-Camp for re-equipping with the Panther. The ten already received had to be handed over to Panzer Lehr Regiment already heavily committed in Normandy. On August 1, I. Abteilung was attached to Panzer Brigade 10 on which date its strength was only seven Panthers out of a nominal seventy-three, and the I. Abteilung never actually saw service in Normandy.

ON THE ODON

II. Abteilung, SS-Panzer Regiment 10 went into action on June 29 in the attack along the Odon. The 7. and 8. Kompanies made for Gavrus with the division's SS-Panzergrenadier Regiment

Above: **Although positive identification of the unit that once owned this pile of scrap is not forthcoming, one can hazard a guess by its location — le Bény-Bocage — that it once belonged to SS-Panzer Regiment 10. 'It' was once a PzKpfw IV type G but Sergeant Seer** *(left)* **modified it from fifty yards range with a shell from his Sherman. (IWM)** *Below:* **The architecture of the village square has changed little and makes a good comparison.**

22; one gun-layer in 7. Kompanie, SS-Sturmmann Menzel, adding 5 Shermans to his tally of 11 Russian tanks. Gavrus was taken, but it was impossible to advance as far as Baron-sur-Odon.

During the early evening, near Evrecy, the tanks took Point 113 on the right. II. Abteilung now had 28 tanks destroyed to its credit, against the loss of 2 PzKpfw IVs. It looked doubtful, though, that they would be able to push on up to Point 112 or towards Esquay-Notre-

Dame. Flanking fire from Avenay and St Martin was holding back the grenadiers. Avenay would have to be taken. That night the attack was renewed; the tanks followed the grenadiers and, under cover of darkness, they crossed the Guigne river between Avenay and Vieux. They were now in a good position for climbing the slopes of Point 112 from the south. The tanks which were following up attacked simultaneously from Point 113. Advancing from the east were PzKpfw

146

IVs of II. Abteilung, SS-Panzer Regiment 12 and towards midday on July 30 the tanks were on the summit of Point 112.

On July 3 a British counter-attack came in on Point 112, and II. Abteilung again made its way up there amidst a mass of divisional units. When, on July 10, no less than twenty-five enemy tanks approached, it looked as if the hill would undoubtedly be lost. Under cover, facing them as they came on, were SS-Hauptscharführer Borrekott and three other tanks from SS-Hauptsturmführer Hauser's 5. Kompanie — the tactics being that whilst one section advanced the bulk of the tanks stayed hidden, coming into action one section at a time as the fighting progressed, and thus presenting less of a target for Allied aircraft than an entire company. Accordingly, Borrekott and his three tanks opened fire, causing the advancing tanks to come to a halt and return fire at them. Borrekott's tank was destroyed and its crew killed, but in the meantime SS-Oberscharführer Leven's platoon had duly entered the battle. Again the platoon leader's tank was hit, and Leven killed, as 6. Kompanie under SS-Obersturmführer Hegemann, 7. Kompanie under SS-Oberstürmführer Riedel and 8. under SS-Oberstürmführer Alius then moved forward between Points 112 and 113, striking at the Allied spearhead from the flank. On the hill, the enemy had already reached the top. All the time the battalion's medical officer SS-Hauptsturmführer Handrick, went unhurriedly about his business . . . two days later he was killed at Vieux.

On July 26 the division was in the process of being relieved and sent westwards, as was the Hohenstaufen, when orders came through from corps headquarters for II. Abteilung to hold itself in readiness to repulse an attack between Bougy and Point 113.

SS-Obersturmbannführer Otto Paetsch. Born Rheinhausen August 3, 1909; died Altdamm an der Oder March 16, 1945. Was awarded the Ritterkreuz on August 23, 1944 in his role as commander of SS-Panzer Regiment 10. (Bundesarchiv) (Incidentally his uniforms were found in the US in 1977.)

AUNAY-SUR-ODON

On August 1 a divisional Kampfgruppe led by SS-Obersturmbannführer Paetsch, the commanding officer of SS-Panzer Regiment 10, was heading for Aunay-sur-Odon, twenty-eight kilometres south-west of Caen, with II. Abteilung's PzKpfw IVs in its second echelon. When the outskirts of town were reached at about 10.00 p.m., a company of engineers had to be called up to clear a way through the ruins for the panzers to get through.

Deploying his forces, Paetsch ordered II. Abteilung to drive hard for the N177 (the main road south from le Bény-Bocage) and follow it down to about three kilometres north of Vire. By 4.00 a.m. on August 2 reconnaissance showed that the British had infiltrated a number of villages to the west and north-west and, facing them, the Kampfgruppe organised its defences. The greater part of II. Abteilung's strength was at Point 301, two kilometres south of Ondefontaine, scene of some of the most bitter fighting, where it destroyed twenty Allied tanks.

The next day the division made a thrust north-west towards St Georges d'Aunay with tanks in support of its SS-Panzergrenadier Regiment 21; la Valleé and Courcelles were cleared and they clung on at Point 188. In the meantime the bulk of its tanks went in at la Bigne to the south-west — going onto the defensive after encountering stiff opposition.

During the night of August 7-8 the Frundsberg relieved an infantry division between Mortain and Domfront. For the attack on Barenton on the 9th II. Abteilung could muster only twelve tanks. Progress was slow; Allied air activity incessant. . . .

RETREAT

During the morning of August 12 a powerful American assault was launched against the 10. SS-Panzer Division in the Barenton/St Georges-de-Rouelley sector (twenty-six kilometres south of Vire between Mortain and Domfront). With just eight tanks remaining, orders came through in the afternoon for the division to fall back four kilometres or so under cover of darkness and take up fresh positions along a line running through Lonlay-l'Abbaye. The following night it withdrew again and by August 14 encirclement was an immediate danger.

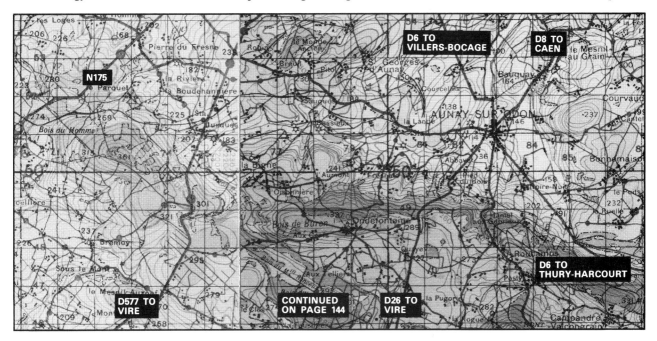

CONTINUED ON PAGE 144

Domfront had been taken by the Americans, but in the hills north of the town the eight PzKpfw IVs and grenadiers were assembled by the GOC, SS-Brigadeführer Harmel, for a limited attack, with assistance from 2. SS-Panzer Division and 17. SS-Panzergrenadier Division. With their superstructures loaded with grenadiers, the tanks went so far as to drive the Americans back — although in the end it made little difference.

Overnight on the 14th the division fell back east on St-Bomer-les-Forges; the tanks taking part in a fierce clash during the afternoon. After reaching the area

Le Tourneur lies just north of le Bény-Bocage. Royal Scots in their Churchill pay scant attention to the wreckage of a PzKpfw IV Ausf G. (IWM)

north of Argentan, it too was confronted with the chaotic bottleneck between Trun and Chambois.

SS-PANZER REGIMENT 12

Generalfeldmarschall Gerd von Rundstedt reviews 12. SS-Panzer Division 'Hitlerjugend' at manoeuvres in March 1944. (Bundesarchiv)

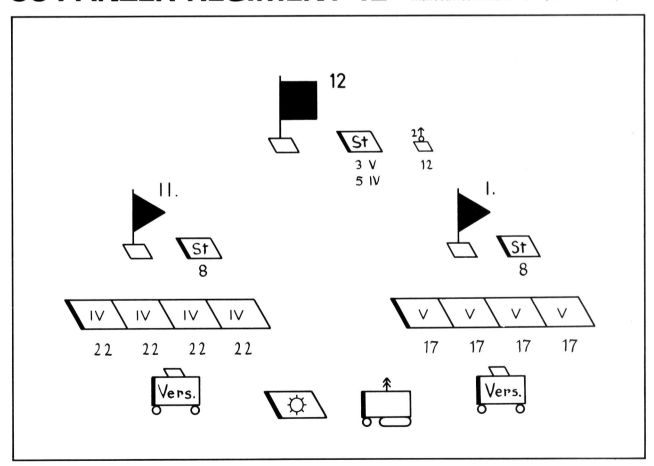

Theoretical organisation chart of SS-Panzer Regiment 12 in June 1944. On the 1st, SS-Panzer Regiment 12 (commander SS-Obersturmbannführer Wünsche) had 91 PzKpfw IVs in its II. Abteilung (commander SS-Sturmbannführer Prinz) and 48 Panthers in its I. Abteilung (commander SS-Sturmbannführer Jürgensen). A company of engineers, 9. Kompanie, had just been created as part of the regiment. The regiment had 12 SdKfz 10/4 20mm Flak half-tracks. The SS-Panzerjäger Abteilung 12 had 10 of the new Jagdpanzer IVs. By July 8 the regiment was down to 32 PzKpfw IV and 24 Panthers.

A leather-coated SS-Standartenführer Kurt Meyer, when commander of SS-Panzer Grenadier Regiment 25 of the 12. SS-Panzer Division, confers with Generalfeldmarschall von Rundstedt. Behind is SS-Brigadeführer Fritz Witt, the division's commander. When Witt was killed at his HQ by naval gunfire on June 14, 'Panzermeyer' took over. Witt's grave No. 1027 can be found in Row 12, Block 8 of the German war cemetery of Champigny-St. André-de-l'Eure. (Bundesarchiv)

SS-OBERSTURMBANNFÜHRER MAX WÜNSCHE

Max Wunsche was born on April 20, 1914 at Kittlitz, Saxony. In 1934 he joined the new SS-Verfügungstruppe and in 1936 passed out of the SS Junkerschule Bad Tölz in Bavaria as an SS-Untersturmführer. The personification of an SS officer, Wünsche was selected in 1938 to join Hitler as an aide. In 1940 he took command of a motorcycle company in the Leibstandarte SS Adolf Hitler which he led in France, where he was wounded; being awarded the Iron Cross I and II Class.

With the rank of SS-Hauptsturmführer, Wünsche served as adjutant at the Leibstandarte divisional headquarters during the Balkans campaign. He was soon given command of an assault gun group, and after being sent to the Kriegsakademie he took over I. Abteilung of the division's panzer regiment at the end of 1942 and went with it to Russia the following year. On February 28, 1943, having been awarded the German Cross in Gold, he received the Knight's Cross to the Iron Cross and promotion to SS-Obersturmbannführer.

In July 1943, as Operation Zitadelle was about to be launched and cadres from the LSSAH were being brought back to Germany to form the nucleus of the new Hitlerjugend Division, Wünsche, at 28, was recalled to take over its new panzer regiment.

On August 11 Wünsche was awarded the Oak Leaves to his Knight's Cross. He was badly wounded and taken prisoner in the Falaise pocket by British forces on August 24 and was not released until February 27, 1948. In the late 1960s he was residing in Wuppertal-Barmen.

An award for valour on the field of battle. SS-Obersturmbannführer Max Wünsche decorates SS-Oberscharführer Stempel on July 20, 1944 with the Eisernes Kreuz (a Second Class in the hand of his adjutant) for having destroyed five enemy aircraft. Wünsche wears one of the Italian cloth uniforms. (Bundesarchiv)

The Hitlerjugend Division was raised as a panzergrenadier division in July 1943 from members of the Hitlerjugend. Its cadre was drawn principally from the Leibstandarte SS Adolf Hitler and to a small extent from the army. Unit selection and the basic training of recruits was carried out at Beverlo military camp in northern Belgium between July and September 1943 with a three-month course at Lauenburg for those selected as NCOs. In October it was redesignated a panzer division: 12. SS-Panzer Division Hitlerjugend.

The division's tank regiment, SS-Panzer Regiment 12, was formed on November 3 at the Mailly-le-Camp training area in eastern France, through which most of the tanks which fought in Normandy must have passed at some stage. The core of the regiment was from the LSSAH, including its commanding officer, SS-Obersturmbannführer Wünsche, who had been a battalion commander in the LSSAH until his recall from Russia in July. Shortages among the tank crews were made up from among the repair company.

To begin with, Wünsche had just four PzKpfw IVs and four Panthers on which to train his young crews — and these eight tanks had been acquired from the Eastern Front through unofficial channels. For the time being, the division was provided with vehicles commandeered from the Italians.

A radical improvement in the equipment situation enabled full-scale divisional training exercises to take place in the early spring of 1944, when SS-Panzer Regiment 12 was based in the Hasselt area, south of Beverlo. In February Guderian paid the division a visit followed by von Rundstedt the next month.

Contrary to popular opinion in Germany — and to what the Allies believed until June 1944 — the Hitlerjugend Division rapidly attained a higher than average level of training, and the fanatical aggression of its troops was to make it a formidable fighting force.

In April 1944 the division was moved into the area between Caen and Paris bordered by Dreux, Evreux, Bernay and Vimoutiers. As yet, however, only 1. Kompanie of SS-Panzer Regiment 12 was considered operational, and there were complaints about the regiment's lack of command tanks and equipment for vehicle maintenance. On June 6 divisional headquarters was at Acon, just south of the Route Nationale 12 between Dreux and Verneuil-sur-Avre.

NORMANDY

At dawn on D-Day, 12. SS-Panzer Division Hitlerjugend passed into the control of Rommel's Army Group B, having been until then in the OKW reserve. Its orders were to assemble east of Lisieux. SS-Panzer Regiment 12 was to be split in two: I. Abteilung going with SS-Panzergrenadier Regiment 26; II.

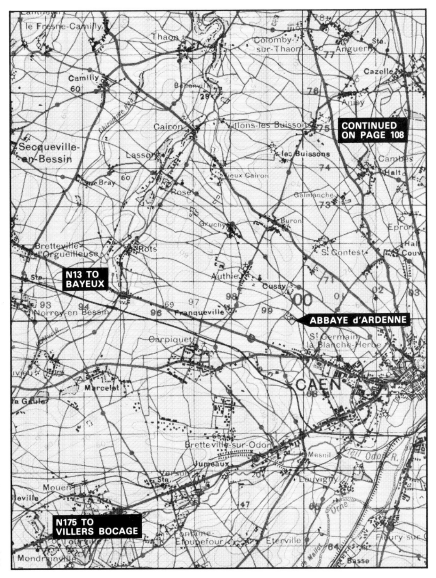

CONTINUED ON PAGE 108

Abteilung joining up with SS-Panzergrenadier Regiment 25.

Towards 3.00 p.m. the division was ordered to regroup west of Caen to carry out a counter-attack, passing under the command of LXXXIV Panzer Korps (whose HQ was at St Lô). The various units took up positions that evening and the following night, with II. Abteilung of SS-Panzer Regiment 12, under SS-Sturmbannführer Prinz, not arriving until the following morning — and then with only fifty tanks as the rest were in a second echelon. With columns being harried from the air, delays were becoming a fact of life. Meanwhile, I. Abteilung's Panthers, commanded by SS-Sturmbannführer Jürgensen, were stranded on the far side of the Orne for lack of petrol.

FRANQUEVILLE

The remaining PzKpfw IVs arrived west of Caen during the night. Wünsche was at the Abbaye d'Ardenne, some two or three kilometres north-west of Caen, headquarters of SS-Panzergrenadier Regiment 25, commanded by SS-Oberführer Kurt Meyer — better known

as 'Panzermeyer'. To their left, Canadian armour was making its way from Buron towards Authie, apparently totally unaware of the presence of the Hitlerjugend panzergrenadiers and armour.

One Kompanie of PzKpfw IVs was near the abbey; another was one-and-a-half kilometres to the west, to the south of the hamlet of Franqueville — each in constant radio contact. The Canadian tanks were obviously aiming for the airfield at Carpiquet and were now just a few hundred metres from Franqueville, but not until they were through the few tumbledown buildings that comprised the hamlet did 'Panzermeyer' at last give Wünsche the signal.

'Achtung! Panzer . . . maaarsch!' Wünsche ordered the tanks forward. The sky over Franqueville began to light up as the leading tank burst into flames, its crew baling out at the double. Allied infantry were dug in at the edge of Authie yet the ambush had been well laid and so far there had not been a sound from the Allied artillery. Authie was taken as was Franqueville as the panzergrenadiers pressed forward for Buron and St Contest. More PzKpfw IVs

were burning outside Buron — but not on their own — and then an artillery barrage reminiscent of 1914-18 drenched the village.

Meyer was aware that on the right Panzer Regiment 22's tanks were still stuck at Couvre-Chef. Troops of Panzergrenadier Regiment 25 were at Mâlon (where a PzKpfw IV had planted itself in one of the regiment's own anti-tank ditches) but they were pulling back. To the left, west of the little River Mue, Allied armour was advancing nose to tail towards Bretteville l'Orgueilleuse.

At nightfall the reckoning for SS-Panzer Regiment 12 was six tanks destroyed, of which two were completely written off. Opposite them, the Sherwood Rangers Yeomanry had lost twenty-eight.

Around midnight, SS-Obersturmführer von Ribbentrop reported at the Abbaye d'Ardenne. Rudolf Ribbentrop, the son of the Reich Foreign Minister, was one of the officers from SS-Panzer Regiment 1 who had followed Wünsche into the Hitlerjugend Division. He had been awarded the Knight's Cross in July 1943 and now had his arm in a sling as a result of being wounded in the shoulder a few weeks previously. Ribbentrop had come to re-assume command of his company in I. Abteilung — which was not yet in sight.

BRETTEVILLE-L'ORGUEILLEUSE

One of I. Abteilung's Kompanies finally arrived on June 8, and was put into a night attack on the left flank

Above: On the night of June 8/9, the Panthers of I. Abteilung advanced westwards along the N13 into Bretteville-l'Orgueilleuse. Just as the leading tank reached the centre of the town it was knocked out, according to 'Panzermeyer' their only loss for that day. Three weeks later the Ausf G was still lying outside No. 75 rue de Bayeux where it was photographed by Sergeant Leeson. (IWM) *Below:* An historic spot: where the first Panther was destroyed in the Battle of Normandy.

against Bretteville-l'Orgueilleuse to relieve I. Bataillon, SS-Panzergrenadier Regiment 26. The attacking formation included a reconnaissance company, with Kurt Meyer in overall command. At dusk, the Panthers moved off towards Franqueville, directed forward with precision over the reconnoitered ground and travelling in wedge formation with panzergrenadiers clinging on behind the protection of their turrets. Among them was Wünsche who had insisted on accompanying his men personally.

After the column had passed a battery of 88s in position around the N13, there was nothing ahead except the enemy. The Panthers pushed forward on the right of the road with the reconnaissance unit and 'Panzermeyer' on the left. Forcing the pace, they planned to reach Rots before it got completely dark. It was the reconnaissance unit which entered the village first, halting until the Panthers arrived a few minutes later. There the reconnaissance panzergrenadiers dismounted to continue on

foot. Meanwhile the tanks filed through the village and reformed in a wedge at the western end, two abreast on the road itself. By now it was pitch dark and only the flames of the exhausts were visible. Norrey was over to the left with Bretteville-l'Orgueilleuse 200 metres ahead.

Using one of the tactics employed on the Eastern Front, the two leading tanks broke the still night air with a salvo from their long-barrelled 75s and moved forward determinedly into Bretteville. Every one of them now opened up. From the village short bursts of Bren gun fire came back in reply. The Panthers that were following on, with their panzergrenadiers still aboard, moved forward and spread out into the whole village.

Surprise tactics had paid off, as they had the previous day at Franqueville. There was no sign, however, of SS-Panzergrenadier Regiment 26, and at daybreak 'Panzermeyer' decided to turn around and withdraw to a hill east of Rots. The leading Panther, which had been knocked out, was abandoned in the middle of the village. Several officers had been killed and Wünsche himself was among the wounded.

The Panther was hit on the rear of the turret: a devastating shot which snapped the 45mm-thick armour like a child's chocolate Easter egg. (IWM)

Hitlerjugend zum Front! The 12. SS thunder through the streets of Caen. (Bundesarchiv)

Above: **A spectacular kill on the outskirts of Norrey-en-Bessin. Although the floor plate has been pierced, it would need far more than a land mine to do this to a Panther. To overturn the 45-tons of an Ausf A would need a hit or near miss from an aircraft bomb or naval shell, or possibly an internal explosion of the magazine. The triple exhaust is worthy of note as this modification was adopted on certain type As to overcome a** fire hazard. The two side pipes sucked fresh air onto the middle pipe, preventing excessive heat reaching the oil filter and petrol pump. (IWM) *Below:* **We established the location as just north of the village. The road in front of the old shack is the new N13, the Caen-Bayeux highway which bypasses both Rots and Bretteville, the old main road through the centre of the town (pages 152-153) now reduced to the D83c.**

COUNTER-ATTACK

General Geyr von Schweppenburg, commanding Panzergruppe West, joined Meyer at the Abbaye d'Ardenne. He planned an offensive to gain the coast which would start at 11.00 p.m. on June 10 and be made by three panzer divisions: the Hitlerjugend, Panzer Lehr and 21. Panzer Division. Daylight attacks had already become impossible, not so much because of the difficulties faced by the fighting units themselves but because of the problems posed for the petrol and ammunition supply columns; nor could an offensive such as this be launched a second time. In the event, it was not to be launched at all, the Allies having taken the initiative on the left against the Panzer Lehr.

The Hitlerjugend continued to defend the sector west of Caen. At Carpiquet the airfield was still being held by a divisional flak battery of 88s and the remainder of I. Bataillon, SS-Panzergrenadier Regiment 26 plus a company of Panthers, fifteen strong, sent from I. Abteilung, SS-Panzer Regiment 12.

At the end of June, the tank regiment was still complaining about the continuing lack of command tanks and Flakvierling 38s as well as of personnel carriers for the engineers and tank recovery vehicles.

North of Caen, the 16. Luftwaffen Feld Division (like all such units, made up of Luftwaffe personnel who had become infantry by chance) was very much ill at ease. II. Abteilung, SS-Panzer Regiment 12 was sent to the north-east of the city while the majority of I. Abteilung were in action directly to the north. Meanwhile Caen went on being pounded by heavy bombers.

Near Buron the Canadians ended up by breaking through, taking St Contest in their stride, and most of II. Abteilung reeled back. The Canadians later

The concerted German counter-attack west of Caen aimed at cutting through the enemy forces to reach the coast before the Allies could consolidate the bridgehead. Three panzer divisions were involved: 12. SS, Panzer Lehr and 21. Panzer Division. This Panther Ausf G at Fontenay-le-Pesnel, fifteen kilometres west of the city, could have belonged to either the Hitlerjugend or Panzer Lehr. (IWM)

Above: Another Panther type G in the middle of the village advancing in the direction of Caen. The grenadier is checking the road to Cristot — the Italian camouflage material of his uniform identifies him quite probably as a member of SS-Panzer Regiment 12. (Landrien Collection) *Below:* The church bell tower was never rebuilt and the house has been extended, making an exact comparison impossible.

There is another identification problem with these shots, taken in the same general area, as it was fought over by both SS-Panzer Regiment 12 and Panzer Regiment 3 at the end of June. On the rear left side of this Panther Ausf A can be seen the entry hole by the projectile that pierced the 40mm armour plate which overhangs the track, setting the fuel alight. A hit such as this might well have been deflected had the tank been an Ausf G where the upper sides were thicker and at an increased angle. SS-Panzer Regiment 12 had its headquarters' tanks numbered –04 and –05 with the adjutant in the former and commanding officer in the latter, '204' being the mount of the adjutant of 2. Kompanie. (IWM)

withdrew, but without letting go of St Contest.

Authie and Franqueville fell in turn. North of Caen only von Ribbentrop's fifteen Panthers remained in position, where they were joined by 'Panzermeyer' who, as the division's new commanding officer following the death of SS-Brigadeführer Witt, wanted to be right up with the action himself. Von Ribbentrop's Panthers were exchanging shot for shot with Shermans established at St Contest. The ancient towers of the Abbaye d'Ardenne were now no more than stumps and the surrounding orchards completely uprooted. Unless Buron was relieved, III. Bataillon of SS-Panzergrenadier Regiment 25 faced annihilation. Every available tank was brought up but stalemate resulted, both sides suffering heavy losses. Von Ribbentrop's Panthers now turned their guns towards the Shermans coming from

The pictures were taken by Sergeant Christie on June 27 when men of the Durham Light Infantry paused to be photographed beside the tank. The location is the junction of the D139 and 173a between Fontenay-le-Pesnel, Tessel, Rauray and Cheux.

the direction of Authie. SS-Oberführer Meyer was making for Cussy, half-a-kilometre to the east, with a Panther. The north of Caen was now in Allied hands and withdrawal to the south of the city was becoming vital. The Orne running through its midst was crossed for the last time.

TO THE SOUTH

On July 11 the division was relieved by 272. Infanterie Division and was sent back to recuperate around Potigny, thirty-odd kilometres north of Falaise, while several Kompanies of SS-Panzer Regiment 12 were sent to the le Neubourg area, over 100 kilometres to the east between Rouen and Evreux.

On July 17 the division was recalled; the British and Canadians having overrun its old positions. After the defensive battles that followed the division was again relieved by the 272. Infanterie Division with the intention of letting it rest south-east of Falaise — although, in fact, it remained in readiness to the north of the town. By this time it had been split into two battle groups — Kampfgruppe Krause and Kampfgruppe Waldmüller — which together fielded a total of about fifty various armoured vehicles.

On August 7 II. Abteilung of SS-Panzer Regiment 12 was in support of Kampfgruppe Krause near Grimbosq, on the Orne fifteen kilometres south of Caen. Next day (August 8) several of SS-

This Ausf A was reported as being hit by a 17-pdr anti-tank gun — virtually the only Allied weapon able to destroy a Panther under normal battle conditions. A second tank lies in a ditch behind. Most probably 12. SS as the location is Norrey-en-Bessin on June 27 but could also have belonged to Panzer Regiment 3. (IWM)

Panzer Regiment 12's tanks were brought into reserve in Quesnay Wood, on the Caen-Falaise road, where there were already some Panthers. They finished re-assembling at about 3.00 a.m. on the 9th. In the early morning Wünsche put his men on the alert although Kampfgruppe Waldemüller was nowhere to be seen. The tanks were astride the road. Wünsche was to make two concentric drives for Point 140, three kilometres to the east, with a few of schwere SS-Panzerabteilung 101's Tigers approaching from the west and fifteen of I. Abteilung's Panthers from the east. The Panthers moved off along the road but were suddenly caught in a pincer and were fired on from either side. Allied fighter-bombers, after seeming to hesitate, joined in, but shot up their own tanks in error. Point 140, wreathed in smoke, was captured by the Germans. The Canadian Columbia Regiment had lost twenty-eight tanks — SS-Panzer Regiment 12 none.

On August 10 other tanks from the regiment took part in the fight for Point 195, three kilometres south-west of Quesnay and on the other side of the N158. To the north-east, the Poles were trying to force a crossing over the River Laison near Condé-sur-Ifs, turning the flank of Kampfgruppe Krause, and some of the tanks had to be moved across from Point 195 to the right — about a dozen of them heading for Condé . . .

As the division's battle-worn remnants and various service units regrouped around Evreux and Bernay, its operational strength returns on August 13 included no more than twenty tanks, although among them were a few of the formidable Jagdpanzer IVs.

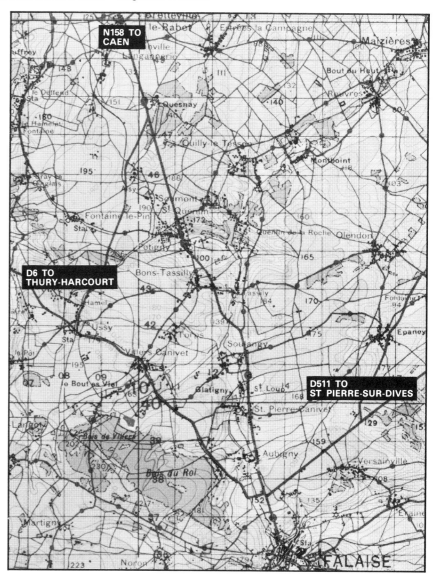

FALAISE

On the morning of August 14 'Panzer-meyer' and Wünsche headed north-west to establish new positions. Point 159, just north of Falaise, was the fulcrum, and underwent a tremendous bombardment the following day. The tank crews were under orders not to move until the opposing tanks appeared. This brought some success, and the Allied tanks were halted. The pressure was maintained to the right, however, on the River Dives, at Jort and Perrières, and there the few remaining tanks were put out of action.

At Point 159 the attacks were coming in again, and SS-Sturmbannführer Karl-Heinz Prinz, commanding II. Abteilung, who had been awarded the Knight's Cross on July 11, was killed. To the right of the hill Typhoons were again harrying some of the regiment's tanks. Wünsche, at the point of exhaustion, reported to Meyer that it was impossible to hold out any longer. When Meyer was wounded a few tanks continued to cling to the reverse slopes of Point 159, but on the afternoon of August 15 it had to be abandoned.

On August 17 SS-Hauptsturmführer Hans Siegel, in charge of 8. Kompanie, was awarded the Knight's Cross to the Iron Cross.

During the night of August 18-19 the remains of the division left their heavy vehicles behind and a group led by Wünsche crossed enemy lines although he was taken prisoner six days later.

Death of a prinz! SS-Sturmbannführer Karl-Heinz Prinz (with binoculars) was killed at Point 159. Today he lies buried in the German Soldatenfriedhof at La Cambe — Block 36, Row 9, Grave 327.

Spoils of war. A Cromwell recovery vehicle of the 11th Armoured Division with a PzKpfw IV Ausf H which appears to be largely intact. The turret has been turned backwards and the divisional sign on the rear right clearly shows it to be 12. SS-Panzer Division. Being a PzKpfw IV it must belong to the II. Abteilung and the number 837 further identifies it as being tank number seven from the third platoon of the eighth company. Photo by Sergeant Hardy on July 6. (IWM)

Sturmgeschutz 40 of SS-Panzer Abteilung 17. During the German counter-attack on Carentan on June 13, they got to within 500 yards of the town before being repulsed by elements of the 2nd Armored and 101st Airborne Divisions. (US Army)

SS-PANZER ABTEILUNG 17

The 17. SS-Panzergrenadier division Götz von Berlichingen was created in France on November 15, 1943. From December it was stationed between Tours, Angers and Parthenay in western France carrying out working up exercises. Its SS-Panzer Abteilung 17 was equipped with StuGs, and it was the only panzergrenadier division to take part in the Normandy fighting — its baptism of fire.

On D-Day, 17. SS-Panzergrenadier Division was quickly called upon and was brought into the line to the south of Carentan less than a week after the first Allied landings. The division fought in this sector until the American break-out on July 18, after which it fell back, little by little, towards the base of the Cotentin Peninsula before being driven back east into the Falaise pocket.

SS-STURMBANNFÜHRER LUDWIG KEPPLINGER

Kepplinger was born on December 31, 1911, at Linz in Austria. Because of his political views he was discharged from

the Austrian army — he belonged to a mountain regiment — whereupon he crossed into Germany and joined the SS-Verfügungstruppen in Bavaria in 1935.

In 1940 Kepplinger was SS-Hauptscharführer in 11. Kompanie, Standarte 3 Der Führer, the third infantry regiment in the SS-Verfügungstruppen Division. In Holland that year his Knights Cross of the Iron Cross was one of the first to be awarded in the Waffen-SS and the first to be awarded to an NCO or warrant officer (September 4). He was soon promoted to SS-Untersturmführer and went to Russia with SS-Regiment Westland of the SS-Division Wiking.

The commanding officer of SS-Panzer Abteilung 17 of the 17. SS-Panzergrenadier Division Götz von Berlichingen, Kepplinger, by then holding the rank of SS-Sturmbannführer, was reported missing in September 1944 and is believed to have been killed by the Maquis near Laval on August 6/7, 1944. He now lies in Vault 68, Room 168 at Mont-de-Huisnes, one of the 11,956 interred there from the Second World War.

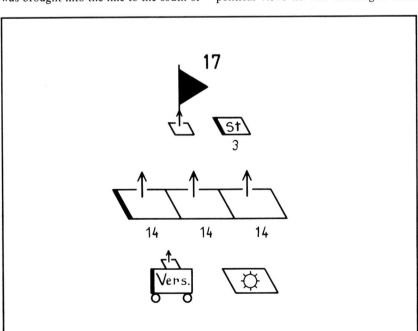

Organisation table (theoretical) of SS-Panzer Abteilung 17. In June, 17. SS-Panzer Grenadier Division had 37 StuGs (paper strength 42) but none of the 3 Befehlspanzer IIIs it was supposed to have in the staff company of its SS-Panzer Abteilung 17.

SCHWERE
SS-PANZER ABTEILUNG 101

Untersturmführer in December 1942, and early in 1943 he was given command of a Tiger I in 13. Kompanie of the Leibstandarte's SS-Panzer Regiment 1. Thereafter his victories began to mount up, and his tally stood at 66 tanks alone on January 9, 1944. The day before he received his Knights Cross (awarded on the 14th) he destroyed a further 19 tanks and 3 heavy assault guns; and when he was promoted to SS-Obersturmführer on January 20 his tank kills amounted to 117. He was awarded the Oak Leaves to the Knights Cross, awarded only two weeks previously, on the 30th.

In April Wittmann became a company commander in schwere SS-Panzer Abteilung 101, with which his most notable exploit was at Villers-Bocage on June 13, 1944, against the British 7th Armoured Division. On June 22, he added the Swords to his Knight's Cross (the 71st holder of this award) and shortly afterwards received promotion to SS-Hauptsturmführer and was made commanding officer. When he was killed on August 8, near Cintheaux, Wittmann had been credited with destroying 138 tanks and assault guns and 132 anti-tank guns in less than two years.

The theoretical organisation chart for schwere SS-Panzer Abteilung 101. On June 1 the battalion (commanded by SS-Obersturmbannführer von Westernhagen) had 37 Tigers (theoretical strength 45) and 3 SdKfz 7/1 quadruple 20mm Flak half-tracks. Only 11 Tigers remained serviceable on July 1, but the total on the strength of the unit had increased to 20 by August 1.

SS-HAUPTSTURMFÜHRER MICHAEL WITTMANN

Michael Wittmann was born on April 22, 1914, at Vogelthal, in the Oberpfalz. He joined the army in 1934 and was stationed at Freising with 10. Kompanie, Infanterie Regiment 19. In 1937 he enrolled in the Leibstandarte SS Adolf Hitler. By the outbreak of war he was an SS-Unterscharführer, and commanded an armoured car in Poland and France.

In the Balkans campaign in 1941 he was in command of an assault gun and was awarded the Iron Cross II Class in July. His first successes date from the Leibstandarte's thrust into Russia. Coming under attack by eight Soviet tanks, he put six of them out of action. In September he earned the Iron Cross I Class during the advance on Rostov, having been wounded for the second time.

After being sent to the SS-Junkerschule (officer cadet school) at Bad Tölz, Wittmann passed out an SS-

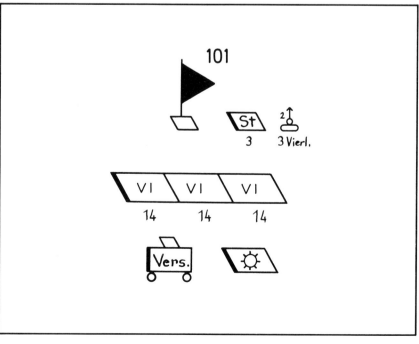

The elite of the Waffen-SS, and members of the crack I. SS-Panzer Korps, move up to the front. The schwere (heavy) SS-Panzer Abteilung 101 were equipped with Ausf E Tigers and this series of pictures was taken around June 10 east of Rouen.

Travelling south-westwards on the N316 from Gournay-en-Bray to les Andelys, the unit has just passed through the Forêt de Lyons and is beginning the climb out of the Levrière valley towards Morgny. (Bundesarchiv)

Not only was the 101 renowned in its own right, it had as its second company commander the famed Michael Wittmann. What von Richthofen was in the air in the First World War so Wittmann became to the Panzertruppe in the Second. This is his company grinding up the hill. His personal tank should have borne the number 200, '0' indicating that it belonged to the Stab of the 2. Kompanie. Unfortunately a Tiger with this number does not appear in the photos. (Bundesarchiv)

The figures on the turrets would have been in red outlined in white on a camouflage background of sand, olive green and reddish brown. The 221 identifies this Tiger as that of the commander of the second platoon, second company. Although these Tigers appear brand new, some have the old type of dished wheels with rubber rims. (Bundesarchiv)

On reaching Morgny, the driver of a Schwimmwagen parked in the entrance to the D13 Longchamps road in the manner of a military policeman to keep the convoy on the correct route. From an examination of the photographs taken of schwere SS-Panzer Abteilung 101 in Normandy it would appear to indicate that each company had its insignia painted on the front of its tanks in a different way. 1. Kompanie carried the battalion shield on the left front with a tactical sign on the right; the 2. Kompanie had the shield on the right-hand side with no tactical symbol, and the 3. Kompanie also omitted this symbol but had the crossed key insignia on the left front. Unfortunately in both these pictures one cannot prove this theory as the tankers are covering the position where the insignia was painted with their legs. (Bundesarchiv)

No. '131' indicates SS-Hauptsturmführer Möbius' 1. Kompanie. As a general rule, steel helmets were no longer issued to tank crews in 1944. This shot makes a striking comparison with the Morgny of today although the gentleman who lettered the war memorial would appear to have been slightly intoxicated at the time. (Readers wishing to visit the village should take care to select the correct one — there is another Morgny about twenty-five kilometres north-west. (Bundesarchiv)

'Our' village is the one on the N316. A better match for the comparison is given by the previous frame in the series reproduced on page 161. (Bundesarchiv)

Schwere SS-Panzer Abteilung 101 (renumbered 501 in October 1944) was the heavy tank component of I. SS-Panzer Korps, which came into being during the summer of 1943, consisting of the LSSAH, then fighting in Russia, and the 12. SS-Panzer Division Hitlerjugend, which was being formed in Belgium. Schwere SS-Panzer Abteilung 101 was formed in France at this time, at Mailly-le-Camp.

At the time of the invasion the commander of I. SS-Panzer Korps, SS-Obergruppenführer 'Sepp' Dietrich, had his headquarters at Septeuil, south of Mantes-la-Jolie, west of Paris, and schwere SS-Panzer Abteilung 101 was stationed in the Beauvais area.

To reach Normandy it was routed via Paris, where, on June 8 near Versailles, its Tigers were caught in an air raid which damaged several of them — at least in Wittmann's 2. Kompanie.

The Abteilung did not really reach the battle zone before June 12. In the vicinity of Villers-Bocage 2. Kompanie found cover in a small wood to the north east of the village (minus four tanks which had to be left with SS-Obersturmführer Stamm, in charge of the workshops company), while 1. Kompanie under SS-Hauptsturmführer Möbius was to their right. Corps headquarters had moved on June 9 to the little village of Baron-sur-Odon, between Villers-Bocage and Caen, near Point 112, where it remained until June 15.

On the morning of June 13 Wittmann wanted to have a look for himself at the ground to the north-west between him and Balleroy, to check whether a rumour that the British 7th Armoured Division

Preparing for battle. Tactical conference of tank commanders — note the P.08 Luger holsters. (Bundesarchiv)

had pushed into the left flank of the Panzer Lehr, which was holding the front line, was correct. In Wittmann's tank the gun-layer was SS-Oberscharführer Balthasar Woll, with whom Wittmann had gained most of his success in Russia. Woll now had his own tank but it was under repair.

The small yet potent force of four Tigers and one PzKpfw IV approached Villers-Bocage only to spot a British armoured column leaving the town to move eastwards up the N175 towards the high ground of Point 213, which was a strategic position a kilometre or so beyond the town on the northern side of the road. Having left the built-up area the British vehicles halted on the hill past the junction with the road to Tilly. Not having met any opposition, the drivers got down to stretch their legs and, no doubt, enjoy a cigarette and brew up. With the British so occupied, Wittmann decided to cut round behind them and reconnoitre the town to establish the strength of the opposition. Entering Villers-Bocage, which runs steeply downhill to the west towards the river valley of la Seulles, he spotted four Cromwell's parked one behind the other on the main street. Three of the British tanks were quickly knocked out, the fourth managing to reverse off the road and take cover in the garden of a house.

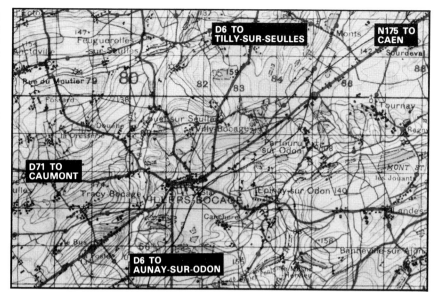

There have been many conflicting accounts published about SS-Obersturmführer Michael Wittmann's almost single-handed battle at Villers-Bocage which successfully stopped a British armoured advance by the 22nd Armoured Brigade — part of the 7th Armoured Division. Thanks to detailed research by American historian Major Gary L. Simpson (a tank commander in the US National Guard), Major W. H. J. Sale, MBE, MC, of the 3rd County of London Yeomanry, and Elisabeth M. Brodie who has researched Wittmann's biography, the actual course of the action has now been resolved to the satisfaction of both German and British survivors. Phase one began when the 22nd Armoured, with the 4th County of London Yeomanry (Sharpshooters) in the lead, were ordered to capture the important road junction of Villers-Bocage and the high ground beyond (Point 213).

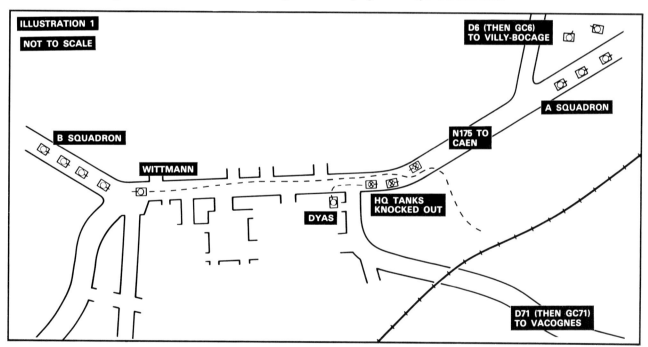

Lieutenant-Colonel Arthur, the Viscount Cranleigh, the commanding officer, had requested time to carry out a proper reconnaissance of the area as German armoured cars had been spotted observing the advance south from Tilly-sur-Seulles. Orders were, however, to push on regardless (which, apart from the immediate aim, accorded with the Allies' overall strategy of keeping the German armour away from the American front). Leaving the four regimental HQ tanks at the top of the main street in Villers, 'A' Squadron was ordered forward to secure Point 213 about two kilometres north-east up the N175. Meanwhile Wittmann's force of four Tigers and one PzKpfw IV from Panzer Lehr Regiment had the same objective in mind — to hold Villers-Bocage, and protect the flanks of the

Panzer Lehr Division. Seeing the British armour leave Villers, he decided to cut in behind them and reconnoitre the town. Entering from the east he spotted the Cromwells parked at the side of the road and opened fire. He immediately knocked out Viscount Cranleigh's tank (he had gone forward in a scout car to Point 213); then that of Major Carr, second in command, followed by the Regimental Sergeant Major's Cromwell. The fourth British tank, commanded by Captain Pat Dyas, backed off the road into a front garden. Although Wittmann failed to spot him, Dyas with his gunner at that moment outside the tank, watched helplessly as the Tiger presented a perfect side shot as it moved past him down the hill into the town (ILLUSTRATION 1).

Above: **One of the Sharpshooters regimental HQ Cromwell IVs lying where Wittmann hit it at the top end of the rue Clemenceau. (Bundesarchiv)** *Below:* **With the old house,** gateway and wall all demolished, it was only with reference to other shots taken at this spot that we were able to pinpoint the location (see *opposite*).

For several days the town, a vital road junction in the Normandy road network, had been the target for fighter-bombers of the Second Tactical Air Force, and Wittmann descended the hill past the rubble of bombed out houses. As he reached the bottom more British tanks came into view parked on the Caumont road. Shots were immediately exchanged, the Tiger receiving at least one hit from a Firefly. At this point Wittmann ordered his driver to reverse out of trouble and proceed back up the hill. However, having turned round he came face to face with the Cromwell which had taken shelter in the garden and which had subsequently driven out behind him and had been stalking him down the street from the rear. The Tiger's frontal armour deflected two shells from the British tank before the Cromwell was knocked out by Wittmann.

The pillars of the gateway on the right are the link — this is the same tank, photographed from the rear. The PzKpfw IV '634' of the Panzer Lehr is not a casualty — just parked with a good view down the street. (Bundesarchiv)

Another of the Cromwells lies just behind the PzKpfw IV and faces towards the high ground of Point 213. The same cement-faced house is visible on the extreme left of the comparison to the top photo. (Bundesarchiv)

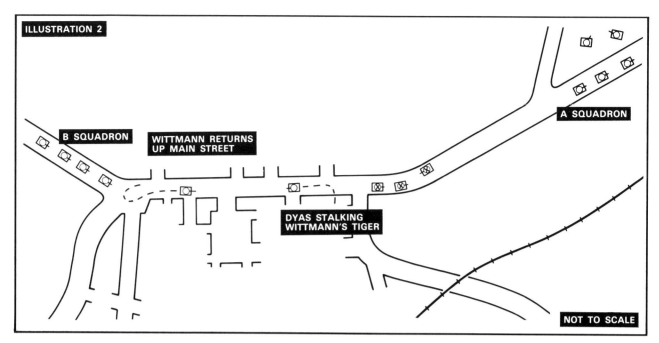

ILLUSTRATION 2

B SQUADRON

WITTMANN RETURNS
UP MAIN STREET

A SQUADRON

DYAS STALKING
WITTMANN'S TIGER

NOT TO SCALE

Wittmann continued down the hill where he came up against the tanks of 'B' Squadron parked on the road to Caumont. He exchanged shots with Sergeant Lockwood in a Firefly and the Tiger received at least one hit. Seeing he was outnumbered, Wittmann turned round and began to climb back up the street which at this point is called the rue Pasteur. Meanwhile Captain Dyas had loaded his gun and had followed the Tiger downhill, stalking Wittmann from the rear. When the Tiger turned round they came face to face (ILLUSTRATION 2). Two shells from the Cromwell failed to penetrate the Tiger and Wittmann returned the fire, knocking out the tank and killing two of the crew, one with his machine gun as he tried to escape. Although wounded Dyas managed to get away on foot and, with the help of a French girl, joined 'B' Squadron.

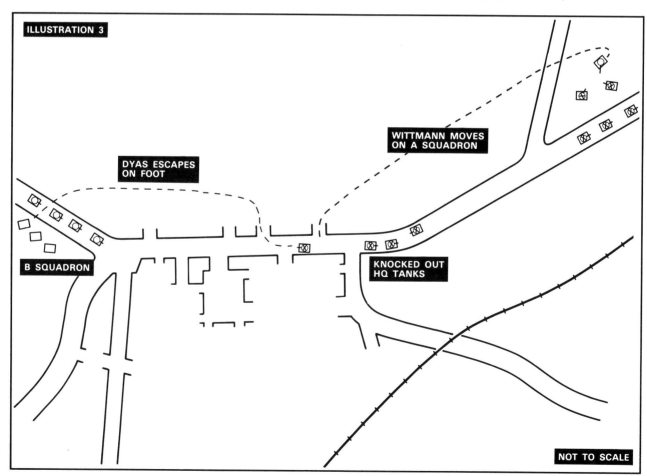

ILLUSTRATION 3

DYAS ESCAPES
ON FOOT

WITTMANN MOVES
ON A SQUADRON

B SQUADRON

KNOCKED OUT
HQ TANKS

NOT TO SCALE

Wittmann left the town and rejoined the other Tigers to replenish his ammunition. He then moved against 'A' Squadron parked on the N175 leading up to Point 213. After first knocking out the British Fireflys with their 17-pdr guns — the only weapon dangerous to a Tiger — he systematically shot up the rest of the squadron. When the crews tried to escape the onslaught, they were either killed or captured by German infantry supporting 2. Kompanie (ILLUSTRATION 3).

Pictures of 'A' Squadron never before identified as such. The road is the N175 leading north-east from Villers — at this point a long hill leading up to Point 213. Here Wittmann and company caught the British vehicles as they were parked on the verge and from the angle of the anti-tank gun it appears the attack came from the northern side of the road. *Above:* This was a Loyd gun carrier loaded with ammunition — exploded shell cases are scattered about. *Right:* The crews must have taken cover in the ditch behind the convoy. After death their pockets were rifled and unwanted papers litter the ground. *Below:* Almost like a time machine the camera jumps ahead to record the same spot in 1983 with nothing to indicate the tragic events of yesterday. (Bundesarchiv)

This shot of the same 6-pdr clearly shows how near the rear of the column was to the town. (Bundesarchiv)

Further up the hill more Cromwells and at least one Sherman, which had gone forward to reconnoitre Point 213, were hit or abandoned. The latter seems a possibility as one of the Cromwells has been moved from the road *above*, which is Frame 1A on the roll, to the verge depicted in Frame 4A *below*. More looted bodies lie in the ditch at this point although it should be appreciated that stealing from the dead is common in all armies in all wars. (Bundesarchiv)

Not far away in the woods on the crown of the hill lie more Sharpshooter Cromwells.

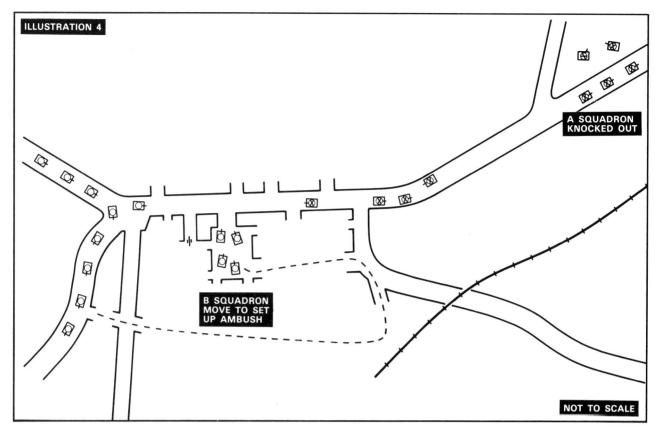

ILLUSTRATION 4

A SQUADRON KNOCKED OUT

B SQUADRON MOVE TO SET UP AMBUSH

NOT TO SCALE

After Captain Dyas made contact with Major Aird commanding 'B' Squadron, he radioed to Viscount Cranleigh outside the town advising him of the destruction of the HQ tanks. Lieutenant-Colonel Arthur replied that they, too, were under attack from Tiger tanks at that moment. No further messages were received from 'A' Squadron — Viscount Cranleigh had been taken prisoner. Unaware of the fate of the squadron, Major Aird despatched a troop of four Cromwells (one a Firefly with a 17-pdr gun), under Lieutenant Bill Cotton, to try to make contact with the squadron. Although they managed to cross the town they were unable to get over the railway embankment and instead turned back to set up a strategic position in the main square to catch any Germans coming back down the rue Clemenceau (ILLUSTRATION 4). This position would enable the Cromwells to catch the Tigers broadside on where they stood a better chance of a kill. Men of the Queen's Regiment also set up a 6-pdr anti-tank gun in an alleyway. The range was so short that each gun was sighted through the barrel at a fixed point on the opposite side of the street.

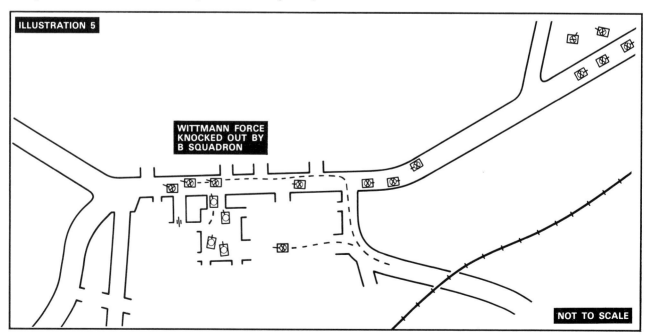

ILLUSTRATION 5

WITTMANN FORCE KNOCKED OUT BY B SQUADRON

NOT TO SCALE

Having eliminated the threat from the high ground, SS-Obersturmführer Wittmann decided to return to the town centre in force, unaware of the trap that had been set. In the company of two Tigers and a PzKpfw IV, he led the way back past the knocked out Cromwells. Bill Cotton's troop let him pass whereupon the Queens sent a fatal shot into his side. The second Tiger was hit by Sergeant Bobby Bramall with his Firefly but Corporal Horne missed his target, the Mk IV. However immediately driving out behind it, he stopped it with a well-placed shot up its rear end. (ILLUSTRATION 5)

Above: Amid the rubble from a subsequent Allied bombing attack, Wittmann's Tiger lies disabled on the right. In the distance is the second Tiger and the PzKpfw IV. Wittmann and his crew managed to escape unharmed. (Bundesarchiv) Below: The close proximity of the bend at the top of the street (page 171) is graphically illustrated in Brana Radovic's 1989 comparison.

The Germans had managed to escape because of the absence of infantry to mop up. Later, in pouring rain, Lieutenant Cotton armed with an umbrella, some blankets and a can of petrol, walked with Sergeant Bramall up to the German tanks. Petrol-soaked blankets were pushed into each and set alight so burning them out and denying the Germans the chance of their repair. Wittmann's tank clearly shows the effects of the blaze. (Bundesarchiv)

During the late afternoon the British force pulled back and RAF Typhoons hit the centre of the town, one report stating that their target was the tanks already destroyed. This is the PzKpfw IV and Tiger in the main street. (Bundesarchiv)

On leaving the town to refuel and rearm, Wittmann returned to attack the British he had spotted earlier below Point 213. Approaching under cover of a wood, he first knocked out the end half-track effectively blocking the escape of the remainder of the vehicles which he then systematically shot up one by one. Proceeding along the length of the column, tanks, lorries, half-tracks and Bren gun carriers went up in smoke spreading wreckage all over the road. Altogether Wittmann destroyed about twenty-five armoured vehicles in the attack.

Having dealt with a possible threat to his rear, Wittmann then returned to the town in the company of two Tigers and a PzKpfw IV. This time, however, the panzers were not to be so lucky. The British squadron which had clashed with Wittmann earlier had now taken up defensive positions around the main square, and an anti-tank gun had been set up to enfilade the main street from a small alley. In this way the lighter gunned British force hoped to catch the Tigers in an ambush side on where the chances of scoring a damaging hit on the tracks was more certain.

Wittmann retraced his former route down the hill, past the hulks of his earlier victims, straight into the trap. Wittmann in the lead was hit by the anti-tank gun, and the following Tiger by a

The third Tiger would appear to have been caught at the crossroads of the rue Jeanne Bacon and rue Emile Samson. The main street is a few dozen yards to the left. (Bundesarchiv)

Firefly. The PzKpfw IV passed by unscathed until one of the British tanks drove out behind it and sent a shell up its rear end. Wittmann and his crew from the Tiger managed to escape on foot as neither side possessed the infantry support which would normally be on hand to mop up or take prisoners.

There is no doubt that Wittmann's largely single-handed initiative stopped a British armoured thrust which could have resulted in the encirclement of Panzer Lehr Division. His action enabled Villers-Bocage to be retaken later in the day by a Panzer Lehr Kampfgruppe and units of 2. Panzer Division and, as a result, Bayerlein, commanding Panzer Lehr, put Wittmann's name forward for the Swords to his Knights Cross.

A few days later Wittmann was able to put up a second pip when he was promoted to SS-Hauptsturmführer. He was also offered a post as an instructor at an officer training school which he refused, preferring to remain with 2. Kompanie.

On June 15 corps headquarters was established at Evrecy, which it left on June 28 for Clinchamps-sur-Orne, to the east. Between July 9 and July 16 the Abteilung regrouped south of Evrecy, entering the line from July 17 to July 24 to the south of Avenay and then around Vieux, further east.

On August 7 schwere SS-Panzer Abteilung 101 was attached to what remained of the Hitlerjugend Division, in position halfway between Caen and Falaise. Wittmann was now in command, and his orders on August 8 were to take Cintheaux, on the Caen-Falaise

It was Air Chief Marshal Sir Trafford Leigh-Mallory (Air Commander-in-Chief, Allied Expeditionary Air Force) who proposed the use of heavy bombers to help the land campaign in Normandy. With the advance bogged down by the stubborn resistance around Caen, Leigh-Mallory suggested that the weight of RAF Bomber Command could be brought to bear decisively on the battlefield. A preliminary rehearsal was fixed for June 30 . . . the target Villers-Bocage. Aircraft from Nos. 3, 4 and 8 Groups, some 250 in all, covered by eight squadrons of Spitfires, dropped 1,176 tons of high explosive, the RAF history stating that it was 'with good effect'. One eye witness reported that he had seen the remains of a German tank strewing the top of a two-storey building. One Tiger is still recognisable as such and so is Wittmann's, further down the rubble on the left, but the Mk IV appears to have received a direct hit. Perhaps this was the one that went skywards. (IWM) *Below:* Comparison by Brana Radovic in 1989. A plaque beside a shop on the left of the street records the destruction and reconstruction which was inaugurated on March 7, 1948.

An interesting shot of a schwere SS-Panzer Abteilung 101 Tiger which appears to have been captured in full working order. The location? That Panther seems familiar . . . the 12. SS Ausf A on pages 156-157. (IWM)

road, in order to protect the division's right flank, and to occupy the heights to the north of the village. When 'Panzermeyer' (SS-Oberführer Kurt Meyer) came up to the Tigers which were hidden behind a hedge to the east of the village, SS-Sturmbannführer Waldmüller of the Hitlerjugend Division was going over the final details of the attack with Wittmann when a solitary bomber flew over the spot several times, sending up coloured flares. Meyer could foresee what was

Left: A little way down the road at Rauray, Lieutenant Handford of the Army Film and Photo Unit found this late production Ausf E (characterised by the periscope-equipped cupola), also from schwere SS-Panzer Abteilung 101. On June 28 it was used as cover by a German sniper. (IWM) *Right:* Technical advisor, Jean Paul Pallud, discusses the action with Gordon Ramsey.

coming and abruptly put forward the attack, which had originally been set for 12.30 p.m. After Meyer had shaken Wittmann by the hand, reminding him again of the importance of the attack, the ace of all tank aces clambered aboard his Tiger.

The Tigers now set off northwards, seeking out any depressions in the ground in order to stop and fire and then crossing the open fields at top speed, while the Hitlerjugend panzergrenadiers followed on. The Tigers were met with artillery fire: Wittmann pushed on ahead even faster and they got through unscathed. Overhead, the sky had come to life — but the Allied aircraft were bombing their own positions. At 1,800 metres, using their superior range, the Tigers began to shoot up the Shermans advancing towards Cintheaux. They were face to face with the Canadian 4th Armoured Division. Wittmann held his ground and the fighting went on for several hours before the few Panthers still possessed by I. Abteilung of SS-Panzer Regiment 12, under SS-Sturmbannführer Jürgensen, made themselves known and Cintheaux was taken.

That evening, as Bretteville-sur-Laize, to the west, had fallen, the Tigers covered the withdrawal of Waldmüller's panzergrenadiers and sheltered for the night six kilometres down the road from Cintheaux in the woods surrounding the Château de Quesnay.

When Wittmann was reported missing 'Panzermeyer' ordered a search to be made everywhere for him. A few eye-witness accounts have since described how Wittmann's Tiger, fighting alone against a group of Shermans east of Cintheaux during the evening, having destroyed two of them and immobilised a third, looked set on fighting its way out when it took the full impact of five Shermans firing from three sides. There were no survivors.

The Abteilung was placed under SS-Obersturmführer Wünsche of Panzer Regiment 12, and next day (August 9) they were called upon to retake Point 140 with the panzer regiment's Panthers. Out from beneath the trees came the Tigers and proceeded along the ridge towards the sector held by Kampfgruppe Krause. Wheeling round to face the Allied flank, two of them took cover in the undergrowth and opened fire. A couple of Shermans were hit, and the two Tigers became the butt of some murderous return fire. Together with three other tanks that had been brought into action they somehow managed to defend themselves long enough until Jürgensen's Panthers were able to start wheeling round on the other flank. Clouds of smoke began billowing upwards from the Canadian tanks as they brewed up. Towards 11.00 a.m. two half-tracks tried to break out northwards but were soon shot up by a Tiger close to Kurt Meyer. In the course of the night, the Canadians managed to get back to

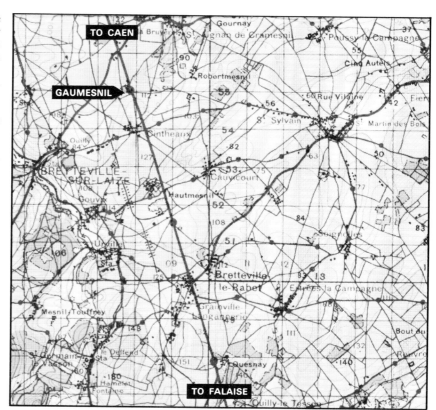

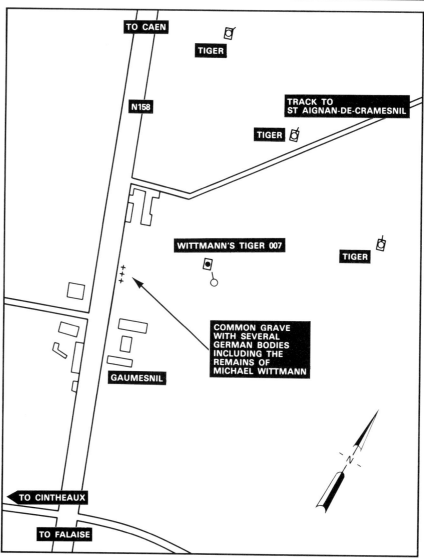

the Poles, leaving behind twenty-eight of their tanks around Point 140.

On August 18 two of the Abteilung's Tigers, though damaged, managed to halt the armoured reconnaissance tanks of the British 53rd Infantry Division at Nécy, south of Falaise. The following morning at about 2.00 a.m. the officer in charge, SS-Obersturmführer Meitzel, was taken prisoner with both crews, all of whom had been wounded . . . .

Right: **The remains of Wittmann's Tiger '007' near Gaumesnil, blasted apart by the combined efforts of five Shermans. Detailed local research early in 1981 enabled Jean Paul Pallud to produce the sketch plan (*opposite*) and to pinpoint the exact spot (*below left*), confirmed by fragments of steel and glass, where Wittmann and his crew met their deaths.**

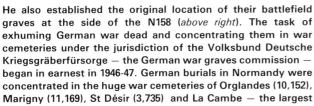

He also established the original location of their battlefield graves at the side of the N158 (*above right*). The task of exhuming German war dead and concentrating them in war cemeteries under the jurisdiction of the Volksbund Deutsche Kriegsgräberfürsorge — the German war graves commission — began in earnest in 1946-47. German burials in Normandy were concentrated in the huge war cemeteries of Orglandes (10,152), Marigny (11,169), St Désir (3,735) and La Cambe — the largest German Second World War cemetery in France with 21,160 graves. Smaller plots are located in the British cemeteries at Bayeux (466), Fontenay-le-Pesnel (59), Hottot-les-Bagues (132), Douvres-la-Delivrande (182), Ranville (323), Ryes-Bazenville (328), Cheux-St Manvieu (556), Secqueville-en-Bessin (18), Tilly-sur-Seulles (232) and Tourgeville (33). The graves in British cemeteries were basically original burials at the time by the British Graves Registration Service and these were not touched.

SS-Hauptsturmführer Michael Wittmann was not recorded as being buried in any of these cemeteries and so we passed the location of the temporary roadside graves we had found to the German authorities in September 1982 with the assumption that they had been re-interred in one of these cemeteries — most probably La Cambe — as 'unknown'. In March 1983 two investigators discovered the remains — not at La Cambe but still buried beside the N158! Jean Paul's evidence had been a crucial factor and thanks to his dedicated effort, the hero of the panzertruppe was accorded a decent burial at La Cambe (*photo left*). Of the remains of the five crewmen, Michael Wittmann, Rudolf Hirschel and Heinrich Reimers alone could be identified and their names now mark their communal grave (Block 47, Row 3, Grave 120). A 6.35mm self-loading pistol found with the remains was retained by the Volksbund.

SCHWERE SS-PANZER ABTEILUNG 102

Schwere SS-Panzer Abteilung 102 was the heavy tank component in Normandy of II. SS-Panzer Korps. This corps, which was formed in the spring of 1942, comprised 9. SS-Panzer Division Hohenstaufen and 10. SS-Panzer Division Frundsberg and was, in effect, the first SS armoured corps, only becoming II when 'Sepp' Dietrich's I. SS-Panzer Korps came into being in 1943. Established in Germany, the corps was sent to France in the middle of 1942 to oversee the SS divisions that were being reorganised. The following winter, it was sent to the Eastern Front, where it was at the heart of the battles of Kharkov and Kursk. During the summer, it went to northern Italy, with only the LSSAH Division under its wing, and then back to France — to the Alençon area — where it took in the new Frundsberg and Hohenstaufen Divisions. In March 1944, II. SS-Panzer Korps was moved to the Lemberg region, near the frontier between Poland and Russia, returning again a month later to the Eastern Front, on the Tarnopol sector in the western Ukraine. Then, in June, the corps was ordered to Normandy. From its formation II. SS-Panzer Korps had been commanded by SS-Obergruppenführer Hausser, but on June 28 SS-Gruppenführer Bittrich took over when Hausser was given command of the 7. Armee following the sudden death of General Dollmann.

On D-Day schwere SS-Panzer Abteilung 102 was still stationed in Holland, at the camp at Wezep where it had been formed at the beginning of the year. In charge of 1. Kompanie was SS-Obersturmführer Kalls; 2. Kompanie was led by SS-Hauptsturmführer Endemann and 3. Kompanie by SS-Obersturmführer Siebenlist. As usual, they had a long wait for their tanks. By mid May, only 1. and 3. Kompanie had taken delivery of theirs, and it was June 6 itself before 2. Kompanie received its Tigers.

Some of the NCOs and men came from the heavy tank unit which should have been part of III. SS-Germanische Panzer Korps, and mostly the Abteilung consisted of Germans who came from Romania, in keeping with the Waffen-SS policy of filling out its ranks with Volksdeutschen. Their commanding officer, SS-Sturmbannführer Weiss had come from 2. SS-Panzer Division Das Reich.

On June 13, the Abteilung was moved to the vicinity of St. Pol, south of Calais. Although the German High Command still believed that the Normandy landings were just a diversion and that the real blow was about to fall in the Pas-de-Calais, on June 15 the Abteilung was ordered to join up with II. SS-Panzer Korps via Paris, where the Tigers were stationed in the grounds of the palace at Versailles.

VERSAILLES TO NORMANDY

On the evening of July 1 the Tigers set out for Normandy under their own steam, one platoon at a time leaving every hour. A haze of oil and petrol fumes wafted around the column and the drivers had to fight to stay awake. Every ten or fifteen kilometres a halt was called to inspect the engines, and maintenance and tank crews slaved alongside one another to maintain the momentum of the journey. The tracks were supposed to go 45 kilometres without attention, but the road surface was particularly hard on them. Towards 3.00 a.m. the first Tigers made a halt at Rambouillet. The tanks were concealed under the trees before the crews turned in for the night.

They started off again the following day around dusk. On some of the tanks the thermostats were registering 100° centigrade, but the thought of losing the rest of the column was enough to keep them all moving forward; and so they pushed on with flames shooting out of the exhausts and smoke coming off the armour-plate above the engines. Finally, on a hill out of Châteauneuf (on the N839) the inevitable happened — one caught fire. The driver stopped immediately; everyone grabbed a fire extinguisher, and the engine sizzled in clouds of smoke. When, at dawn, the tank at last reached the next repair point it had its cooling fan changed. Ten

metres up the road the engine stalled and they had another look at it. Three kilometres further on, it burst into flames once again. It took quite some time to fit a second fan: in the rush the first had been fitted in back to front, and instead of extracting the hot air it had been drawing it back in again!

On July 4 the schwere SS-Panzer Abteilung 102 reassembled around Cauville, south-west of Thury-Harcourt, and a few days later went into readiness at Vacognes, south-west of Evrecy. Corps HQ was at Hamars, six kilometres north of Cauville.

POINT 112

On July 9, the Abteilung was ordered up to Point 112, a few kilometres further north (four kilometres north-east of Evrecy), which had already been the scene of some violent fighting. At 11.00 p.m. the Tigers lay in wait two kilometres south-east of the hill at the northern exit of St Martin. The attack that had been planned was to take place at the juncture of the Frundsberg Divison on the left and the Hitlerjugend Division on the right.

Next morning the hill was pounded by Allied artillery fire. SS-Sturmbann-

The theoretical organisation of schwere SS-Panzer Abteilung 102. On June 1 the battalion commander, SS-Sturmbann-führer Weiss, had only 28 Tigers at his disposal as opposed to the 45 he should have possessed. He had 3 SdKfz 10/4, 20mm Flak half-tracks.

Left: Evrecy lies a mile south-west from Point 112 — the location of schwere SS-Panzer Abteilung 102's baptism of fire in Normandy. This Tiger I came to a sticky end just outside the village. As there seems no evidence of an aerial bombardment, possibly an internal explosion has ripped off the turret, splitting the 80mm-thick armour in two, and separating it from the 88 barrel which weighs nearly 1½ tons. (Bundesarchiv) *Above:* We established that the picture had been taken looking south from the D8.

führer Weiss received the order to attack, and 2. Kompanie advanced from St Martin with seven tanks. In front of them, the hill lay under a smokescreen that enveloped everything. Then, as the

Tigers began their ascent, the smoke suddenly dispersed and they opened fire. With SS-Untersturmführer Schroif's platoon on the left and SS-Untersturmführer Rathsack's on the

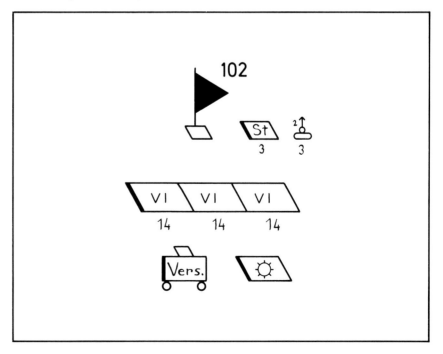

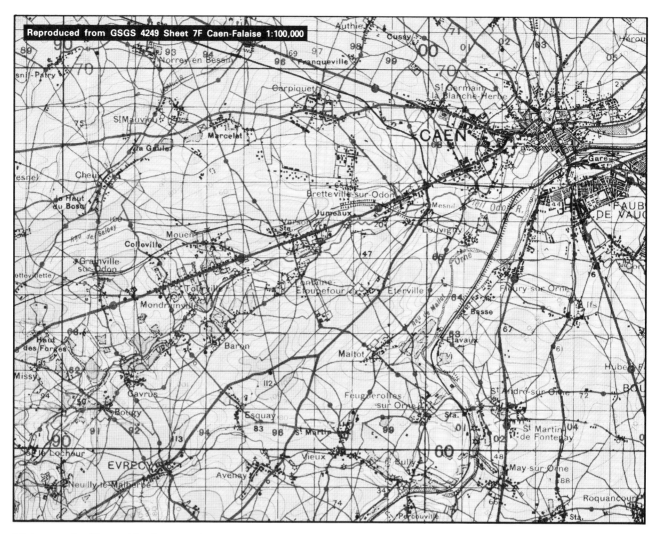

High ground military objectives are always referred to by the spot height and, as most military maps are based on the original national surveys of the countries concerned — Continental maps using the metric system — this is invariably given in metres. Thus Point 112 is 367 feet high. It is important, however, to remember when reading accounts of battles that these are above-sea-level measurements — without a map one pictures an enormous hillock when in actual fact Point 112 is a very slight prominence only thirty feet or so above the surrounding countryside. Most army maps of the period — referred to as GSGS (standing for Geographical Section General Staff) number so and so — leave a lot to be desired as

right, the tank commanders' eyes were trained mainly towards a copse on the south-east slope. The first anti-tank shell to hit tank 213 slewed it round in a half-circle. Tank 212 managed to destroy an anti-tank gun. The company commander, SS-Hauptsturmführer Endemann, veered off to the right and was lost to view. Radio contact had been non-existent since the start of the attack.

Towards 10.00 a.m. 2. Kompanie's Tigers managed to occupy the whole of the eastern slope of the hill and gave continuous supporting fire to the troops of SS-Panzergrenadier Regiment 21 from the Frundsberg Division. Weiss ordered his tanks to withdraw to the south of the hill. Shells and pockets of smoke marked where they had been.

On the right 1. Kompanie had advanced towards Maltot, where at dawn they had reported the presence of British troops. To protect the Abteilung's right flank SS-Hauptscharführer Baral's platoon was ordered to make its way towards the village. The tanks left St Martin at top speed, coming under fire

at Maltot as they reached the first houses. Unscathed, the Tigers pushed on, harried when they stopped beside walls and hedges, but able to come right up to the enemy head-on. SS-Unterscharführer Fey, in tank 134, came across four Shermans just in front of his gun: 'Panzer . . . halt! On the left-hand tank, 200 metres range, fire at will!' It took two shells each for the first two. Baral fired at the third. The fourth Sherman turned away and made off to the north.

By the evening of July 10, the Allied artillery had not let up. In the confused situation, the Germans gave up the hill. The following afternoon SS-Unterscharführer Baral led the recapture of Maltot and that night, preceded by artillery fire, the British retook Eterville.

At about 5.00 a.m. on the 12th, the Tigers were again ordered in support of the panzergrenadiers to re-occupy Point 112. 1. and 3. Kompanie took part in the attack and at 5.20 a.m. precisely SS-Untersturmführer Schroif reached the copse on the south-east slope once more

— to come across three Shermans and eight anti-tank guns. A light aircraft (undoubtedly a spotter) hung about overhead. The first shells landed ten minutes later, causing little damage to the Tigers, which managed to destroy several Churchills, but forcing the panzergrenadiers to go to ground. The Tigers' main concern was for hidden anti-tank guns — a threat only until their discovery, for the Tiger's '88' could blow them apart. Another smokescreen came down, and the Tigers halted just below the summit of the hill. A hundred metres ahead, scout cars were ferrying back and forth in an attempt to evacuate men and equipment. Two Churchills that were covering them were brewed up. Down the hill went the scout cars, behind a fresh layer of smoke.

The Tigers were brought back to St Martin, but they had to move out smartly on July 14 when British radio signals were picked up requesting artillery support and bombing. One solitary tank was left protecting Point 112.

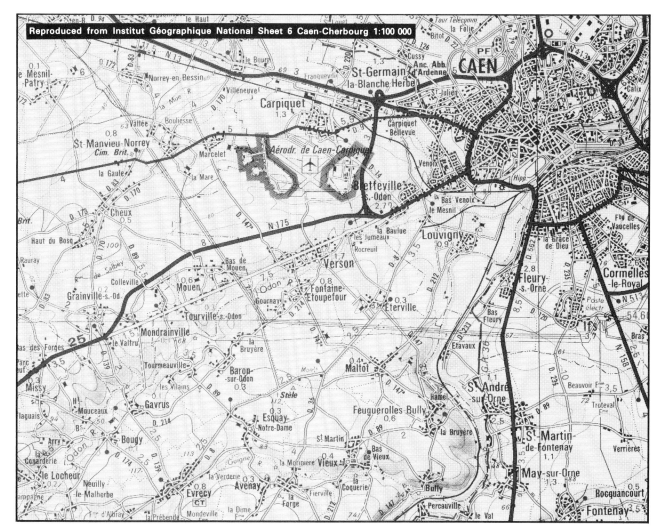

far as clarity and typography are concerned. Even the quality is sometimes poor as lithography printing, if not in its infancy, was much more primitive compared to today's photographic emulsions and presensitised printing plates. Nevertheless they enable us to understand the battle more clearly in the light of the terrain as it was at the time and so extracts from GSGS 4249 have been used throughout this book. Schwere SS-Panzer Abteilung 102's battle at Point 112 is a prime example. Look at the expansion of Caen, the most important town during the Normandy campaign, since 1944 with new suburbs, roads and bypasses, which would confuse the issue had we used modern maps. (Both extracts reproduced to the same scale.)

An Allied attack on Maltot with flamethrowing tanks during the night of July 15/16 brought 1. Kompanie into action, and at one stage SS-Oberscharführer Rodinger saw a British captain approaching his tank and making theatrical gestures. In a Viennese dialect, he called on Rodinger to surrender. Rodinger — a Viennese himself — talked with the officer for about twenty minutes before suggesting that he ought really to return to his own lines!

SS-Oberscharführer Kall's tanks occupied Point 112 for a second time, with III. Batallion of SS-Panzergrenadier Regiment 21.

On July 17, the Abteilung was again pulled back to St Martin and Feuguerolles-sur-Orne for essential maintenance, but one Tiger was kept constantly on the hill. At 5.00 p.m. on July 21, orders were received at the Abteilung's HQ at Amayé-sur-Orne, four kilometres to the south of Point 112, that SS-Sturmbannführer Weiss was to get his tanks ready to move. At 6.00

p.m. he was to advance on Maltot from St Martin — virtually a repeat performance — through countryside that was becoming all too familiar.

South-west of Maltot, 2. Kompanie had to undergo some unpleasant flanking fire from British infantry and anti-aircraft guns from the western heights leading to Point 112. When the Frundsberg Division assault guns arrived, 2. Kompanie's Tigers veered off to the right in the direction of Feuguerolles and one platoon which was confronted by anti-tank guns put three of them out of action. Throughout the night 2. Kompanie and the panzergrenadiers held the line from Maltot to Feuguerolles. The field guns that opened up on them at dawn were not able to make much impression against the Tigers' armour-plate, but a lucky shot was enough to break a track, which is what happened to tank 214, belonging to SS-Unterscharführer Kuhlmann.

Still in position on July 23, 2. Kompanie asked for and got two artillery strikes on Maltot after hearing the

rumble of tank engines. Towards 8.30 a.m. British tanks emerged from Maltot on both sides of the road. Of the six knocked out, three were hit by SS-Untersturmführer Schroif (tank 241), two by SS-Oberscharführer Rodinger (tank 231) and one by SS-Unterscharführer Münster (tank 212). The Tigers held the sector until the infantry were able to dig themselves in, then pulled back 200 metres to the rear, along the hedgerows, with two tanks remaining as look-outs at the northern exit of Feuguerolles.

On July 24, the British and Canadians increased their pressure on the right bank of the Orne, near May-sur-Orne, only three kilometres as the crow flies from Feuguerolles. 2. Kompanie was in position to the north and the north-east. Against this threat, reconnaissance showed that on the left bank it was only possible to offer support from the hamlet of Hamel, adjoining the northern part of Feuguerolles, and No. 2 Platoon was sent there without delay. . . .

On July 25, the Allies broke through

on the right of the Orne between St-Martin-de-Fontenay and Bourguébus. Once more schwere SS-Panzer Abteilung 102 supported the Hohenstaufen Division's counter-attack from the left bank, with 2. Kompanie again destroying much of the equipment that faced it. Sent as an observer, tank 222 commanded by SS-Untersturmführer Oberhuber was hit by an anti-tank gun at about 11.30 a.m. and the radio operator was killed.

The Tigers stuck at it south of Point 112 up to August 1, when orders came through assigning the Abteilung to the Hohenstaufen Division and ordering it to move southwards during the night. In twenty minutes that evening the Abteilung vacated the positions it had been holding around Maltot and Point 112 and set off via la Caine, Hamars, Campandré and then north-east in the direction of Roucamps, just north of Mont Pinçon. Along the Orne valley the dust that rose above their columns attracted some shelling and it was a tiring night-time move for the crews.

VIRE

Just before 8.00 a.m. on August 2, 2. Kompanie reached the sector three kilometres north-east of St Jean-le-Blanc, to the south-west of Mont Pinçon. A kilometre to the south, 2. Kompanie was in support.

SS-Obergruppenführer Bittrich, commanding II. SS-Panzer Korps, ordered the Abteilung into the Vire-Chênedollé-Estry sector. The Tigers were to push north-east and along the road leading towards Villers-Bocage, and to achieve this a Kampfgruppe was formed from the Abteilung and the Hohenstaufen's armoured reconnaissance group which was to be led by SS-Sturmbannführer Weiss himself.

Near Chênedollé 1. Kompanie, under SS-Obersturmführer Kalls met up with an enemy armoured spearhead. Weiss's orders, however, were to push on to Vire, where the situation was uncertain, and he left Kalls and pressed forward with 2. Kompanie, making contact with paratroops of 3. Fallschirm Division that evening at about 8.30 p.m.

The following day, Weiss was able to attack north-eastwards. SS-Untersturmführer Loritz's platoon were up front, followed on foot by troops from the Hohenstaufen reconnaissance group, with most of the rest of the unit including 1. Kompanie following on. Six kilometres north of Vire, Loritz, in tank 232, destroyed three Cromwells but the Tigers were in countryside that was all hedgerows and sunken lanes — ideal for defence not for attack — and Loritz thought it best to await the infantry. Meanwhile the British opened fire. Now the Tigers had to keep in close contact with each other as they moved forward. At 1.00 p.m. the hamlet of la Bistière was reached and raked with fire. Soon afterwards tank 232 shot up a Sherman.

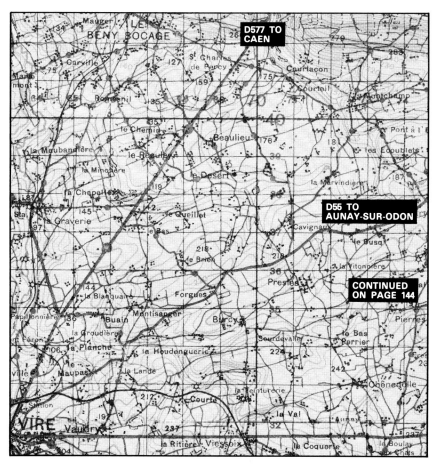

D577 TO CAEN

D55 TO AUNAY-SUR-ODON

CONTINUED ON PAGE 144

The 2. Kompanie had passed Point 119, when Loritz took on two more Shermans. SS-Hauptsturmführer Streng did likewise, but his tank was hit in the tracks and had to be taken in tow. The 1. Kompanie, coming up behind, forked left at la Papillonière, at the crossroads north of Vire, heading for la Graverie.

Having fully accomplished his mission, Weiss deployed his tanks and troops in defensive positions overnight. On Point 119 two Tigers faced in opposite directions: one on the lookout towards the north, the other keeping watch to the east.

The attack upon the hill by armour and infantry on all sides next morning failed. The approach was not difficult but, close to, the fighting was brutal. NCOs Rodinger, Harlander, Piller and Kuhlmann managed to destroy seven tanks between them. Only one Tiger was knocked out — tank 233 which suffered no less than seven shots at point-blank range. For the whole Abteilung, the tally that day was seventeen Allied tanks, two armoured reconnaissance vehicles and two anti-tank guns.

During the night the Tigers returned to la Bistière to fill up with petrol and re-ammunition.

Next day (August 4) the position worsened. The area all around was infiltrated and two more attacks were mounted on the hill at 2.00 p.m. and 4.00 p.m. which were both repulsed. It looked as if Allied armour was prowling towards la Bistière, and SS-Unterscharführers Rodinger and

Münster, who were sent there, managed to destroy three tanks. At 10.30 p.m. Kampfgruppe Weiss received orders to fall back to the north of Vire.

Just before daybreak on August 5, 2. Kompanie left the town for Pierres, ten kilometres to the north-east, and then moved south to Chênedollé at about 6.00 p.m. Most of the Tigers had suffered the effects of the incessant fighting, and 2. Kompanie gave up three of its tanks to 1. Kompanie whilst the others went on to the repair company, which was set up along the road between Vire and Tinchebray further south.

Vire fell during the afternoon of August 7. The 1. Kompanie helped bolster the defence near Chênedollé, where at dawn on the 8th SS-Unterscharführer Fey's Tiger was to the north of the village with a group of sappers. Fifteen Allied tanks advanced towards their positions. The first of them was hit at 600 metres and in half an hour Fey managed to destroy fourteen. As night fell and the last Sherman of the day put in an appearance, Fey had two rounds left . . . and they took care of the fifteenth.

Amidst the carnage of tanks and vehicles, the damage to Fey's Tiger amounted to a broken track caused by an anti-tank round, and under cover of darkness two of the Abteilung's tanks towed him as far as the tank workshops at Vassy. With his tally added to the others, the grand total for schwere SS-Panzer Abteilung 102 for August 8 came to twenty-four Allied tanks.

FALAISE

At 7.00 a.m. on August 9 schwere SS-Panzer Abteilung 102 changed sector for the second time, being sent to the north of Falaise, where its tanks arrived via Condé-sur-Noireau towards midday. Over the next two days 2. Kompanie was in action on the N158 from Caen. Whilst the other two Kompanies were astride the road Loritz's Tiger 231 added four more tanks to its score.

The Falaise pocket spelt death and destruction for so many of the panzer regiments in Normandy. Gradually squeezed towards the east, the jaws of the Allied pincer closed around Chambois where the first link was forged between the British, Canadian and Polish forces in the north, and the Americans to the south, on Saturday, August 19. This is the main street down which the vast majority of panzers trying to escape must have passed. Unlucky were a PzKpfw IV type H of the 8. Kompanie of Panzer Regiment 3 and an m.Zgkw 8t (SdKfz 7) eight-tonne medium prime mover. (US Army)

On August 12 the Allies broke through at Barbery about five kilometres to the west of the road. The 2. Kompanie was quickly called up: one Tiger took the approach road through Espins, another went through Fresney-le-Vieux, six others went off towards Barbery and, as they reached the outskirts of the hamlet

The horrors of the 'corridor of death'. One crewman, trapped by his feet, was burned alive; the other was shot as he climbed out of the tank. (IWM)

of Cingal, swung round to the east. Loritz, Rodinger and Münster succeeded in knocking out five tanks. Tank 232, commanded by SS-Unterscharführer Moldenhauer, caught fire after being hit by two anti-tank rounds and none of the crew got out.

There were further encounters during the afternoon and tank 211 had to be taken in tow. Then came the order to withdraw. At 7.00 p.m. at the Château de la Motte, south of Acqueville, 2. Kompanie could muster only four runners.

Two days later, on August 14, SS-Unterscharführer Münster's tank took an anti-tank round in the turret which wounded several of the crew, but there were no survivors from Loritz's tank 231 when it met its end. Tank 222 had rejoined its depleted Kompanie at 2.00 p.m. — just when Allied bombers were pounding Potigny on the N158 about nine kilometres north of Falaise. The handful of Tigers pulled back, but later occupied Point 183, to the north of the village. The 2. Kompanie now had only three Tigers left. The maintenance company was working all hours, though spare parts were no longer reaching them, under the constant threat of an Anglo-Canadian spearhead arriving at any time and overrunning their improvised workshops.

On August 15, the front line ran through Potigny where, at midday, the Tigers were still putting up a stout defence. SS-Unterscharführer Oberhuber destroyed another Allied tank. One Tiger had stationed itself in the middle of the road but under a cloud of smoke shells the Allied tanks veered to the right. The Tigers were firing on sight now, and at about 7.00 p.m. SS-Unterscharführer Oberhuber's tank was hit. With the Canadians bearing down on Falaise en masse, the Tigers fell back to the south at nightfall.

About 500 metres north of Falaise on the morning of August 16, 2. Kompanie consisted of two Tigers with the other two Kompanies about the same. By now the town was in ruins, with house-to-house fighting going on and, in the afternoon, the remaining tanks making a stand to the north were sent to join forces with the troops still holding out in that part of the town. At the École Supérieure sixty Hitlerjugend troops fought on to the end. . .

The amount of Allied equipment destroyed by schwere SS-Panzer Abteilung 102 between July 10 and August 20, 1944, included 227 tanks, 28 anti-tank guns, 19 half-tracks, 4 Bren gun carriers and 35 lorries. In the process, however, the Abteilung paid a heavy price: the vast majority of its tanks were lost; the last of them on the banks of the Seine, near Elbeuf on August 25.

SS-STURMBANNFÜHRER HANS WEISS

Hans Weiss was born on August 28, 1911 at Vöhringen. He decided to become a brewer like his father, but in 1933 joined up in the SS-Verfügungstruppe at Ellwangen. In Poland, in September 1939, he was already commanding a company in the SS reconnaissance group attached to Panzer Division Kempf. He was wounded and awarded the Iron Cross II Class, being awarded the Iron Cross I Class a year later whilst serving in the West.

In the Spring of 1941, in the Balkans, he commanded the mobile machine gun company of the reconnaissance group of SS Division Reich and afterwards in Russia where his unit took part in every action with the division. He was wounded several times.

In February 1943, he took part in the retaking of Kharkov, this time at the head of the whole reconnaissance group, and his attacking spirit earned him the Knights Cross of the Iron Cross, awarded on April 6. By then he was an SS-Hauptsturmführer. He already held the German Cross in Gold, whilst the silver bar of the Close Combat Badge was soon to follow.

Known to his men as the 'Brown Bomber', doubtless because of his typical boxer's head, Weiss was in command of the heavy tank unit in II. SS-Panzer Korps, at the time of the invasion, and on July 1, 1944, was promoted to SS-Obersturmbannführer.

On August 19 he was severely wounded by a bullet in the head near Trun; another bullet went through his lung and a third lodged in his pelvis. He was taken prisoner whilst unconscious by American troops. He died on October 2, 1978.

After the link up at Chambois the corridor remained open for two more days. Barely 2,000 metres wide, it stretched as far as St Lambert-sur-Dive where this Panther of the third company of SS-Panzer Regiment 1 fought it out behind the Mairie. This has now been rebuilt a few metres away from its original position. (IWM)

DER RÜCKMARSCH

The Rückmarsch — the retreat — for those that managed to extricate themselves from the pocket led east and north-eastwards across France. One major obstacle lay in the way — the Seine. Unfordable and with all bridges down, the Germans were forced to rely on boats and rafts. The main crossing point was at Rouen and Bourgtheroulde was the last big town before reaching the river. There a German war cameraman recorded the scenes of an army in defeat. (Bundesarchiv)

Tank 213 from the 2. Kompanie, schwere Panzer Abteilung 503, passes along the Grand Rue of Bourgtheroulde, the N138, in the direction of Rouen. The Seine is only seven kilometres away. Little do the crews realise that they will find no heavy rafts and no way of crossing. Their efforts to save their Tigers to fight another day will have been in vain. (Bundesarchiv)

Even post-war tourists must have been confused by this corner. Picture *above* taken in 1977 and *below* in 1980. The war memorial has been moved to make way for car parking space.

Which way now? A profusion of signs at the junction with the D313. Several panzer division emblems can be made out: the 'master key' of the LSSAH, the trident of the 2. Panzer Division, and the Kampfrune of the Das Reich Division. (Bundesarchiv)

Napoleon: 'There is not much difference after a battle in the material condition of the victor and vanquished, but the morale difference is immeasurably great.' Panzertruppe and infantry, NCOs and privates, Bourgtheroulde, August 1944.

An m.Zgkw 8t. (SdKfz 7) eight-tonne medium prime-mover followed by the one-tonne le.Zgkw 1t (SdKfz 10). (Bundesarchiv)

An le.Zgkw U304(f) armoured personnel carrier (ex-French Unic Kegresse P107) and Zündapp KS750 motor-cycle. (Bundesarchiv)

The end of the road — literally — for this armour piled up beside the Seine on the dockside at Rouen.

WHAT NOW REMAINS?

By the end of August 1944 the battle for Normandy was over. For three months the Germans had made supreme efforts to contain the Allied assault on Festung Europa. The German armoured forces, which had played such a decisive part in the victories of 1940, failed in the defensive rôle they were forced to play four years later. Swamped by the enormous numerical superiority of the Allied armour, the heavy German tanks which should have been able to hold their own with ease, were whittled away, one by one. Scattered throughout the length and breadth of Normandy, although more proliferous in the pocket east of Falaise, the panzers lay stricken: immobilised, trackless, blown apart, burned out or simply stranded for lack of fuel.

From the beginning the Allied forces operated an efficient recovery operation for their own damaged tanks and this was extended to retrieving those of the enemy which were of any value. However, as the number of knocked out German tanks increased, so British and American interest in them waned and the majority were thereafter left where they lay. Subsequently the abandoned hulks were made the property of the new French Government which continued to assemble the wreckage in huge dumps. One of the largest in Normandy was situated on the plain just outside St Lambert-sur-Dives consisting of tanks that were caught in the Falaise pocket. Eventually the dump consisted of everything from a Tiger to a horse-drawn cart and included every conceivable kind of field gun — all of which were sold in lots by auction in 1947 to the scrap merchants which seem to proliferate in the aftermath of any war.

There still remained a larger number of hulks which had been left in situ and these were sold off individually. A would-be purchaser first had to apply for

German transport still lining the Pontchardon road, east of Vimoutiers, photographed by Alain Roudeix in 1947. He took us back to exactly the same spot in 1980.

What enthusiast would not like to take up the offer in this REME salvage dump? Sorry no location given! (IWM)

Neatly perforated barrel of a PzKpfw IV Ausf H alongside a type B or C of Panzer Regiment 22. (IWM)

Reconciliation after death in the American sector; US and German vehicles in a dump near Isigny-sur-Mer. Assuming they have been gathered in from the surrounding area, the German items must have belonged to SS-Panzer Regiment 2, Panzer Regiment 3 or the Panzer Lehr Regiment. The two AFVs on the left are French Renault UE/AMX UE tractors used by the German forces as Infanterie Schlepper UE 630(f). These are fitted with four Wurfrahmen 40 projectors for the Wurfgerät 40 rockets. What about the SdKfz 251 half-track with the Allied star?

We can give the location for this one. Leave the N13 in Isigny by the D5 opposite the church. Continue beyond the built-up area and over the crossroads of the D196 and D203 (to Airel and Montfréville). The direction is that of Lison — straight ahead. The field is opposite the water tower which will be seen on the right of the road. (There's nothing left!) (US Army)

At the site of the depot on high ground just outside St Lambert-sur-Dive we did find some relics.

a permit to remove a particular vehicle stating precisely where the tank, etc., stood. He then had to produce a surveyors report on its condition after which an agent would determine the asking price on behalf of the Government. In theory the new owner was given one year to remove it but in practice this extended to as much as seven or eight years. By this method the authorities were able to clear the countryside at no cost to themselves and, in fact, to make a financial gain. Certain wholesale scrap dealers bought up enormous quantities of material — one of them even purchasing on behalf of the Syrian Army which wanted spare parts for PzKpfw IVs with which their own armoured force were equipped!

M. Alain Roudeix (in the familiar checked cap) told us that this particular dump was cleared by 1947. (ECP Armées)

By the mid-1970s virtually everything had been cleared and there remained only two locations where the wreckage of the panzers could still be seen in Normandy. Both sites lay on the outskirts of Trun, a small town eighteen kilometres south-east of Falaise. Madame Maurat's scrapyard became something of a legend — the last tank graveyard — and with the establishment of the French armoured forces museum at Saumur (in the Loire valley between Angers and Tours) in 1965, it was only to be expected that the museum director, Colonel Michel Aubry, would eventually claim the wreckage for the nation. At a time when working examples of the famed Mk IV, the Panther and the Tiger were non-existent, any material which could provide the necessary spare parts was a priceless asset. By 1980 the smaller of the two sites had been completely cleared and it was only a question of time before the second suffered the same fate.

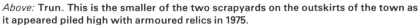

Above: **Trun. This is the smaller of the two scrapyards on the outskirts of the town as it appeared piled high with armoured relics in 1975.**

Five years later, empty. The wreckage has been transported south to the French Musée des Blindés at Saumur.

Above: **By 1983 ploughed up for carrots!** *Left:* **Morsels of a different sort for the hungry.**

The larger of the two Trun yards still remains as it was left after the end of the war— but for how long?

Even in the 1980s it is still possible to find wreckage of the panzers in Normandy. This wheel, apparently from an RSO tracked chassis, still lies in a hedgerow at Norrey-en-Bessin.

Much of the smaller German equipment was bulldozed into holes scooped out of the ground and buried only to be later dug out again by Alain Roudeux forty years later!

A 7.5cm PaK 40 outside the Mairie at le Dézert, defended by the Panzer Lehr Regiment, in memory of Colonel Harry A. Flint, Commander of the US 39th Infantry Regiment, who fought and died in the area with seventy-seven of his men on July 24-25. He was posthumously awarded the Bronze Oak Leaf Cluster to his Distinguished-Service Cross received earlier.

Track link, fuel pumps and turret floor from Michael Wittmann's Tiger recovered and retained by a farmer in the Cintheaux area.

This PzKpfw IV is believed to have served with either Panzer Regiment 22 or SS-Panzer Regiment 12 in the Caen and Cagny area. From the dump at St Lambert-sur-Dive it went in 1948 to a scrapyard on the Route de Paris at Le Mans. Today it can be seen at the Musée Militaire de Dieppe-Pourville having been purchased by M. Jacques Collé in 1976.

And thus, forty years later, there is but one complete German tank left in Normandy today . . . just one reminder of the panzers which once stalked the narrow lanes . . . defended the bocage . . . and clanked their way into the history books. It stands beside Route Nationale 179 from Lisieux to Alençon — the Tiger of Vimoutiers. The tank was originally believed to have been on the strength of schwere Panzer Abteilung 503 in August 1944 although this has not been confirmed. What is known is that on August 19 several German tanks were making their way to a fuel dump which had been set up in the nearby Château de l'Horloge. Forced to detour along the Vimoutiers-Gacé road (N179), several panzers from mixed units which had extricated themselves from the Falaise pocket ran out of petrol. Others were simply abandoned by their crews who possibly thought they had a better chance of escaping on foot. Scattered along and about a short stretch of the N179 were a PzKpfw III, several IVs and three Tiger I Ausf Es — two by the railway embankment and one in the centre of the road. Other tanks, including one of the rare Königstigers were to be found on the narrow D33 which runs in a north-south direction a couple of kilometres to the east of the town, and altogether it has been estimated that sixty German tanks were abandoned around Vimoutiers during the last days of August.

Before the crew left the single Tiger standing in the centre of the road, they made a half-hearted attempt at demolition by placing charges on the engine cover and alongside the turret. The explosions buckled the armour plate above the Maybach engine and jammed the turret. Some time later an American bulldozer pushed the tank off the lower, northern side of the road to clear the route.

In its pre-1975 location, the Tiger outside Vimoutiers was a unique exhibit. Ironically, After the Battle, dedicated to the preservation of WWII relics, was responsible indirectly for its subsequent removal. Publicity given to the tank in the magazine in 1975 resulted in local townspeople demanding action over its restoration.

Alain Roudeix indicates its original position in 1944 before it was dozed into the ditch.

A local scrapman, M. Morat, was not long in making a claim for it yet after the purchase had gone through he made no effort to move it. The gearbox was lifted out but that was all and there it remained for over three decades . . . a plaything for local children, its rusty, moss-covered exterior blending and becoming an accepted part of the local landscape.

When M. Morat died, possession of the Tiger passed to his sister who quickly sold it to a scrapyard in Caen. The new owners wasted no time in claiming their prize and oxy-acetelene cutting gear soon appeared on the scene. However no sooner had they made their first cut (on the right-front mantlet) than the local town council was informed by a well meaning citizen that their local landmark was about to be removed. Eddy Florentin, French historian of the Normandy campaign, offered his support and telephoned the Ministry of War in Paris personally to protest about the loss of a valuable part of the town's history. The upshot of the affair resulted in the town of Vimoutiers making an emergency purchase of the Tiger for NF6000 (then around £600).

In May 1975 *After the Battle* covered the Falaise battle (issue No. 8) and the Tiger was featured on the cover of the magazine. To the nostalgic it was a unique legacy of the Second World War of which there are all too few to be seen in their 'natural' state and part of its special significance lay in it having been left where it was in 1944. However, having now achieved widespread publicity, the feeling of the townspeople was that the Tiger should be restored as befitted its new-found fame, and a decision was taken to remove it from its resting place, repaint it and set it up on level ground. The job of its recovery was given to Alain Roudeix, an ex-Maquis collector-extraordinaire, well suited to carry out the task. Not only had he an intimate knowledge of the fighting in the area, he had taken part in the clearance of both ordnance and vehicles from the local battlefields, and in the early days, before he appreciated their future value as museum pieces, scrapped many tanks himself.

In October 1975 the project began with the removal of the turret to reduce top weight. Then using two rubber-tyred bulldozers so as not to rip up the tarmac, the chassis was bodily dragged up onto the road and onto a specially prepared piece of level ground alongside. After refitting the turret and welding all the hatches shut, the plating was repaired before the whole was sprayed a desert sand colour. The camouflage scheme was added by reference to the colour of

The interior, looking 'fore' and 'aft' courtesy of Dr Jerry Jacobson.

original paint still adhering to pieces of tank armour in M. Roudeix's possession.

And so the sole survivor in Normandy of Hitler's much-vaunted panzer forces remains almost as a memorial . . . a Tiger tamed at the roadside . . . and in the words of the *Panzerlied:* 'Our Panzer will become an honourable grave'.

GLOSSARY

A
Abteilung (Abt.) battalion, detachment.
Abteilungskommandeur battalion commander.
Adjutant ADC, aide-de-camp.
Ausfürung (Ausf) model, mark or design.

B
Befehlspanzer command tank.
Befehlshaber commanding officer of a formation such as a corps or army.
Bergepanzer armoured recovery vehicle.
Betriebstoff petrol, fuel.
Beutepanzer captured tank.

D
Dienstgrad rank.
Dienstgradabzeichen badges of rank.

E
Einheitsfeldmütze standard peaked soft field cap worn between 1943 and 1945, copied from the cap worn by mountain troops and also the Afrika Korps.

F
Feldgrau the grey-green colour of the standard clothing worn in the German Army and Waffen-SS.
Feldjacke the double-breasted battle blouse worn by tank crew members.
Feldmütze side cap, similar to that worn in the British Army.
Feuerwerker artificer.
Flak (Fliegerabwehrkanone) anti-aircraft gun.
Flakvierling quadruple anti-aircraft gun.
Funker radio operator, especially one in a tank.
Funklenkwagen radio-controlled vehicle.

G
Gasschützunteroffizier NCO in charge of anti-gas defence precautions.
Gepanzerter (gp) armoured.

H
Heer army.
Hilfswillige (Hiwi) Russian auxiliary in the German army.
Hoheitsabzeichen the national emblem (an eagle holding a Swastika in its claws).

I
Instandsetzung/Instandhaltung maintenance.

J
Jagdbomber (Jabo) fighter-bomber.
Jagdpanzer (Jgd.Pz.) tank destroyer.

K
Kampfgruppe task force, literally a battle group.
Kriegsausrüstungsnachweisung (KAN) war establishment table (equipment).
Kette caterpillar track (tank track).
Kettenkrad half-track (specifically a motorcycle with twin tracks at the rear).
Kraftfahrzeug (Kfz) non-armoured vehicle abbreviation which accompanied the ordnance inventory number of all non-armoured (soft-skinned) motor vehicles.
Kompanie company.
Kompanieführer company commander.
Königstiger King or Royal Tiger.
Kraftstoff petrol, fuel.
Kraftwagenführer driver (tank or otherwise).
Krankenpanzerwagen armoured ambulance.
Kriegsstärkenachweisung (KStN) war strength table.
Kubelwagen literally 'bucket car', referring to the bucket seats, not to the vehicle's body, which was that of the Volkswagen Type 82.
Kampfwagenkanone (KwK) tank gun.

L

Ladeschütze loader, e.g. in a tank.
Ladungsträger explosive carrier.
Lastkraftwagen (Lkw) army lorry.
LSSAH abbreviation for the 1st SS Panzer (Armoured) Division, the Leibstandarte SS Adolf Hitler.

M

Melder message carrier or runner.
Maschinengewehr (MG) machine gun.
Mittlerer Schützenpanzerwagen (mSPW), medium armoured semi-tracked personnel carrier (basic type) for riflemen.

O

OKH, Oberkommando des Heeres Army High Command.

P

Panzerabteilung (Pz.Abt.) tank battalion.
Panzerabwehrkanone (PaK) anti-tank gun.
Panzerfunkwart tank radio mechanic.
Panzergranate (Pzgr) armour-piercing shell.
Panzer Grenadier Division (Pz.Gren.Div.) motorised infantry division 1942-1945.
Panzerjäger tank destroyer.
Panzerkommandant tank commander.
Panzerkompanie (Pz.Kp.) tank company.
Panzerkorps tank or armoured corps.
Panzeroberschütze senior private in the tank arm.
Panzerregiment (Pz.Rgt.) tank regiment, armoured regiment (mixed).
Panzerschlosser derogatory term for a person working on vehicles, in this case tanks.
Panzerschütze private in the tank arm.
Panzerwart tank mechanic.
Pionierpanzerwagen (Pi.Pz.Wg.) armoured engineers vehicle.
Personenkraftwagen (Pkw) a vehicle for carrying personnel.
Piat acronym of Projector, Infantry, Anti-Tank, i.e. a hand-held launcher firing a hollow-charge grenade.
Panzerdivision (Pz.Div.) tank or armoured division.
Panzerkampfwagen (PzKpfw) tank.

R

Regimentskommandeur regimental commander (in peacetime usually a lieutenant-colonel.
Richtschütze gun-layer.
Rommelkiste nickname for the containers for storing kit placed on the rear of tanks.

S

Saukopf/Saukopfblende sow's head cast gun mantlet.
Schwere heavy.
Schreiber company clerk.
Schirmmütze peaked cap for service use and for walking out.
Schirrmeister technical quartermaster sergeant.
Schulterklappe shoulder-straps as worn by NCOs and privates.
Schulterstücke officer's shoulder-strap.
Schürzen supplementary armour plates (skirts).
Schwimmwagen amphibious vehicle, specifically the Volkswagen Type 166.
Sonderkraftfahrzeug (SdKfz) abbreviation of 'special purpose motor vehicle' used as a prefix for the ordnance inventory number given to armoured vehicles and vehicles standardised and accepted into military service.
Spiess slang for company sergeant major in the German Army.
Sprenggranate (Sprgr) high explosive shell.
Stab (St) staff or headquarters.
Stabskompanie staff or headquarters company.
Sturmgeschütz (StuG) self-propelled assault gun.

T

Tross baggage convoy.
Turm cupola or turret.

V

Versorgungskompanie supply company.

W

Waffenmeister armourer.
Waffenoffizier ordnance officer.
Wehrmacht correct name for German Armed Forces as a whole (Heer, Kriegsmarine and Luftwaffe) but often used in Allied terminology as meaning the German Army itself.
Wehrmachtsbeamte military official in uniform.
Werkstattkompanie repair company.

Z

Zimmerit an anti-magnetic cement applied to tanks to prevent the adhesion of magnetic mines.
Zug section.
Zugführer section commander.
Zugmaschine/Zugkraftwagen (Zgkw) tractor or half-tracked tractor.

COMPARATIVE RANK TABLE

A seemingly dispirited machine gunner hitches a ride on a Panther engine deck. (Bundesarchiv)

The problem with presenting comparative rank tables between the various armed services is that the levels of responsibility and authority were not always the same in the different armies. Inaccuracies can also be created if one tries to translate foreign ranks into English, i.e. Head Storm Leader for Hauptsturmführer. The table that follows is based on a comparison of the authority of the rank; thus an American Corporal was junior to a British Corporal in this respect.

German Army	Waffen-SS	British Army	US Army
Generalfeldmarschall		Field-Marshal	
Generaloberst	SS-Oberst-Gruppenführer und Generaloberst der Waffen-SS	General	General of the Army (5 stars)
General der Panzertruppen, etc.	SS-Obergruppenführer und General der Waffen-SS	General	General (4 stars)
Generalleutnant	SS-Gruppenführer und Generalleutnant der Waffen-SS	Lieutenant-General	Lieutenant General (3 stars)
Generalmajor	SS-Brigadeführer und Generalmajor der Waffen-SS	Major-General	Major General (2 stars)
	SS-Oberführer	Brigadier	Brigadier General (1 star)
Oberst	SS-Standartenführer	Colonel	Colonel
Oberstleutnant	SS-Obersturmbannführer	Lieutenant-Colonel	Lieutenant Colonel
Major	SS-Sturmbannführer	Major	Major
Hauptmann Rittmeister*	SS-Hauptsturmführer	Captain	Captain
Oberleutnant	SS-Obersturmführer	Lieutenant	First Lieutenant
Leutnant	SS-Untersturmführer	2nd Lieutenant	Second Lieutenant
Stabsfeldwebel/Stabswachtmeister*	SS-Sturmscharführer	Regimental Sergeant Major	Warrant Officer
Oberfeldwebel/Oberwachtmeister*	SS-Hauptscharführer	Staff Sergeant	Master Sergeant
Feldwebel/Wachtmeister*	SS-Oberscharführer	Sergeant	Technical Sergeant
Unterfeldwebel/Unterwachtmeister*	SS-Scharführer	Lance Sergeant	Staff Sergeant
Unteroffizier	SS-Unterscharführer	Corporal	Sergeant
Obergefreiter	SS-Rottenführer	Lance Corporal	Corporal
Gefreiter	SS-Sturmmann		
Oberschütze (ditto as below)	SS-Oberschütze, etc.		Private First Class
Schütze, Grenadier, Kanonier, Pionier, etc.	SS-Schütze, etc.	Private	Private

* Cavalry, artillery, signals, flak and transport troops (Fahrtruppen) used the rank title Wachtmeister instead of Feldwebel, whereas captains in cavalry and transport troops were addressed as riding master.